COGNTIVE 2019

The Eleventh International Conference on Advanced Cognitive Technologies and Applications

May 5 - 9, 2019

Venice, Italy

COGNITIVE 2019 Editors

Marta Franova, CNRS, LRI & INRIA, France

Charlotte Sennersten, CSIRO Mineral Resources, Australia

Jayfus T. Doswell, The Juxtopia Group, JUICE-Lab, USA

Printed from e-media with permission by:

Curran Associates, Inc.
57 Morehouse Lane
Red Hook, NY 12571

Some format issues inherent in the e-media version may also appear in this print version.

Printed by Curran Associates, Inc. (2019)

International Academy, Research, and Industry Association (IARIA)
412 Derby Way
Wilmington, DE 19810

Phone: (408) 893-6407
Fax: (408) 527-6351

petre@iaria.org

Additional copies of this publication are available from:

Curran Associates, Inc.
57 Morehouse Lane
Red Hook, NY 12571 USA
Phone: 845-758-0400
Fax: 845-758-2633
Email: curran@proceedings.com
Web: www.proceedings.com

Table of Contents

Few-Shot Learning Using Supervised Non-Associative Autoencoders and Correlation Techniques 1
Ehsan Sedgh Gooya and Ayman Al Falou

Cognitive Decision Support for Industrial Product Life Cycles: A Position Paper 3
Stefan Thalmann, Heimo Gursch, Josef Suschnigg, Milot Gashi, Helmut Ennsbrunner, Anna Katharina Fuchs, Tobias Schreck, Belgin Mutlu, Juergen Mangler, Gerti Kappl, Christian Huemer, and Lindstaedt Stefanie

EEG Based Valence Emotion Recognition by the Cognitive Model of Emotion 10
Jun-Su Kang and Minho Lee

Smart Shopping Cart Learning Agents Modeling and Evaluation 12
Dilyana Budakova, Lyudmil Dakovski, and Veselka Petrova-Dimitrova

VoxelNET's Geo-Located Spatio Temporal Softbots - Including Living, Quiet and Invisible Data 20
Charlotte Sennersten, Craig Lindley, and Ben Evans

Importance of Coordination and Cultural Diversity for an Efficient and Flexible Manufacturing System 28
Kashif Zia, Alois Ferscha, and Dari Trendafilov

Neural Computation of Perceived Relative Size and Depth in Complex 2D Image Configurations 32
Birgitta Dresp-Langley and Adam Reeves

Resonance Thinking in Cartesian Systemic Emergence 37
Marta Franova and Yves Kodratoff

Multimodal Interactions Viewed as Dual Process on Multi-Dimensional Memory Frames Under Weak Synchronization 44
Muneo Kitajima, Jeome Dinet, and Makoto Toyota

A Framework for Tutoring Computational Thinking: Learning Environment and Task Analysis 52
Kazuhisa Miwa and Kazuaki Kojima

Delivering Comprehensive Knowledge of the World to the Computer: How to Make the Computer Understand Meaning 56
Victor Raskin and Julia Taylor Rayz

Cognitive Products: System Architecture and Operational Principles 62
Dari Trendafilov, Kashif Zia, Alois Ferscha, Ali Abbas, Behrooz Azadi, Johannes Selymes, and Michael Haslgrubler

Wearable Augmented Cognition for Improving Medic Performance: An Adaptive Transcranial Cognitive 71

Augmentation Device with Wearable Augmented Reality
Jayfus Doswell and Kenneth Wilson

A Position for Proactive Cybersecurity Policies for Military BCIs 76
Ashley Boykin and Jayfus Doswell

Algorithm for Classification of EEG Signals in Astronauts 78
Victor Ortiz and Jayfus Doswell

Neural Network-Based Reasoning for Solving the Tower of Hanoi 83
Sanghun Bang and Charles Tijus

Capturing Knowledge for Multimodality Processing: Interpreting Brain Vascular Imaging and its Description 85
Julia Rayz, Vitaliy Rayz, and Victor Raskin

COGNITIVE 2019

Forward

The Eleventh International Conference on Advanced Cognitive Technologies and Applications (COGNITIVE 2019), held between May 5 - 9, 2019 - Venice, Italy, targeted advanced concepts, solutions and applications of artificial intelligence, knowledge processing, agents, as key-players, and autonomy as manifestation of self-organized entities and systems. The advances in applying ontology and semantics concepts, web-oriented agents, ambient intelligence, and coordination between autonomous entities led to different solutions on knowledge discovery, learning, and social solutions.

The conference had the following tracks:

- Brain information processing and informatics
- Artificial intelligence and cognition
- Agent-based adaptive systems
- Applications

Similar to the previous edition, this event attracted excellent contributions and active participation from all over the world. We were very pleased to receive top quality contributions.

We take here the opportunity to warmly thank all the members of the COGNITIVE 2019 technical program committee, as well as the numerous reviewers. The creation of such a high quality conference program would not have been possible without their involvement. We also kindly thank all the authors that dedicated much of their time and effort to contribute to COGNITIVE 2019. We truly believe that, thanks to all these efforts, the final conference program consisted of top quality contributions.

Also, this event could not have been a reality without the support of many individuals, organizations and sponsors. We also gratefully thank the members of the COGNITIVE 2019 organizing committee for their help in handling the logistics and for their work that made this professional meeting a success.

We hope COGNITIVE 2019 was a successful international forum for the exchange of ideas and results between academia and industry and to promote further progress in the area of cognitive technologies and applications. We also hope that Venice provided a pleasant environment during the conference and everyone saved some time for exploring this beautiful city.

COGNITIVE 2019 Chairs

COGNITIVE 2019 Steering Committee

Po-Hsun Cheng, National Kaohsiung Normal University, Taiwan
Jose Alfredo F. Costa, Federal University - UFRN, Brazil
Om Prakash Rishi, University of Kota, India
Kazuhisa Miwa, Nagoya University, Japan
Olga Chernavskaya, Lebeved Physical Institute, Moscow, Russia
Paul Smart, University of Southampton, UK
Ryotaro Kamimura, Tokai University, Japan
Olivier Chator, Ecole Nationale Supérieure de Cognitique, France

COGNITIVE 2019 Industry/Research Advisory Committee

Jayfus Tucker Doswell, The Juxtopia Group, Inc., USA
Tiago Thompsen Primo, Samsung Research Institute, Brazil
Galit Fuhrmann Alpert, computational neuroscientist, Israel

COGNITIVE 2019

Committee

COGNITIVE 2019 Steering Committee
Po-Hsun Cheng, National Kaohsiung Normal University, Taiwan
Jose Alfredo F. Costa, Federal University - UFRN, Brazil
Om Prakash Rishi, University of Kota, India
Kazuhisa Miwa, Nagoya University, Japan
Olga Chernavskaya, Lebeved Physical Institute, Moscow, Russia
Paul Smart, University of Southampton, UK
Ryotaro Kamimura, Tokai University, Japan
Olivier Chator, Ecole Nationale Supérieure de Cognitique, France

COGNITIVE 2019 Industry/Research Advisory Committee
Jayfus Tucker Doswell, The Juxtopia Group, Inc., USA
Tiago Thompsen Primo, Samsung Research Institute, Brazil
Galit Fuhrmann Alpert, computational neuroscientist, Israel

COGNITIVE 2019 Technical Program Committee

Mohammad Abido, King Fahd University of Petroleum & Minerals, Saudi Arabia
Witold Abramowicz, University of Economics and Business, Poland
Thomas Agotnes, University of Bergen, Norway
Jose Alfredo F. Costa, Federal University - UFRN, Brazil
Piotr Artiemjew, University of Warmia and Masuria, Poland
Petr Berka, University of Economics, Prague, Czech Republic
Gilberto Bernardes, INESC TEC, Portugal
Ateet Bhalla, Independent Consultant, India
Peter Brida, University of Zilina, Slovak Republic
Dilyana Budakova, Technical University of Sofia - Branch Plovdiv, Bulgaria
Albertas Caplinskas, Vilnius University, Lithuania
Facundo Carrillo, Laboratorio de Inteligencia Artificial Aplicada | ICC (UBA/CONICET), Buenos Aires, Argentina
Francesco Carlo Morabito, University Mediterranea of Reggio Calabria, Italy
Yaser Chaaban, Leibniz University of Hanover, Germany
Olivier Chator, Ecole Nationale Supérieure de Cognitique, France
Po-Hsun Cheng, National Kaohsiung Normal University, Taiwan
Olga Chernavskaya, Lebeved Physical Institute, Moscow, Russia
Sunil Choenni, Dutch Ministry of Security & Justice / Rotterdam University of Applied Sciences, Netherlands
Helder Coelho, Universidade de Lisboa, Portugal
Leonardo Dagui de Oliveira, University of São Paulo, Brazil
Darryl N. Davis, University of Hull, UK

Copyright Information

For your reference, this is the text governing the copyright release for material published by IARIA.

The copyright release is a transfer of publication rights, which allows IARIA and its partners to drive the dissemination of the published material. This allows IARIA to give articles increased visibility via distribution, inclusion in libraries, and arrangements for submission to indexes.

I, the undersigned, declare that the article is original, and that I represent the authors of this article in the copyright release matters. If this work has been done as work-for-hire, I have obtained all necessary clearances to execute a copyright release. I hereby irrevocably transfer exclusive copyright for this material to IARIA. I give IARIA permission or reproduce the work in any media format such as, but not limited to, print, digital, or electronic. I give IARIA permission to distribute the materials without restriction to any institutions or individuals. I give IARIA permission to submit the work for inclusion in article repositories as IARIA sees fit.

I, the undersigned, declare that to the best of my knowledge, the article is does not contain libelous or otherwise unlawful contents or invading the right of privacy or infringing on a proprietary right.

Following the copyright release, any circulated version of the article must bear the copyright notice and any header and footer information that IARIA applies to the published article.

IARIA grants royalty-free permission to the authors to disseminate the work, under the above provisions, for any academic, commercial, or industrial use. IARIA grants royalty-free permission to any individuals or institutions to make the article available electronically, online, or in print.

IARIA acknowledges that rights to any algorithm, process, procedure, apparatus, or articles of manufacture remain with the authors and their employers.

I, the undersigned, understand that IARIA will not be liable, in contract, tort (including, without limitation, negligence), pre-contract or other representations (other than fraudulent misrepresentations) or otherwise in connection with the publication of my work.

Exception to the above is made for work-for-hire performed while employed by the government. In that case, copyright to the material remains with the said government. The rightful owners (authors and government entity) grant unlimited and unrestricted permission to IARIA, IARIA's contractors, and IARIA's partners to further distribute the work.

Few-Shot Learning using Supervised Non-Associative Autoencoders and Correlation Techniques

Ehsan Sedgh-Gooya

L@bISEN, VISION Lab, Yncréa ouest
20 rue Cuirassé Bretagne CS 42807
29228 Brest Cedex 2, France
Email: ehsan.sedgh-gooya@isen-ouest.yncrea.fr

Ayman Alfalou

L@bISEN, VISION Lab, Yncréa ouest
20 rue Cuirassé Bretagne CS 42807
29228 Brest Cedex 2, France
Email: ayman.al-falou@isen-bretagne.fr

***Abstract*—Deep learning, while very effective today, traditionally requires very large amounts of labeled data to perform the classification task. In an attempt to solve this problem, the few-shot learning concept, which uses few labeled samples by class, becomes more and more useful. In this paper, we propose a new low-shot learning method, dubbed Supervised Non-Associative Auto-Encoder (SNAAE) to perform classification. Complementary to prior studies, SNAAE represents a shift of paradigm in comparison with the usual few-shot learning methods, as it does not use any prior knowledge neither unlabeled data. SNAAE is based on stacking layers of an autoencoder, which are trained in a supervised way to rebuild a single version representing their inputs. The reconstructed output is then classified outside of the neural network by correlation plane quantification metric. To perform the classification, the rebuilt output is compared with the initial versions used as target to train the SNAAE. We demonstrate empirically the efficiency of our proposed approach on the well known handwritten digits Modified National Institute of Standards and Technology database (MNIST) database.**

***Keywords*–Neural Networks; Few-shot learnong; Semi-Supervised learning; Autoencoders.**

I. Introduction

At a time when unlabelled data is becoming increasingly common, manual labeling of all these data is expensive, time consuming and inefficient. Moreover, when we place ourselves on the side of the humans, we need few data to learn new concepts with very little supervision. Hence, the few-shot learning concept becomes increasingly important. The aim of these concepts is to improve the generalization capabilities of learning models so that they can achieve very good performance using a few labeled samples. For a maximal efficiency, the state-of-the-art few-shot learning algorithms [1] [2] typically make use of prior knowledge and large amounts of unlabeled data. In this paper, we address the above problem, and we propose a new few-shot learning classification method based on Supervised Non-Associative Auto-Encoder (SNAAE). Furthermore, SNAAE does not need at all any prior knowledge neither unlabeled data. We organize our article by first describing a general autoencoder framework. Then in the following section we define and explain our proposed method. Finaly, the efficiency of our proposed approach is tested on MNIST.

II. A General Autoencoder Framework

Autoencoders [3]–[5] are simple learning circuits which aim to transform inputs into outputs with the least possible amount of distortion. While conceptually simple, they play an important role in machine learning. Autoencoders were first introduced in the 1980s by Hinton and the PDP group [6] to address the problem of backpropagation without a teacher, by using the input data as the teacher. Together with Hebbian learning rules [7], autoencoders provide one of the fundamental concepts for unsupervised learning and for beginning to address the mystery of how synaptic changes induced by local biochemical events can be coordinated in a self-organized manner to produce global learning and intelligent behavior. To derive a general framework an $n/p/n$ autoencoder [8] is defined by a tuple $n, p, m, \mathbb{F}, \mathbb{G}, \mathcal{A}, \mathcal{B}, \mathcal{X}, \Delta$ where:

1) $\mathbb{F}, \mathbb{G}$ are sets;
2) n and p are positive integers. Here we consider primarily the case where $0 < p < n$.
3) $\mathcal{A}$ is a class of functions from $\mathbb{G}^p$ to $\mathbb{F}^n$.
4) $\mathcal{B}$ is a class of functions from $\mathbb{F}^n$ to $\mathbb{G}^p$.
5) $\mathcal{X} = \{x_1, \ldots, x_m\}$ is a set of m (training) vectors in $\mathbb{F}^n$. When external targets are present, we let $\mathcal{Y} = \{y_1, \ldots, y_m\}$ denote the corresponding set of target vectors in $\mathbb{F}^n$.
6) Δ is a dissimilarity or distortion function (e.g. L_p norm, Hamming distance) defined over $\mathbb{F}^n$.

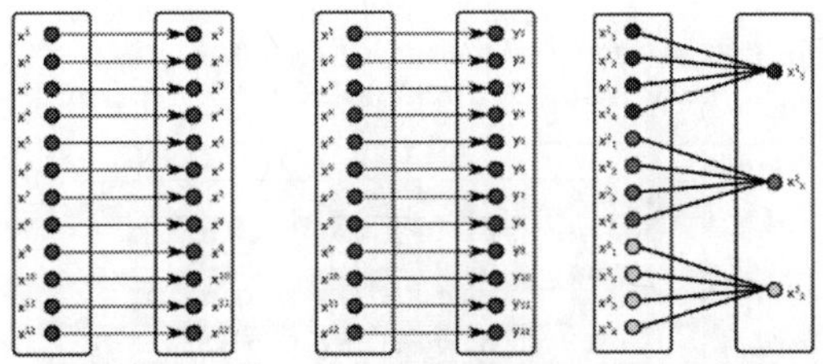

(a) Associative Autoencoder (b) Non-Associative Autoencoder (c) SNAAE

Figure 1. Autoencoders

A. *Associative Auto-Encoder*

For any $A \in \mathcal{A}$ and $B \in \mathcal{B}$, the autoencoder transforms an input vector $x \in \mathbb{F}^n$ into an output vector $A \circ B(x) \in \mathbb{F}^n$ (Figure 1-a). The corresponding autoencoder problem is to find $A \in \mathcal{A}$ and $B \in \mathcal{B}$ that minimize the overall distortion function:

$$\min E(A,B) = \min_{A,B} \sum_{t=1}^{m} E(x_t) = \min_{A,B} \sum_{t=1}^{m} \Delta(A \circ B(x_t), x_t) \quad (1)$$

B. Non-Associative Auto-Encoder

In the non auto-associative case, when external targets y_t are provided, the minimization problem becomes:

$$correct: Figure2 \min E(A,B) = \min_{A,B} \sum_{t=1}^{m} E(x_t, y_t) = \min_{A,B} \sum_{t=1}^{m} \Delta \quad (2)$$

III. SUPERVISED NON-ASSOCIATIVE AUTOENCODERS (SNAAE)

As any system based on neural network, two operations are performed by SNAAE: offline and online phase. In the following subsections, we describe these two phases.

A. Offline phase

Let us consider $X = \{x_1^1 \cdots, x_1^M, \cdots, x_p^1, \cdots, x_p^M, \cdots x_P^1, \cdots, x_P^M\}$ the set of training set where M is the number of labeled images for training phase and P is the cardinality of classes. Among $\{x_p^1, \cdots, x_p^M\}$ (samples images corresponding to class p), a reference image is chosen to be the target image (Figure 1-c). Offline phase is then performed according to 2.

B. Online phase

During online phase, when an input query image x_q is presented, the SNAAE first reconstruct the reference image $\hat{x}$. $\hat{x}$ class is then evaluated by corelation techniques [9] between all reference images and $\hat{x}$.

IV. EXPERIMENTS AND RESULTS

In this set of experiment, we have first evaluated SNAAE on the MNIST datasets [10]. We consider just 1, 3, 5, 10, 100, 500 randomly chosen labeled samples per class. We then evaluated our approach on the test dataset. Table I reports the results. We may observe that on MNIST datasets, our SNAAE proposed model achieve good accuracies, outperforming the ones obtained by the Convolutional Neural Network (CNN) models [11]. In Figure 2, the performance of our approach is compared to CNN more precisely.

TABLE I. FEW-SHOT LEARNING: CLASSIFICATION ACCURACY OF SNAAE AGAINST BASELINE CNN ON THE MNIST

	SNAAE	CNN
1-shot	**49.38** ±4.26	18.83 ±4.26
3-shot	**61.26** ±4.26	20.63 ±2.75
5-shot	**69.99** ±1.15	20.95 ±4.02
7-shot	**76.75** ±2.13	28.33 ±1.87
10-shot	**83.06** ±1.82	31.52 ±5.73
100-shot	**96.49** ±0.19	83.53 ±4.14
200-shot	**97.63** ±0.15	90.54 ±0.54
500-shot	**98.71** ±0.16	94.78 ±0.30
full-shot	**99.37** ±0.05	98.62 ±0.09

As shown in Figure 2, our method greatly exceeds the performance of a convolutional network when few data are available.

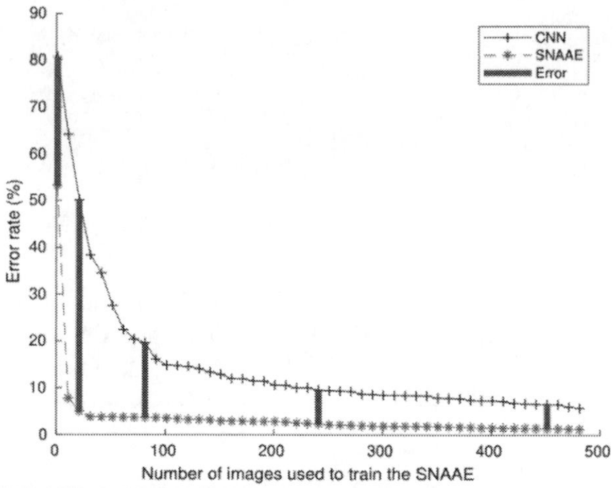

Figure 2. Error rate curve comparing SNAAE to CNN. As illustrated in this figure, for 1, 21, 81, 241, 451 images used to train the SNAAE, the difference between CNN's error rate and SNAAE one are respectively 27.46, 45.14, 15.96, 7.26, 5.16.

V. CONCLUSION

In this paper, we introduce SNAAE (Supervised Non-Associative Autoencoders), taking inspiration from the human world. SNAAE is capable to successfully perform the few-shot learning task, without the need of having prior knowledge neither unlabeled data. When unlabeled data is unavailable, SNAAE offers very good performance. In our proposed method, SNAAE, evaluated on MNIST, need only 500 images per class (less than 10% of the whole dataset) to surpass the cnn's performance.

REFERENCES

[1] G. Koch, R. Zemel, and R. Salakhutdinov, "Siamese neural networks for one-shot image recognition," in ICML Deep Learning Workshop, vol. 2, 2015.

[2] O. Vinyals, C. Blundell, T. Lillicrap, D. Wierstra et al., "Matching networks for one shot learning," in Advances in neural information processing systems, 2016, pp. 3630–3638.

[3] Y. Bengio, P. Lamblin, D. Popovici, and H. Larochelle, "Greedy layer-wise training of deep networks," in Advances in neural information processing systems, 2007, pp. 153–160.

[4] D. P. Kingma and M. Welling, "Auto-encoding variational bayes," arXiv preprint arXiv:1312.6114, 2013.

[5] Y. Pu, Z. Gan, R. Henao, X. Yuan, C. Li, A. Stevens, and L. Carin, "Variational autoencoder for deep learning of images, labels and captions," in Advances in neural information processing systems, 2016, pp. 2352–2360.

[6] D. E. Rumelhart, G. E. Hinton, and R. J. Williams, "Learning internal representations by error propagation," California Univ San Diego La Jolla Inst for Cognitive Science, Tech. Rep., 1985.

[7] E. Oja, "Simplified neuron model as a principal component analyzer," Journal of mathematical biology, vol. 15, no. 3, 1982, pp. 267–273.

[8] P. Baldi, "Autoencoders, unsupervised learning, and deep architectures," in Proceedings of ICML workshop on unsupervised and transfer learning, 2012, pp. 37–49.

[9] A. Alfalou and C. Brosseau, "Understanding correlation techniques for face recognition: from basics to applications," in Face Recognition. InTech, 2010.

[10] Y. LeCun and C. Cortes, "MNIST handwritten digit database," 2010. [Online]. Available: http://yann.lecun.com/exdb/mnist/

[11] F. Chollet et al., "Keras. h ps," github. com/fchollet/keras, 2015.

Cognitive Decision Support for Industrial Product Life Cycles: A Position Paper

Stefan Thalmann[‖]**, Heimo Gursch[†], Josef Suschnigg*, Milot Gashi*, Helmut Ennsbrunner[‡],
Anna Katharina Fuchs[§], Tobias Schreck **, Belgin Mutlu *, Jürgen Mangler[¶], Gerti Kappl[††¶], Christian Huemer [††¶],
and Stefanie Lindstaedt [**†]

*Pro2Future, Graz, Austria
‖University of Graz, Austria
†Know-Center, Graz, Austria
‡Fronius International, Pettenbach, Austria
§AVL List, Graz, Austria
¶Center For Digital Production, Vienna, Austria
** Graz University of Technology, Graz, Austria
†† TU Wien, Vienna, Austria

email: stefan.thalmann@uni-graz.at, josef.suschnigg@pro2future.at, milot.gashi@pro2future.at

Abstract—**Current trends in manufacturing lead to more intelligent products, produced in global supply chains in shorter cycles, taking more and complex requirements into account. To manage this increasing complexity, cognitive decision support systems, building on data analytic approaches and focusing on the product life cycle, stages seem a promising approach. With two high-tech companies (world market leader in their domains) from Austria, we are approaching this challenge and jointly develop cognitive decision support systems for three real world industrial use cases. Within this position paper, we introduce our understanding of cognitive decision support and we introduce three industrial use cases, focusing on the requirements for cognitive decision support. Finally, we describe our preliminary solution approach for each use case and our next steps.**

Keywords–Product Life Cycle; Validation; Big Data Value Chain.

I. Introduction

Manufacturers are experiencing the request for ever more intelligent products in shorter cycles from their customers. At the same time, manufacturers are also facing increasing cost pressures from global supply chains and increasingly complex regulatory requirements. Consequently, a holistic view of the Product Life Cycle (PLC) is a necessity to analyse and to manage these conflicting requirements. PLC management considers information describing the design, development, validation, production, usage, maintenance and disposal phase of a product. The collected data from these stages is not limited to data directly related to the design of the product, e.g., specifications, or material usage. Moreover, it includes aspects related to the product (e.g., change orders, procedures, suppliers, workflows, etc.), as well as aspects related to the product (e.g., change orders, procedures, suppliers, or workflows) [1] [2].

Collecting this data is a first step. Importantly, the data provides the opportunity to extract valuable knowledge from it to derive insights significant enough to trigger improvements on any stage of the product life cycle. Hence, data analytics approaches can help to extract actionable knowledge from the data, laying the foundation for a better understanding of the involved processes. Depending on the complexity, coverage and scale of the product and its life cycle, the extracted knowledge can be complex and manifold. Decision Support Systems (DSS) are intended to refine and present the extracted knowledge, since they select the right information for a person working on a particular task in a given stage of a product life cycle [3] [4]. Based data analytic approaches they are also named data driven DSS [5].

This paper reports from research efforts of a consortium formed by industry and academia to tackle this challenge, specifically, the research center Pro2Future and the industrial partners AVL LIST GmbH (AVL) and Fronius International GmbH (Fronius). Both industrial partners aim to leverage the potential of cognitive DSS based on data analytic approaches. AVL and Fronius are already adopting the Internet of Things (IoT) paradigm by creating connected products, which are constantly collecting data about their usage. This creates the option of new data driven approaches towards cognitive DSS, which we investigate in three different use cases. Each of the use cases offers the option to research various aspects of cognitive DSS, applied to a specific application domain. Due to the importance and the complexity, we investigate novel approaches outlined in this paper. The strategic goal of this joint project is to investigate the potential of cognitive DSS in the context of the PLC in industry.

This paper is organised as follows: The second section gives a brief overview of research conducted in either cognitive DSS and the product life cycle. The third section describes three use cases on how engineers can be supported in their work by DSS. Based on the use cases, the forth section discusses difficulties in integrating such systems into the industry, whereas the last section gives an outlook for future work of the three use cases separately.

II. Background

A. Cognitive Decision Support Systems

The overarching aim of decision support is to give users the support for making better decisions [6]. Decision support is particularly relevant for complex decision making problems, where human deciders cannot process all relevant data in time and in full detail for the decision, due to data volume, velocity or complexity. Current developments, including IoT or Industry 4.0, lead to an overwhelming amount of data available for decision making [7]. Consequently, the demand for decision support, during the whole decision process, also increases [5]. To handle the complexity and volume of such data driven decision problems, the decision making needs to be supported by Information Technology (IT) [8].

DSS aim to help decision makers in utilising data and models in solving unstructured or semi-structured problems, to improve the decision quality [10]. A common approach focuses on understanding the decision problem first, and then breaks down the decision-making process into several subprocesses [11]. These smaller problems can then be addressed by mathematical or algorithmic solutions [12], after the decision has been structured [13]. The disadvantage of this "classical" DSS is, that they are designed for one specific decision problem and that it is difficult to adapt them to new or changed decision problems [14]. However, the digitisation of industrial processes demands a high level of adaptability and flexibility [15]. Hence, more flexible and cognitive approaches, applicable to huge data sets with varying properties and inherent format variety, are needed [16].

Cognitive computing, in general, aims to develop coherent, unified, universal mechanisms, which are able to adapt to new situations and are inspired by the human mind [17]. More specifically, cognitive systems rebuild aspects of human thinking while adding the ability to handle big data sets [18]. Especially, the ability to handle big data sets is crucial for the new emerging data-based decision problems. In the scope of DSS, a cognitive system can give contextual insights from the model, which is able to generate hypotheses in terms of giving possible explanations, and to continuously learn from the input data over time [14]. Summing up, in the context of our work we define:

Cognitive DSS provide universal mechanisms capable of adapting to changing data sets, to improve the decision quality. Thereby, universal mechanisms refer to the ability to continuously learn from the input data and to generate hypotheses based on this learning. Improvement in the decision quality means, that cognitive DSS present insights from big data sets to decision makers in such a way, that the decision quality increases.

B. Product Life Cycle

The PLC is a process describing stages of a product from conceptional design, over production and usage, to the end of life [2]. Due to the so-called forth industrial revolution, *big data* plays an increasingly important role in the modern industry and offers potential benefits for several industry sectors [19]. The usage of data can create value for industry in many ways including increased productivity, better product quality and higher competitiveness, on both the customer and company side [20]. Since each of the process stages are independent, it is necessary to implement a data-value chain for each of the product life cycle stages separately [21]. Figure 1 depicts the relation between the PLC, the big data value chain and how data and knowledge are exchanged between the two processes [9]. This work picks up on these ideas and focuses on the data usage process for the PLC validation stage, the production stage and the in-use/service stage.

III. Use Cases

The following use cases explain data usage in several stages of the specific PLCs of our industry partners, implementing cognitive decision support in different ways.

A. Powertrain Verification and Validation

1) Context: An important aspect of AVL's engineering services is the Verification and Validation (VV) of powertrain prototypes for automotive applications. This VV activity follows the development stage in the PLC. The use case introduced by [9] describes how data usage for VV can be implemented. Verification is a quality assurance process to provide that the product fulfils its intended requirements [22] ("Having developed the right product"). Requirements can be driven by user needs (e.g., fuel or energy consumption, engine performance and durability), but also imposed by legal requirements (e.g., noise emission) [23]. Validation asks, if the intended functionality can be provided over the product lifetime ("Having developed the product right"). VV for powertrains can be either realised in a testing environment, so-called testbeds, or in a customer usage-oriented test, based on customer-oriented usage profiles (e.g., on road). During such tests, hundreds of sensor signals are collected from the powertrain operation as a function of time and/or powertrain controls, like throttle control. These sensors provide data about e.g., engine temperature, exhaust gas composition, pressures, torque and other engineering parameters. Depending on the purpose of a specific VV target, those tests can take thousands of hours for every tested prototype instance under controlled conditions, leading up to a tremendous amount of data. The following use case is located in the early VV stage of the PLC and focuses on functional requirements (mainly verification), but also durability requirements (mainly validation) of an automotive engine. The tests investigated in this use case are all conducted on automotive test beds, where the engine is operated at predefined load conditions.

2) Problem Description: A main challenge in powertrain testing is to support engineers in assessing the condition (health) of engines from large amounts of sensor measurement data taken during test cycles. Many parameters (channels) are measured during testing. A channel contains a value (also called sample point) typically every 100 ms which corresponds to a 10 Hz sample rate, but can have sample rates up to multiple kHz. Depending on the test setup, up to hundreds of channels can be recorded. It is a challenge for engineers, working with this data, to observe every channel and to extract relevant information from it. Depending on the test case, channel measurements may be noisy, or external events may happen which only get captured indirectly in the measurements. As a simple solution, engineers manually select a number of channels based on experience, and define thresholds for simple anomaly detection [24]. The challenge of this approach is, that the thresholds for each sensor need to be defined manually, based on individual experience. This can be done by experienced engineers for some well-known sensors, but not for all sensors. Furthermore, there are complex relationships between the channels, involving correlations and lead-lag relationships, as they are not independent from each other. DSS for powertrain

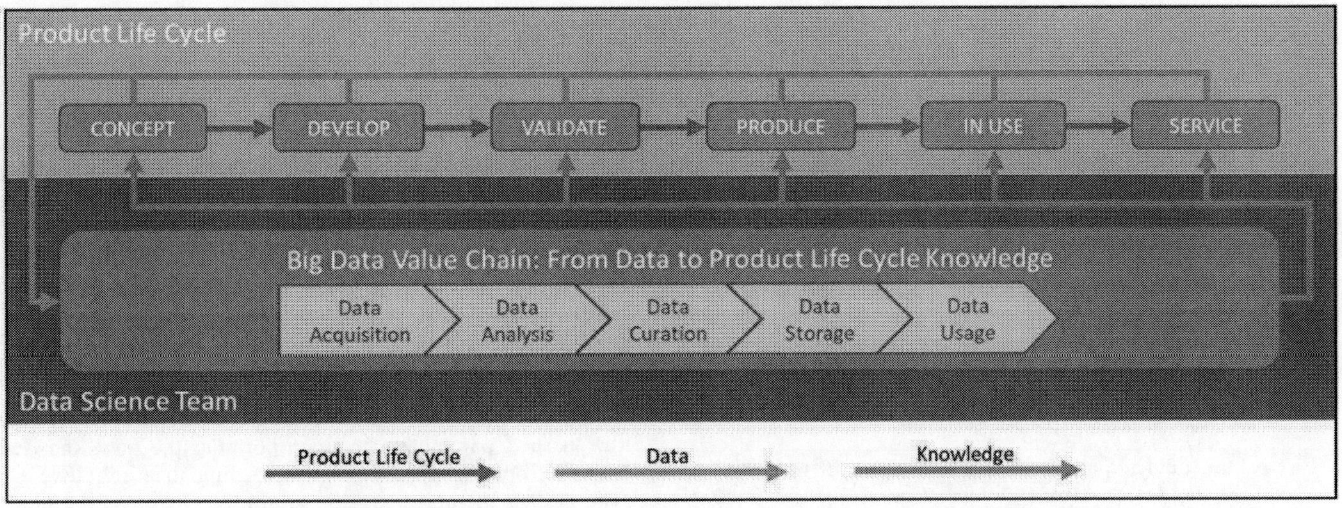

Figure 1. Transfer of knowledge between product life cycle stages and big data value chain by [9].

testing needs to help the test engineer in monitoring relevant channels, guiding her or him to relationships and anomalies as they occur, and predict possible failure cases early on for test intervention, if needed.

3) Solution Approach: Powertrains are increasingly complex systems and the know-how of domain experts is an indispensable resource for a condition monitoring system. Research on time series analysis has provided numerous algorithms to detect trends, patterns and outliers in data [25]. We follow an approach based on interactive visual data analysis (or visual analytics). The idea is to combine data analysis algorithms with appropriate visual representations, from which the expert can efficiently perceive patterns found by the algorithms, and by which he or she can interact with model parameters, and drill down into data details for confirmation and exploration tasks. Visual analytics applications for industrial sensor data have been developed for several applications recently. In [26], a general approach for industrial sensor data has been proposed. [27] focuses on predictive maintenance in the production stage and [28] focuses on the in-use phase of the PLC, describing more specific solutions. The SignalLens system [29] allows to monitor large time series using an efficient focus-and-context visualization and representing features of interest to guide the visual inspection by the expert. Approaches such as these, aim for scalability of the analysis with large amounts of data. In general, it is promising to combine the strengths of human experts (background knowledge, abstract problem-solving, etc.) and of computational data analysis (e.g., fast algorithmic search for well-specified patterns in large data) [30]. To visualise time-dependent data several promising techniques exist, including HorizonGraphs, RiverTheme Graphs or Heat Maps [31], which could support the expert in exploring large amounts of sensor data.

In addition to the visualisation techniques, computational models can be trained for classification, regression, clustering or pattern recognition. Since engineers can have a better understanding about the involved processes and parameters, they should be supported in distinguishing between rare events and true anomalies. In an unsupervised machine learning scenario, the engineer can be supported by visually highlighting potentially interesting outlying data and data patterns which occur frequently. Based on such comparison, the engineer can decide if an anomaly is relevant and needs further inspection, or is transient. We are currently experimenting with showing composite anomaly scores for a sequence of test cycles. By comparing the measurements between cycles, experts can quickly recognise larger differences in measurements, hinting at possible anomalies for further inspection. Figure 2 illustrates a glyph-based design to visualise anomalies in industrial test cycles. It aggregates two different algorithms for anomaly detection (top and bottom circular sector) and encodes the anomaly scores by the intensity of red for visual perception of humans. This design can be adapted for other datasets, as long as they are collected from cyclic data, since those cycles has been identified to be suitable as the granularity level for data visualisation and analysis. However, cyclic data is reasoned by the repetitive behaviour of many industrial tasks. Therefore, the concept could be applicable on other industrial domains as well.

The interaction of a domain expert with the visualisation can be learned by the model in terms of parameter refinement and future decision support. This learning of domain expertise in a cognitive model is also the key to make the desired DSS, based on visual analytics, cognitive. At the end of the workflow new knowledge is discovered, can be applied to new products and lead to a constantly improving condition monitoring system.

B. Welding Machine End Of Line

1) Context: The Final Test System (FTS), at the end of the manufacturing process, is a crucial stage concerning the PLC. In our application, every produced device must accomplish a successful quality check by the FTS before it is sent to the customer. In other words, each produced device has to undergo a quality test as a final inspection by the FTS.

The FTS fully automatically measures about 300 different parameters and the process is supervised by an experienced employee. For the test, three possible results are specified:

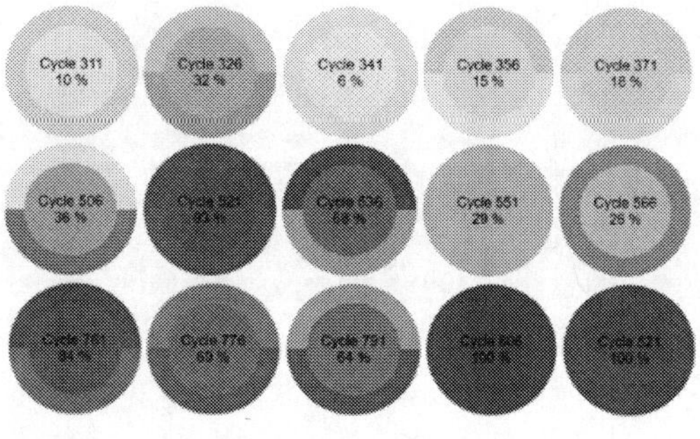

Figure 2. Glyph-based visualisation of anomaly scores. The outer segments show different anomaly scores, while the center shows an aggregate score.

Firstly, the device passes all measurements in the first run. Secondly, the device passes the test successfully after multiple iterations of the test and revisions. Thirdly, the device fails, even after possible re-takes of measurements. In the first and the second case, the device is declared to work properly and is ready for shipping to the customer. In the third case, the device will be handed over to the repair centre for further investigations. Hence, the FTS collects a large amount of data about the devices and their conditions when passing or failing the test.

2) Problem Description: When a device has an incident, which cannot be solved by the customer, no FTS is at hand to investigate the actual cause of device failure. Instead, a maintenance procedure is started, and a repair team is sent to the customer to identify the cause of the failure. Once, a diagnosis is made the identified parts causing the failure will be replaced with new ones.

This diagnosis process is not trivial, since the repair team is obligated to recognise the cause direct in the field with far less sophisticated equipment than the FTS. The process of failure identification is complex and requires a knowledgeable and experienced repair team as the amount of the reliable information is small. Moreover, if the failure cause is unknown, also the needed resources (e.g., spare parts and repair time) cannot be known in advance. But particularly in our case, the number of products in the field and especially the product variants are very high. Therefore, the repair team often needs to anticipate the required resources in advance, which is time-consuming, error-prone and in turn, leads to higher costs. The objective is the creation of a cognitive DSS, which analyses the FTS data and provides decision support for the repair team in the field. The DSS should use the identified knowledge from production data to identify possible failures, based on the known device behaviour and to recommend suitable repair strategies. This system should learn from past cases, improve over time by feedback and be able to transfer the learned to new products or product variants.

3) Solution Approach: The process of the final inspection is complex regarding both the significant number of measurements and the variety of variants and options, respectively. This means, that there is only a small set of comparable measurements throughout all devices. This reduces the amount of usable data and makes the learning more difficult. Only for a small set of common device features, there is a large volume of data, but for the different options and variants there is only a small sample available. Moreover, to provide solutions that reflect the reality it is essential to consider the interdependence between multiple components required to assemble the system. Therefore, considering multi-component system challenges [32] [33] and handling these properly could grant advantages. By employing advanced applied machine learning approaches (e.g., unsupervised learning methods [34]), common behaviour amongst different variants and options can be recognised. Next, rule-based machine learning methods [35] will be applied to identify associations within the maintenance data. This step will extract additional knowledge about the service activities, which will also be incorporated in the DSS. Finally, apply acquired knowledge to recognise failures also in previously unseen devices with similar error patterns, thus supporting the repair team. Moreover, this approach will adapt the learned parameters by incorporating the new knowledge gained from the upcoming data leading to a cognitive DSS. The DSS is therefore capable to aid the worker in the field by predicting the failure causes. Hence, the repair team can better plan the needed resources thus reducing the repair costs.

C. Welding Machine Maintenance and Service

1) Context: In a modern industrial welding process, maintenance actions are required to keep the process operating at its optimal conditions. Within the welding devices, multiple sensors are integrated providing a condition monitoring of process critical parameters. Commonly the monitored parameters include information about the voltage, current, or power of each individual welding. Furthermore, information such as the configuration settings of the welding device, identification numbers of the welded component, etc. are also collected during this process. While the collection of this process data is commonly automated, collection of data about the maintenance actions taken, often require the involvement of workers. For an immaculate data collection, a data collection system is provided, which protocol the maintenance action performed on the welding device. Due to the involvement of the worker during this process, this data collection is more laborious and error-prone compared to a fully automated data collection.

2) Problem Description: A common maintenance procedure is conveyed by monitoring the welding device in-use by multiple integrated sensors. The readings from those sensors can identify the possible need for maintenance actions of various components, like changing the contact tip, cleaning the air filter, etc. These necessary maintenance actions are conducted by a worker in the manufacturing process and the execution of the maintenance action is recorded. The benefit now lies in the combined recordings of the welding processes' parameters and the recorded maintenance actions. The objective is to support the user in finding the perfect time to conduct a specific maintenance activity so that the productivity and quality of the welding process is optimal balanced. The cognitive DSS analyses the process and maintenance data to identify possible patterns within the data. These patterns are used to assist the worker by recommending suitable maintenance activities.

The main challenge in the creation of the cognitive DSS is the automated detection of the need for maintenance activities, based on data-driven solutions, considering the variety of variants and options. The product variants and options make almost all devices different, hence also potentially requiring different maintenance actions. These systems consist of multiple components, which are non-identical and dependent on each other, leading to a multi-component system.

This high variety decreases the amount of data remarkably regarding individual systems (variants and options), leading, on the one hand, to a huge amount of data on the base core of variants, and on the other hand, to small amounts of data concerning the specific variants or options.

3) Solution Approach: Both, the small data challenge and the various dependencies within multi-components need a careful handling while preparing the data. Next, the knowledge extracted from this data is used to improve the cognitive DSS, which in turn will support the workers during the decision-making process. Thus, to increase both the reliability and the performance of the devices, we propose one approach based on data mining techniques [36], such as temporal pattern mining [37] and supervised learning methods [38]. First, assuming that various variants and options are not entirely different, the aim is to identify a relevant variant by applying exploratory data analysis methods [39]. In this case, the aim is to deploy a solution for a specific variant, or subgroup, and later generalise it over all variants and options. Second, recognise patterns (e.g., temporal patterns), within the process data, and relate them to maintenance actions. Third, use the extracted knowledge from previous step, to predict perfect timing for maintenance actions. Finally, improve the prediction accuracy by considering the interdependences between components. Moreover, the DSS will learn from the actions taken and update the optimal maintenance relevant parameters regarding each component separately, leading to the creation of a dynamic optimal maintenance activities strategy over time.

IV. Discussion

The success of the project highly depends on the acceptance of the proposed cognitive DSS by the involved employees. To ensure this, we involved the potential end users from an early stage onward consciously in the project applying a participatory design approach. One important aspect to engage the end users was that the cognitive DSS is designed to support the human experts, and not to replace them [5]. Also, both our industry partners are convinced that, in the foreseeable future, humans cannot be replaced in their core processes, but need more support as work tasks become more complex. The cognitive DSS provides assistance and support by presenting insights from the analysed data, so that the domain experts can develop a better understanding of the PLC. This is an opportunity for the companies and their customers alike by improving productivity, product and support quality and, hence, increased competitiveness.

The participatory approach is not only applied during the design and roll out of the first version of our cognitive DSS itself, rather it was also very important to collect and clean the data in a participatory way. The strong engagement with the end users was necessary to build the required domain knowledge and to receive high quality feedback. This engagement created awareness of the fact, that the quality data collected during the execution of the PLC determines the decision quality and thus is the secret to the success of the DSS. The DSS can only be as good as the data it is built upon. Hence, the end users need to understand that data collection is a key activity and not only another administrative duty. Relying on strong awareness building activities, we developed well-defined data capturing processes for collecting relevant process and quality data from the end users. In doing so, we capture domain knowledge to improve the DSS over time and closing the feedback loop between the PLC and the DSS by two links. Firstly, the data from the PLC going into the DSS and, secondly, the information provided by the DSS to the workers is linked to the PLC. As a result of this cognitive element, users benefit by improved decision support in return for their efforts they spend in data collection activities.

All use cases deal with complex multi-component systems, or even systems of systems creating an immense complexity by all interactions and connections between the components. Such complex systems need to be divided into smaller parts to handle the complexity in a meaningful way. The proposed multi-component analysis is doing this by the individual estimation of the component's wear, modelling interdependences between components, and transferring of insights to different but comparable sub systems.

The described project is ambitious, complex and requires a high invest by all involved partners. Thereby, the investment is not primary in software or servers, rather than in human resources needed to achieve the required understanding and awareness for introducing cognitive DSS. This is due to the fact that continuous high-quality feedback from end users is needed to ensure the continuous learning of the cognitive DSS. Despite of these remarkable efforts, the company partners are convinced that improved decision support will pay off. Even more they believe that this is key to be successful in a globalised and digitised world.

V. Outlook and Future Work

We plan to further investigate different promising directions within our industrial use cases described above. Therefore, in this section we briefly discuss the future work on each of the three use cases separately.

A. Powertrain VV use case

It is a common approach in powertrain VV to define test cycles with given engine speed and engine torque over time. In these test cycles, the engine usage is simulated and repeated until the required total test time is reached. For example, in a durability test, such cycles take two hours and will be repeated till the total time of two thousand hours is reached. We base our design idea on the assumption that those cycles are highly comparable and elaborate on this in future research. In theory, all sensors should return similar measurements for constant engine speed and engine torque. However, some uncertainties need to be investigated in more detail. Over time, the measurements of channels can differ by wearing of the powertrain, environmental changes like temperature, exchanging parts, faulty sensors or different undocumented calibrations. Recognition of many of those anomalies should be done by data analysis. For this purpose, we will investigate if test cycles can be defined as a granularity model for the visualisation and the subsequent data analysis approach. This combination seems promising to highlight anomalies and to further identify if the conditions of the powertrain worsen over time. To judge the conditions correctly, the system needs to learn from user feedback so that the systems capture domain knowledge over time. An idea for user feedback is to allow experts to select and label data patterns corresponding to certain events. The labels can be taken as training data to train supervised data analysis methods, e.g., classifiers to apply to new data.

Preliminary findings show promising results in applying correlation-based anomaly detection. In this first version, a visualisation depicts the correlation matrix for every channel combination of every cycle. By subtracting the matrices from the reference cycle's correlation matrix, the deviation of two cycles can be visualised as a heat map. Also, deviating channels can be intuitively identified by engineers and further analysed. Another task for future work, is to investigate and apply several anomaly detection algorithms. Finding the best model, regarding predictability of data, for different applications, is a hard task. Visual analytics offers the capability of engineers to interact with data through information visualisation and the underlying data analysis. Suitable techniques need to be reviewed, and through design studies [40] in collaboration with the end user engineers, further investigated and developed. Consequently, the design needs to be evaluated, whereas pair analytics [41], seems to be a feasible approach to evaluate visual analytics applications.

B. End of line use case

The small data challenge in our end of line use case, i.e., the high variety of products and the small data sets of reference measurements is a challenge for data driven approaches. In the solution approach, we aim to identify common parameters and values behaving similar of all different components of product variants which are comparable. Finding the right level of detail for the multi-component systems in the project is also described as a major challenge in the literature [32]. Our approach based on exploratory data analysis first aims to identify relationships and interdependencies. Next, the aim is to recognise common error and fault indicators amongst different product variants by applying unsupervised learning approaches. Moreover, rule-based approaches are considered to recognise patterns within the available data extracting additional knowledge about the components and the service activities. Lastly, over the time the decision variables will be adapted every time new information is provided so that the DSS learns.

C. Welding use case

The small data challenge also applies to the welding use case. To solve this challenge for this use case, also similarities between individual components and modules are identified with the same means used in the other two use cases. Hence, the first step is to identify relevant variant, or group of variants by applying exploratory data analysis methods. Next, within an appropriate group of variants, so called clusters, machine learning approaches will be performed to extract indicators to predict the wear of different components. These indicators are based on monitoring information obtained automatically and maintenance action logs provided by the workers conducting the maintenance. Both data is jointly analysed by frequent pattern mining approaches to find sequences of maintenance actions on the component and cluster level. Lastly, the learned parameters (e.g., maintenance strategy) will be adapted every time new information describing the current health state of the system and components are provided, respectively. Another important aspect of our future work is to investigate how the insights we gain can be used for process improvement. More specifically, how these insights can be used to improve business processes representing a concrete PLC during design and run time. For this purpose, we want to create an interface to the process management tool CENTURIO developed in the research center CDP [42].

ACKNOWLEDGMENT

This research work is done by Pro^{2}Future, AVL List and Fronius International. Pro^{2}Future is funded within the Austrian COMET Program-Competence Centers for Excellent Technologies- under the auspices of the Austrian Federal Ministry of Transport, Innovation and Technology, the Austrian Federal Ministry for Digital and Economic Affairs and of the Provinces of Upper Austria and Styria. COMET is managed by the Austrian Research Promotion Agency FFG.

REFERENCES

[1] M. Eigner and R. Stelzer, Product Lifecycle Management, 2nd ed. Berlin, Germany: Springer, 2009.

[2] S. Terzi, A. Bouras, D. Dutta, M. Garetti, and D. Kiritsis, "Product lifecycle management from its history to its new role," Int. J. Product Lifecycle Management., vol. 4, no. 4, 2010, pp. 360–389.

[3] S. LaValle, E. Lesser, R. Shockley, M. S. Hopkins, and N. Kruschwitz, "Big data, analytics and the path from insights to value," MIT Sloan Management Review, vol. 52, no. 2, 2011, pp. 20–31.

[4] Y. Zhang, S. Ren, Y. Liu, T. Sakao, and D. Huisingh, "A framework for big data driven product lifecycle management," Journal of Cleaner Production, vol. 159, 2017, pp. 229–240.

[5] S. Thalmann, "Data driven decision support," it-Information Technology, vol. 60, no. 4, 2018, pp. 179–181.

[6] S. Alter, "A work system view of dss in its fourth decade," Decision Support Systems, vol. 38, 12 2004, pp. 319–327.

[7] F. Kache and S. Seuring, "Challenges and opportunities of digital information at the intersection of big data analytics and supply chain management," International Journal of Operations & Production Management, vol. 37, no. 1, 2017, pp. 10–36.

[8] S. Thalmann, Decision Support Framework for Selecting Techniques to Prepare Knowledge Elements for Adaptive Use. Innsbruck: Innsbruck University Press, 2012.

[9] D. Stanisavljevic, M. Rosenberger, G. Lechner, S. Körner, R. Kern, B. Jeitler, and A. Stocker, "Ein Industrie 4.0-Use Case in der Motorenproduktion," Mensch und Computer 2018 - Workshopband, 2018.

[10] R. H. Sprague, "A framework for the development of decision support systems," Management Information Sciences Quarterly, vol. 4, 12 1980, pp. 1–26.

[11] M. Carter and C. C. Price, Operations research: A Practical Introduction. Crc Press, 2000.

[12] V. L. Sauter, Decision Support Systems for Business Intelligence: Second Edition. Wiley, 2014.

[13] M. A. Eierman, F. Niederman, and C. Adams, "DSS theory: A model of constructs and relationships," Decision Support Systems, 1995, pp. 1 – 26.

[14] J. Hurwitz, M. Kaufman, and A. Bowles, Cognitive Computing and Big Data Analytics, 1st ed. Wiley, 2015.

[15] M. Hermann, T. Pentek, and B. Otto, "Design Principles for Industrie 4.0 Scenarios," in Proceedings of the 2016 49th Hawaii International Conference on System Sciences (HICSS), ser. HICSS '16. Washington, DC, USA: IEEE Computer Society, 2016, pp. 3928–3937.

[16] S. Thalmann, J. Mangler, T. Schreck, C. Huemer, M. Streit, F. Pauker, G. Weichhart, S. Schulte, C. Kittl, C. Pollak et al., "Data analytics for industrial process improvement a vision paper," in 2018 IEEE 20th Conference on Business Informatics (CBI), vol. 2. IEEE, 2018, pp. 92–96.

[17] D. S. Modha et al., "Cognitive computing," Communications of the ACM, vol. 54, no. 8, 2011, pp. 62–71.

[18] Y. Chen, E. Argentinis, and G. Weber, "IBM Watson: How Cognitive Computing Can Be Applied to Big Data Challenges in Life Sciences Research," Clinical Therapeutics, vol. 38, no. 4, 2016, pp. 688–701.

[19] S. Yin and O. Kaynak, "Big Data for Modern Industry: Challenges and Trends," Proceedings of the IEEE, vol. 103, no. 2, 2015, pp. 143–146.

[20] James et al., "Big data: The next frontier for innovation, competition, and productivity," McKinsey Global Institute, 2011, p. 156.

[21] E. Curry, "The big data value chain: Definitions, concepts, and theoretical approaches," in New Horizons for a Data-Driven Economy: A Roadmap for Usage and Exploitation of Big Data in Europe, 2016.

[22] P. G. Maropoulos and D. Ceglarek, "Design verification and validation in product lifecycle," CIRP Annals - Manufacturing Technology, vol. 59, no. 2, 2010, pp. 740–759.

[23] E. Armengaud, "Industry 4.0 as Digitalization over the Entire Product Lifecycle: Opportunities in the Automotive Domain," 2017. [Online]. Available: http://link.springer.com/10.1007/978-3-319-64218-5

[24] V. Chandola, A. Banerjee, and V. Kumar, "Anomaly detection: A survey," ACM computing surveys (CSUR), vol. 41, no. 3, 2009, p. 15.

[25] M. Gupta, J. Gao, C. C. Aggarwal, and J. Han, "Outlier detection for temporal data: A survey," IEEE Transactions on Knowledge and Data Engineering, vol. 26, no. 9, 2014, pp. 2250–2267.

[26] S. Kimani, M. Leva, M. Mecella, and T. Catarci, "Visualization of multidimensional sensor data in industrial engineering," in 2013 17th International Conference on Information Visualisation, July 2013, pp. 156–161.

[27] W. Wu, Y. Zheng, K. Chen, X. Wang, and N. Cao, "A visual analytics approach for equipment condition monitoring in smart factories of process industry," in 2018 IEEE Pacific Visualization Symposium (PacificVis), April 2018, pp. 140–149.

[28] G. Sharma et al., "Multi-sensor visual analytics supported by machine-learning models," in 2015 IEEE International Conference on Data Mining Workshop (ICDMW), 2015, pp. 668–674.

[29] R. Kincaid, "Signallens: Focus+context applied to electronic time series," IEEE Transactions on Visualization and Computer Graphics, vol. 16, no. 6, Nov 2010, pp. 900–907.

[30] Keim et al., "Visual analytics: Definition, process, and challenges," in Information visualization. Springer, 2008, pp. 154–175.

[31] W. Aigner, S. Miksch, H. Schumann, and C. Tominski, Visualization of Time-Oriented Data, 1st ed. Springer, 2011.

[32] K.-A. Nguyen, P. Do, and A. Grall, "Multi-level predictive maintenance for multi-component systems," Reliability Engineering & System Safety, vol. 144, 2015, pp. 83–94.

[33] A. Van Horenbeek and L. Pintelon, "A dynamic predictive maintenance policy for complex multi-component systems," Reliability Engineering & System Safety, vol. 120, 2013, pp. 39–50.

[34] T. Hastie, R. Tibshirani, and J. Friedman, "Unsupervised learning," in The elements of statistical learning. Springer, 2009, pp. 485–585.

[35] B. Liu, W. Hsu, and Y. Ma, "Integrating classification and association rule mining," in Proceedings of the Fourth International Conference on Knowledge Discovery and Data Mining, ser. KDD'98. AAAI Press, 1998, pp. 80–86.

[36] D. J. Hand, "Data mining," Encyclopedia of Environmetrics, vol. 2, 2006.

[37] I. Batal, D. Fradkin, J. Harrison, F. Moerchen, and M. Hauskrecht, "Mining recent temporal patterns for event detection in multivariate time series data," in Proceedings of the 18th ACM SIGKDD international conference on Knowledge discovery and data mining. ACM, 2012, pp. 280–288.

[38] M. Kuhn and K. Johnson, Applied predictive modeling. Springer, 2013.

[39] C. H. Yu, "Exploratory data analysis," Methods, vol. 2, 1977, pp. 131–160.

[40] M. Sedlmair, M. Meyer, and T. Munzner, "Design study methodology: Reflections from the trenches and the stacks," IEEE Transactions on Visualization and Computer Graphics, vol. 18, no. 12, Dec 2012, pp. 2431–2440.

[41] R. Arias-Hernandez, L. T. Kaastra, T. M. Green, and B. Fisher, "Pair analytics: Capturing reasoning processes in collaborative visual analytics," in Proceedings of the 2011 44th Hawaii International Conference on System Sciences, ser. HICSS '11. IEEE Computer Society, 2011, pp. 1–10.

[42] F. Pauker, J. Mangler, S. Rinderle-Ma, and C. Pollak, "centurio.work - modular secure manufacturing orchestration," in Proceedings of the Dissertation Award, Demonstration, and Industrial Track at BPM 2018 co-located with 16th International Conference on Business Process Management (BPM 2018), Sydney, Australia, 2018., 2018, pp. 164–171.

EEG based Valence Emotion Recognition by the Cognitive Model of Emotion

Jun-Su Kang and Minho Lee*
School of Electronics Engineering
Kyungpook National University
Taegu, South Korea
E-mails: {wkjuns, mholee}@gmail.com

Abstract—**In this study, we propose a valence emotion recognition model based on the cognitive model of emotion. The cognitive model of emotion consists of a perceptual system, body response system, schematic system, and propositional system. In the implementation, we build the computational model without the perceptual system. To demonstrate our proposed method, we design an experiment on valence emotion task. From the results, we confirm that the proposed model gives the best results with the most significant electrode pairs (MSP) 15 at the theta band.**

Keywords-EEG; emotion; cognitive model of emotion; phase locking value.

I. Introduction

In day to day life, humans encode their emotional state in activities such as writing, drawing, speaking, etc. Therefore, decoding or understanding their emotional state plays an essential role in creating social linkages and supporting efficient service [1]. The encoded information of emotion is represented through explicit and implicit expressions [2].

Proposed method uses an EEG signal which is a kind of implicit expressions to recognize human valence emotion as two classes (positive and negative). EEG signal is acquired from the scalp-level of the brain non-invasively and provides good temporal resolution. It is important to identify the differences in brain activities in different regions of the brain to understand brain cognition in EEG analysis. Connectivity analysis can identify the differences in brain activities in different sensor locations of EEG device [3]. Among several connectivity calculations, Phase Locking Value (PLV) method [4] has an advantage over other methods because it is more discriminative. EEG phase differences are used to estimate conduction velocity and synaptic integration time [5]. Phase information is also robust to fluctuation in amplitude. PLV is a possible means to represent the synchronization of EEG signals. In our previous work [6], we successfully classify the human intention using PLV which only considers the relative phase between two different sensors.

The proposed emotion understanding system is based on Leventhal's cognitive model of emotion processing [7], which is primarily derived from the perceptual motor model of emotion. We apply the PLV extraction as the body response system, Fuzzy C-Means clustering (FCM) [8] and Adaptive Neuro-Fuzzy Inference System (ANFIS) [9] are applied for the schematic system and the propositional system, respectively. ANFIS is the implementation of the fuzzy inference system to adaptive networks for developing fuzzy rules with suitable membership functions given the inputs and outputs. This paper is organized as follows. In Section 2, the proposed method is presented. In Section 3, the experimental setup is represented. Results and conclusion are presented in Section 4 and 5, respectively.

II. Proposed Method

In the proposed hierarchical and multilevel process theory, Leventhal attempted to incorporate biological as well as conceptual aspects of emotion processing. Figure 1 shows the cognitive model of emotion which consists of four systems, and Figure 2 shows the computational model of emotion corresponding to Figure 1. First, the stimuli are perceived through senses (sight, hearing, touch, etc.) in Perceptual system. Then body responds implicitly (feeling, thought, etc.) or explicitly (facial expression, voice, tone, gesture, etc.) to stimuli in Body response system. Third, in the Schematic system the emotional clusters for building abstracts of current emotional states are made. Finally, in the last system, called Propositional system, labels are given to these emotional clusters.

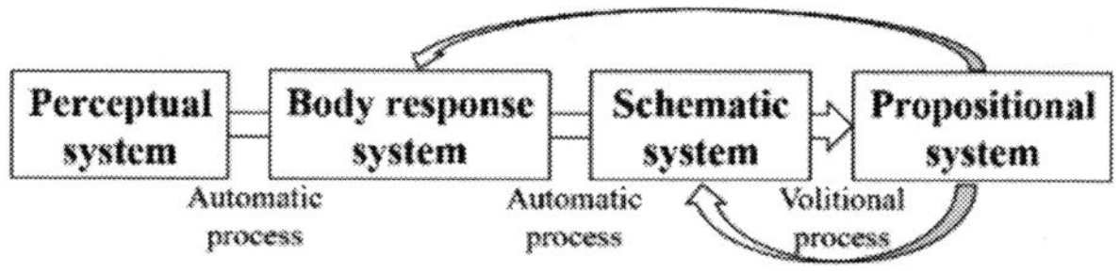

Figure 1. Cognitive model of emotion

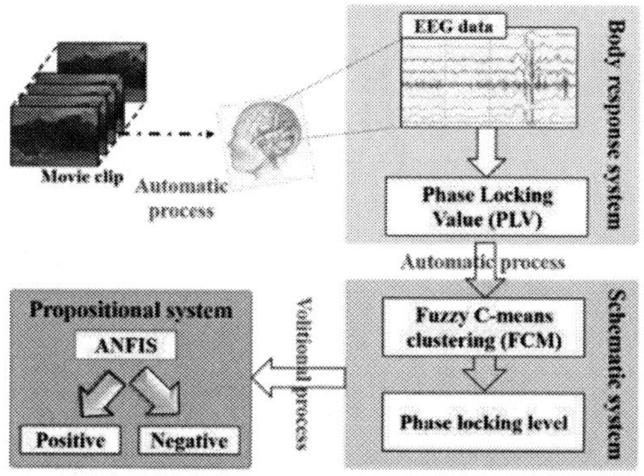

Figure 2. Overall structure of the proposed model

In this study, implementation of the perceptual system remains as future work. In the body response system, which is the first system in our model, the EEG signal is recorded when participants are watching a movie clip. From the acquired EEG signal, the emotional features are extracted by using PLV, which calculates the phase stability between two different EEG sensors. After extracting the PLV feature, MSP are selected [6]. We then build the PLV tensor to represent the dynamics of brain state. The second system in our model is called schematic system wherein the abstract representations of emotional features such as the belongingness of each representation (level of phase stability) are formed by FCM. The PLV descriptor is clustered in three clusters using FCM. The last system of our model is called propositional system wherein the decision process is performed by ANFIS.

III. Experimental Setup

A. Dataset description

Twenty-five healthy university students (twenty-four males and one female) participated in the study. Their mean age was 22.70 years (±2.01 years). Data of 7 participants could not be analyzed because of missed-trigger information (1 participant, male) and noise in EEG signals (6 participants, 5 males and 1 female). There are total 6 blocks for emotion task. Figure 3 shows experiment procedure of this study.

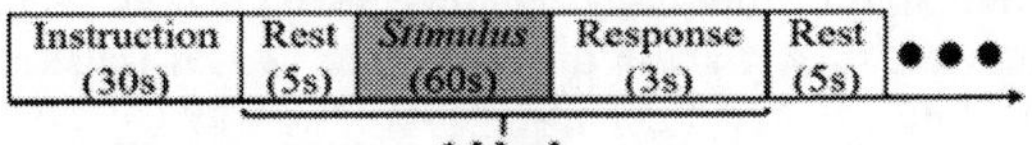

Figure 3. Experiment procedure

After watching the emotion eliciting movie, the subjects were asked to rate the video on a discrete scale ranging from 1 to 7. If the response score of a subject is over 4, we consider it as positive status, otherwise, it is considered as negative status.

B. Preprocessing of EEG data

EEG Data is acquired by Biosemi ActiveTwo system. Total 32 channels (Fp1/2, AF3/4, F3/4/7/8, Fz, FC1/2/5/6, C3/4, Cz, T7/8, CP1/2/5/6, P3/4/7/8, Pz, PO3/4, O1/2, and Oz) are used, and the sampling rate is set as 2048Hz. Notch filter is applied to remove the electric line noise, and bandpass filter is applied to extract the 3 to 50Hz frequency representation.

C. Data processing

PLV feature is extracted using 2.5 seconds window from the preprocessed EEG data, and FCM is applied to set the PLV level to the three membership. The output of FCM is used as an input to ANFIS. Parameters of ANFIS are default setup of MATLAB R2018b, namely the number of nodes is 12, the number of fuzzy rules are 2, etc.

IV. Results

Based on the cognitive model of emotion processing, the proposed system attempts to determine the negative and positive emotional states by EEG signals while participants watch movie clips. For the performance evaluation, subject-wise Leave-One-Out cross validation was used. In Figure 4, average results of the proposed system are summarized, and white and gray bars are average train and test accuracy, respectively.

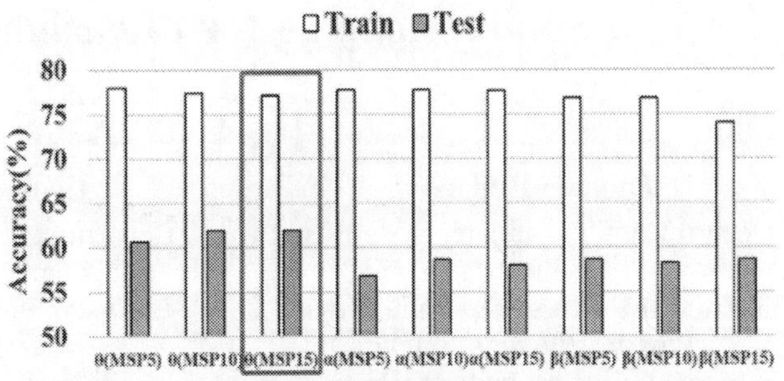

Figure 4. Average train and test performance of the proposed method according to the number of MSP

The best test accuracy (61.904%) in criteria of average accuracy is given with MSP 15 at theta frequency band.

V. Conclusion

In this study, we implemented the computational model of valence emotion classification based on the cognitive model of emotion. The proposed model was successfully implemented and the best test performance is given from MSP 15 at the theta frequency band. In the future work, we will implement the perceptual system and link this to the current computational model.

Acknowledgment

This work was supported by the National Research Foundation of Korea (NRF) grant funded by the Korea government (MSIP) (No. NRF-2016R1A2A2A05921679).

References

[1] A. Esposito, A. M. Esposito, and C. Vogel, “Needs and challenges in human computer interaction for processing social emotional information,” Pattern Recognition Letters, vol. 66, pp. 41-51, 2015.

[2] A. Wood, M. Rychlowska, S. Korb, and P. Niedenthal, “Fashioning the face: sensorimotor simulation contributes to facial expression recognition,” Trends in cognitive sciences, vol. 20, no. 3, pp. 227-240, 2016.

[3] J. Dauwels, F. Vialatte, T. Musha, A. Cichocki, “A comparative study of synchrony measures for the early diagnosis of Alzheimer’s disease based on EEG,” NeuroImage, vol. 49, no. 1, pp. 668-693, 2010.

[4] J. P. Lachaux, E. Rodriguez, J. Martinerie, and F. J. Varela, “Measuring phase synchrony in brain signals,” Human brain mapping, vol. 8, no. 4, pp. 194-208, 1999.

[5] H. Suzuki, “Phase relationships of alpha rhythm in man,” The Japanese journal of physiology, vol. 24, no. 6, pp. 569-586, 1974.

[6] J. S. Kang, U. Park, V. Gonuguntla, K. C. Veluvolu, M. Lee, “Human implicit intent recognition based on the phase synchrony of EEG signals,” Pattern Recognition Letters, vol. 66, pp. 144-152, 2015.

[7] H. Leventhal, "A perceptual-motor theory of emotion," Advances in experimental social psychology, pp. 117-182: Elsevier, 1984.

[8] J. C. Bezdek, R. Ehrlich, and W. Full, “FCM: The fuzzy c-means clustering algorithm,” Computers & Geosciences, vol. 10, no. 2-3, pp. 191-203, 1984.

[9] J. S. Jang, “ANFIS: adaptive-network-based fuzzy inference system,” IEEE transactions on systems, man, and cybernetics, vol. 23, no. 3, pp. 665-685, 1993.

Smart Shopping Cart Learning Agents Modeling And Evaluation

Dilyana Budakova
Department Of Computer Systems and Technologies
Technical University of Sofia, Branch Plovdiv, Plovdiv, Bulgaria
email: dilyana_budakova@tu-plovdiv.bg

Lyudmil Dakovski
Department of Communication & Computer Technologies
European Polytechnic University
Pernik, Bulgaria
email: lyudmil.dakovski@epu.bg

Veselka Petrova-Dimitrova
Department of Computer Systems and Technologies
Technical University of Sofia, Branch Plovdiv, Plovdiv, Bulgaria
email: vesi_s_petrova@yahoo.com

Abstract—**The paper describes the design, implementation and user evaluation of utility and goal-based intelligent learning agents for smart shopping cart. In keeping user's shopping list, they guide visitors through the shops and the goods in the shopping center or according to new promotions in the shops, respectively. It is envisaged that concrete implementation of the shopping agents will be running on each shopping cart in the shopping centers. The k-d decision tree and reinforcement-learning algorithm are used for agents learning. The task environment is partially observable, cooperative, deterministic, and a multi - agent environment, with some stochastic and uncertainty elements. It incorporates text-to-speech and speech recognizing technology, Bluetooth low energy technology, holographic technology, picture exchange communication system. Machine learning techniques are used for agents modeling. This kind of intelligent system enables people with different communication capabilities to navigate in large buildings and in particular to shop in the large shopping centers and maximize user comfort. Some initial user opinions of the shopping cart agents are presented.**

Keywords – Smart shopping cart virtual learning agent; machine learning; reinforcement learning; decision tree; Ambient intelligence; holographic technology; beacon-based technology; assistive technologies.

I. INTRODUCTION

In big and unfamiliar indoor spaces, such as shopping centers, airports, stadiums, hotels, office buildings, people may have difficulties with finding the desired destination. Many categories of people – the elderly, the children, the people with visual or hearing impairment, with difficulties in communication etc. – need specialized ways of communication [2][20][21]. This paper presents modeling, implementation and user evaluation of two intelligent learning agents for smart shopping cart. They guide visitors through the shops and the goods in the shopping center according to user's shopping list or according to new promotions in the shops, respectively. It is envisaged that concrete implementation of the shopping agents will be running on each shopping cart in the shopping centers.

The task environment incorporates text-to-speech and speech recognizing technology, Bluetooth low energy technology, holographic technology, information kiosks, picture exchange communication system.

The rest of the paper is structured as it follows: in Section II the technologies that the task environment incorporates are briefly discussed; in Section III the task environment specification, including performance measure, properties, environment actuators and sensors description is presented; the agent programs realization of the goal-based learning agent and utility goal-based learning agent by means of a decision k-d tree and reinforcement-learning are explained in Section IV; the degree of development of the proposed cognitive architecture components is explained in Section V; an empirical survey about the interest of end customers to the used technologies and a survey about the way the customers perceive the two developed agents are considered in Section VI; in the VIIth Section a number of conclusions are drawn.

II. BACKGROUND TECHNOLOGY USED FOR TASK ENVIRONMENT

Beacons are used to mark the location of objects and navigate people in indoor spaces [10][25][26][33][34]. They work on the principle of lighthouses by emitting signals at short intervals based on Bluetooth Low Energy (BLE) technology. The distance to the Beacon can be defined depending on the signal strength [3]. In addition to emitting advertising or other types of announcements, it is also possible to locate beacons [10][26][34].

Holograms are made of light and sound, appear in the around space and reply to gestures, voice and gaze commands [9]. A hologram can be placed and integrated in the real world or can tag along with user as an active part of user's world helping for navigation in indoor spaces.

Another possible solution to the problem of orientating people in indoor spaces is the use of embodied conversational information kiosks [27][31]. These systems use the information they have both about their own location and about the layout of the building and give instructions to the users how to find the desired place in the building.

The information kiosks are a collection of different technologies such as video processing from face detection, speaker-independent speech recognition, array microphone for noise cancellation, a database system, and a dynamic question answering system [16][31].

The Picture Exchange Communication System (PECS) [1][30] allows people with little or no communication abilities to communicate using pictures. People using PECS are taught to approach another person and give them a picture of a desired item in exchange for that item [4][5].

Screen readers [7][11][17] and text-to-speech (TTS) systems [6][14] enable blind and vision impaired people to use computers and provide the key to education and employment.

According to [13], the first step in designing an agent must always be to specify the task environment as fully as possible. That includes performance measure, environment actuators and sensors description. That's why we will consider smart shopping problems, task environment specifying and shopping learning agents modeling in the next section.

III. Specifying the Task Environment

It is envisaged that shopping agents will be implemented on the shopping cart. The consumers will run their cart following the directions given by the agents. In the future, the shopping agents can be implemented on a robotic shopping cart like an autonomous Kuka robot that can be controlled by gestures [8][22][23][28][29] to follow the user. Then, the environment will become very complex and similar to the environment of the automated driver.

The modulus of the system prototype is given in Figure 6. The task environment consists of four main blocks: input, output, shopping, and navigation.

The technologies, used in the input block, are face detection and speech recognition. The equipment comprises a camera, a microphone, a keyboard, a mouse, and a touch screen. The general object detection algorithm consisting of a cascade of classifiers proposed by Viola and Jones [35] is used to detect faces. For video processing, C# and Intel OpenCV library [15] is used.

The output block uses speech synthesis and virtual character visualization for giving information to the user.

The shopping block includes: drag and drop pictures for creating the shopping list (Figure 4); pictures-to-speech convertor;

The navigation block includes: Beacons/iBeacons or/and Holograms for smart buildings, smart shopping mall navigation. Using of Google Beacon Platform or/and Microsoft HoloLens respectively is needed.

Agent programs include goal-based learning agent and utility goal-based learning agent realization by means of a decision k-d tree and reinforcement-learning.

A. *Performance Measure*

The performance measure to which the shopping agents are aspired include getting to the correct shop in the shopping mall; getting to the new promotion in the shopping mall; minimizing the path when going through the shops from the shopping list; maximizing passenger comfort; maximizing purchases; and enabling people with different communication possibilities to navigate in big buildings and in particular to shop in the big shopping centers.

B. *Environment*

Any shopping agent deals with a variety of shops in the shopping malls; the newest promotion could be in each and any of the shops in a mall; the agents can recommend visiting the shops in a mall in various sequences. An option is to visit all desired shops following the shortest possible way. Another option is to go around the shops in accordance with the arrangement of the items on the shopping list. A third option is to go to the shops in accordance with the availability of sales or new promotions. The location of the shops in an exemplary Mall is given in Figure 1. The model of the environment in Figure 3 is presented in the form of a graph. The nodes are the shops and the edges are the connecting corridors.

Figure 1. Exemplar location of eight shops in a shopping center

C. *Actuators*

The shopping agents are visualized on the display screen. Only the head of an agent is modeled by means of the program Crazy Talk. Face animation includes synchronization of the lip movement with the pronounced text and expressed emotions. The agents' faces normally express friendliness and calmness and when a new promotion or sale is announced they express excitement and joy. The emotions of elevation are realized through changing the strength and the height of the speech and by visualizing a model of the emotion "joy" on the face.

D. *Interaction and Sensors*

For interaction both with the intelligent agents and the consumers are used: Keyboard entry; Microphone; Touch Screen; Camera – OpenCV, Face Detecting; Natural Language Understanding; Speech recognizing; drag-and-drop pictures, pictures to speach convertor; Beacons/iBeacons or/and Holograms for smart shopping mall navigation.

E. *Properties of a Task Environment*

The behavior of the two intelligent agents is mutually complementary. They aim at facilitating the user access to the desired commodities and increasing the number of purchases, made by him/her, as well as at offering information about promotions and sales, in which he/she is interested.

The agent does not know when a new promotion or a new customer will appear. Therefore he/she periodically checks on the site of the mall if there are files, containing information about new promotions or sales and reads them if available. Then, he/she transmits this information to the customers, planning to visit the corresponding shops. Whenever a new customer appears, the agent receives his/her shopping list and defines the sequence for visiting the shops in the mall. That's why task environment is partially observable, cooperative and a multi-agent environment.

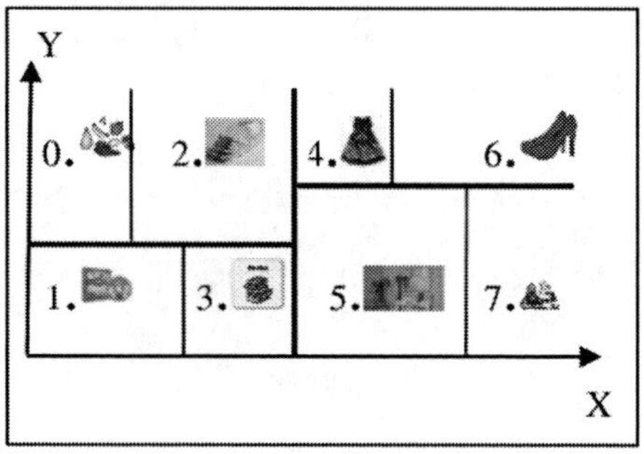

Figure 2. Shop k-d decision tree

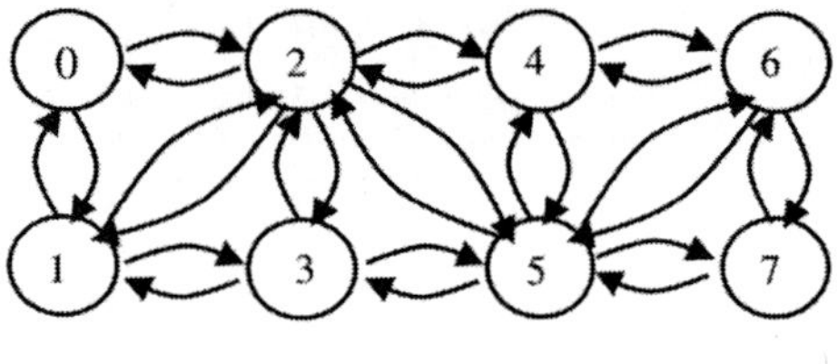

Figure 3. Presentation of the location of the shops in an exemplary mall by an orientated graph

The shopping world is also deterministic with some stochastic elements and contains elements of uncertainty of the environment. The task environment is episodic and it can be realized either as static or as semi-dynamic environment. The environment can be regarded as static as the location of the shops in the mall is known. The agent receives the whole shopping list and suggests a certain path around the shops. Whenever there is information about a new promotion or sale appearing during the shopping, the agent can dynamically recommend a change in that shopping sequence.

The environment can be regarded as both known and sequential because every next shop to visit is determined by the current location of the user and by the items he/she has pointed at as important to buy.

IV. SMART SHOPPING LEARNING AGENTS MODELING

Two software agents have been realized. The first one is a Utility Goal–based learning agent, while the second is a Goal-based learning agent.

A. *Utility Goal-Based Learning Agent*

One of the agents can be regarded as a Utility goal-based agent. That is because it feels happy when discovering that there is a promotion or a sale in a shop, in which the customer is interested to go.

The utility goal-based agent uses a decision k-d tree to quickly find where (in which shop) the customer is located according to his/her coordinates. The theory of building and implementing a decision k-d tree is given in [18]. The customer is depicted in Figure 1 by means of an emoticon, which can be moved using the mouse and placed everywhere on the shown map of the shops in the shopping center. Another way of finding the location of the customer is by using estimate beacons sensors or holograms.

The Utility goal-based agent checks if there are new files about promotions or sales published on the site of the shopping center. In case there are such files, it withdraws them and informs the customer about those of them, which are related to the shops the customer intends to visit.

The information about promotions and sales is given to the customer also in the case when it can be seen from the shopping list that the customer has planned to visit a particular shop where there is a promotion or a sale.

The customer receives notifications about promotions/sales when he/she goes past a beacon as well.

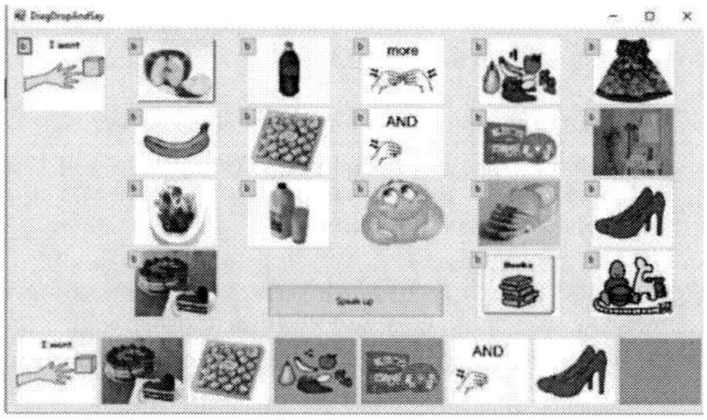

Figure 4. Making a shopping list by dragging and dropping pictures

1) Decision k-d Tree Realization

In order to build the decision tree, the location of the eight shops in the exemplary shopping mall, given in Figure 1, is considered. As it is described in [18][24] all shops are divided first by width alone into two sets, each with an equal number of shops. Next each of the two sets is divided by heights alone. Finally, each of those four sets is divided by width alone, producing eight sets of just one block each. The shop sets are divided horizontally and vertically until only one block remains in each set as it is shown in Figure 2. The overall result is called a k-d tree, where the term k-d is used to emphasize that the distances are measured in k-dimensions.

Finding the nearest block is really just a matter of following a path through a decision tree that reflects the way the objects are divided up into sets. As the decision tree in Figure 2 shows, only three one–axis comparisons are required to guess the shop in which the user is positioned.

In general [18], the decision tree with branching factor k=2 and depth d=3 will give $2^3 = 8$ leaves (shops in our task). Accordingly, if there are n shops (or goods, or users) to be identified, d will have to be large enough to ensure that $2^d \geq n$. Then, the number of comparisons required, which corresponds to the depth of the tree, will be of the order of $\log_2 n$.

B. *Goal-Based Learning Agent*

According to [12][19][32], Reinforcement learning is a method of learning, by which what to do is taught, i.e., how to match a situation to an action, so that a numerical reward received as a signal, is maximized. The teacher does not point at the actions to be undertaken. Instead, the trainee has to find out those, leading to the greatest reward and try to realize them. In the most interesting and challenging cases, not only the immediate reward could be taken into account when choosing an action, but also the further situations and the future rewards.

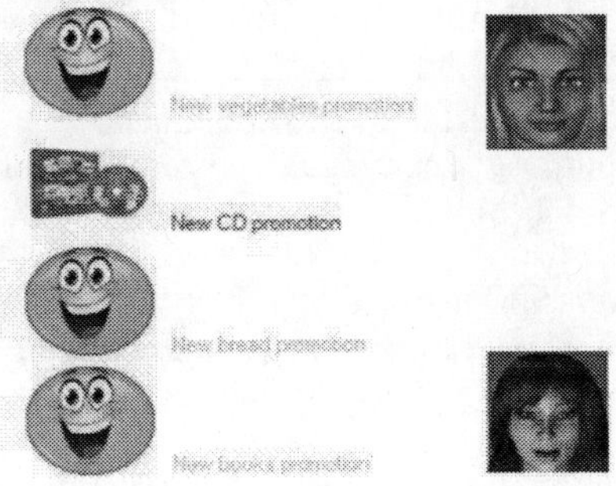

Figure 5. Message about a promotion of a new Compact Disk

All reinforcement learning agents have explicit goals, can sense aspects in their environment and choose actions, which influence it. The agent is realized by a program, matching the way the agent perceives reality and the actions it undertakes.

A reinforcement learning algorithms is used for the second Goal-based learning agent. The agent receives the shopping list from the customer (this is what the agent perceives) and informs the customer about the sequence of shops he/she can visit in order to buy all the goods needed (these are the actions the agent undertakes). The shortest possible route is suggested, in accordance with the particular shopping list.

Since the goal is to visit all the shops from the shopping list, the particular shopping list can be regarded as a plan or a sequence of goals to achieve in order to fulfill the task completely.

It is also possible for the agent to get the exact location of a customer and a particular shop to get to. The shortest possible path to the desired shop is suggested in this case as well.

In order to realize the agent's learning process the following is to be developed: Environment model; Rewards model; Agent's memory model; Agent's behavior function; Value of the training parameter.

The environment model is a graph (Figure 3) of the different environment conditions. The nodes in the graph (Figure 1) are the shops in the exemplary shopping mall. The edges point at the shops, between which there is a transition. Then, this graph is presented by an adjacency matrix. The number of rows and columns in this matrix is equal to the number of shops in the mall. Zero is put in the matrix in a place where there is a connection between the number of a shop, set by a number of a row, and the number of a shop, given by a number of a column. Values of -1 are placed in the other positions of the adjacency matrix.

The rewards model is needed to set a goal for the agent. Reaching every shop from the customer's shopping list is such a goal. Since the agent is a goal-based one, it behavior can be changed by just setting a new goal, changing the rewards model [12]. A reward is only given when the agent gets to a particular shop.

The agent's memory is modeled by presenting it with the help of an M-matrix (Memory of the agent). The rows in the M-matrix represent the current location of the customer, while the columns are the shops, where he/she can go. It is assumed at the beginning that the agent does not have any knowledge and therefore all elements in the M-matrix are zeros.

The rule for calculating the current location of the customer at the moment of choosing the next shop to visit is as it follows:

M (cuurent location of the customer, chosen shop to visit next) = **R**(current location of the customer, next shop) + **Υ. Max**[**M**(next shop, all possible shops where the customer could go from the next shop)].

The following is taken into account in the above formula:

The immediate reward, obtained when the customer decides from the current location to go to a next shop: **R**(current position, chosen shop to go next);

The biggest possible future reward. This is the biggest reward, chosen from among the rewards, which would have been obtained when the customer goes out of the next shop and enters any possible shop: **Max**[**M**(next shop, all possible shops where it is possible to go from the next shop)].

The value of the learning parameter **Υ** defines the extent to which the agent will take into account the value of the future reward. The value of the learning parameter **Υ is** within 0 to 1 ($0 \leq \Upsilon < 1$). If Υ is closer to zero, then the agent will prefer to consider only the immediate reward. Experiments have shown that in this case it is impossible to teach the agent to achieve the goal. If **Υ** is closer to one, then the agent will consider the future reward to a greater extent. This is the better option for successful training of the agent. The value of the learning parameter was experimentally chosen to be **Υ=0.8**. At this value, the obtained weights for all possible actions are clearly identifiable and the process of training is reliable. A random initial position is chosen for the customer in the algorithm for training the agent. The following steps are realized until the target shop is reached:

One of all possible shops is chosen, where it is possible to go from the current position. The shop to which the customer would go next is considered. For this next position now all the shops, to which it is possible to go further are considered. The value of the highest reward is taken. The next position is then set as a current one.

V. Degree of Development of the Proposed Cognitive Architecture Components

The goal-based learning agent and the utility goal-based learning agent are fully developed. The head of each agent is modeled and visualized. We have used Crazy Talk 6 for emotion modeling. The decision k-d tree and reinforcement-learning algorithm are completed and used for agents function realization. The program for creating a shopping list by using key combinations and drag and drop pictures is ready. The picture to speech converter program can pronounce all the existing pictures and the created shopping list. The agents can recognize and react to a few speech commands. They start communication with the users when detecting a face in front of themselves. A number of experiments are conducted with some Estimote beacons and a notification program [14]. The complete beacon based navigation system and the corresponding software are not ready yet, however. The holograms and holographic computer have not been used for now. We hope to obtain and use the holographic computer soon. Experiments in a real shopping center are planned as well.

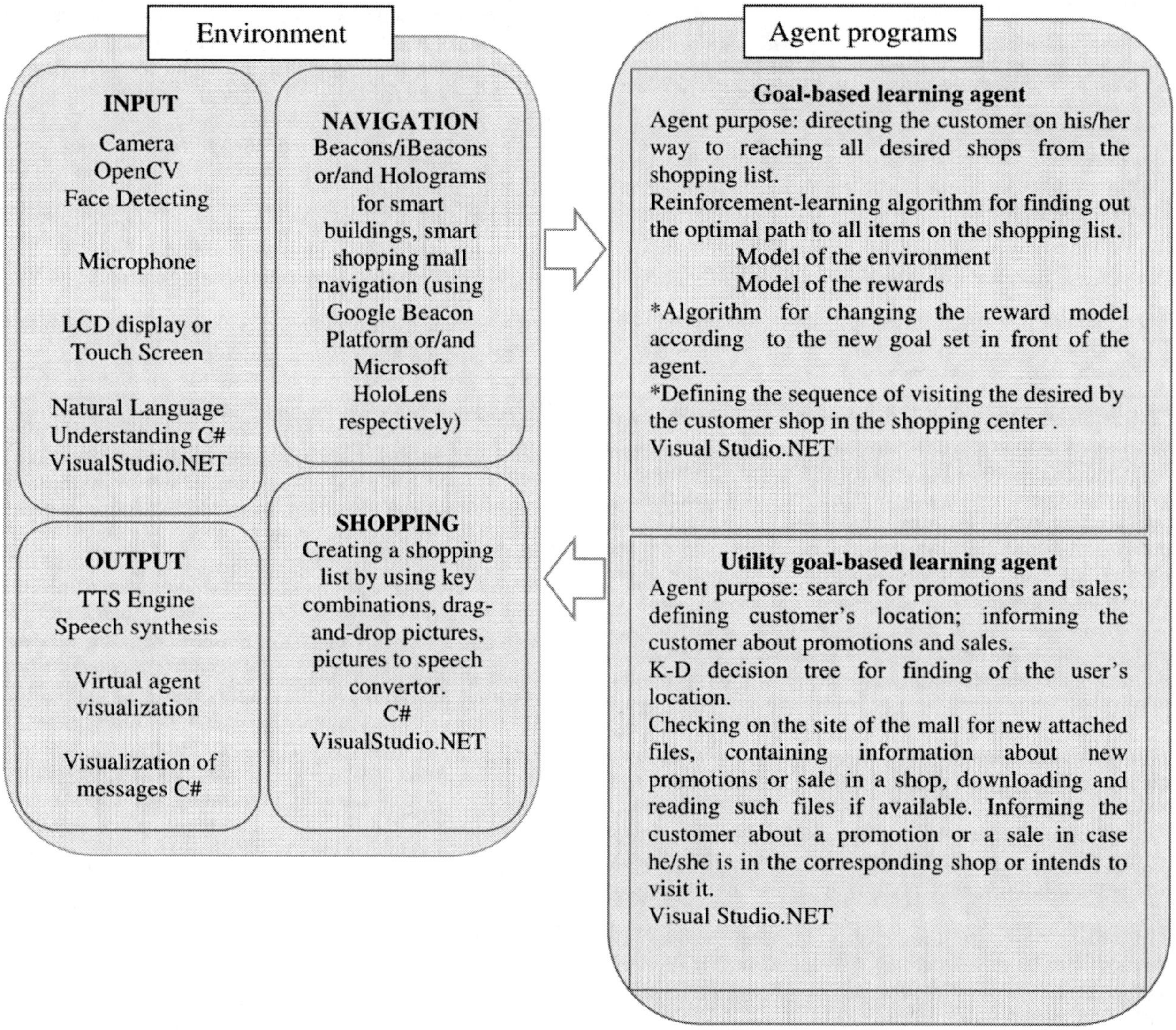

Figure 6. Specifying the task environment and smart shopping learning agents modeling.

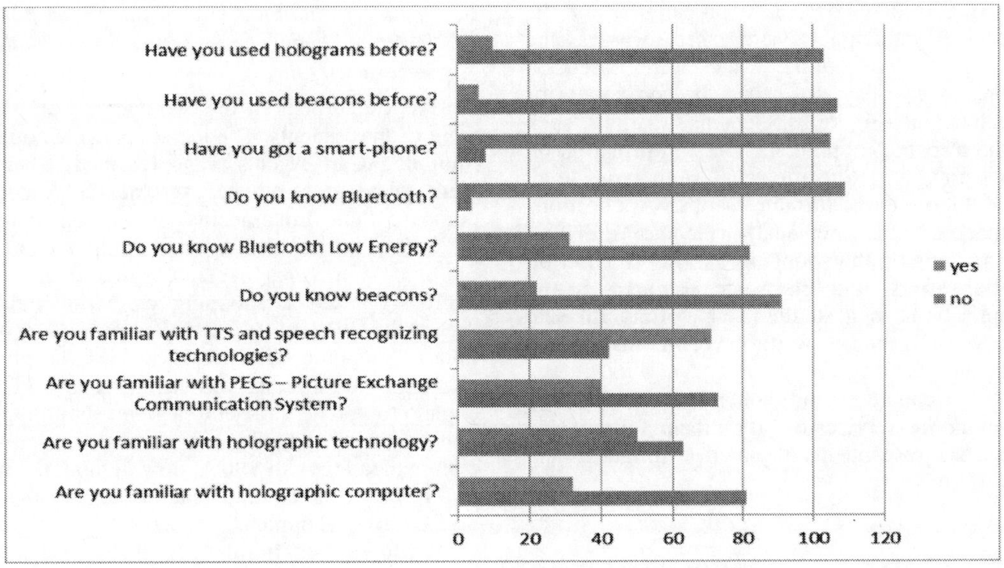

Figure 7. A survey about the interest of end customers in beacon-based services, holographic technology, PECS, TTS and Speech Synthesis technologies.

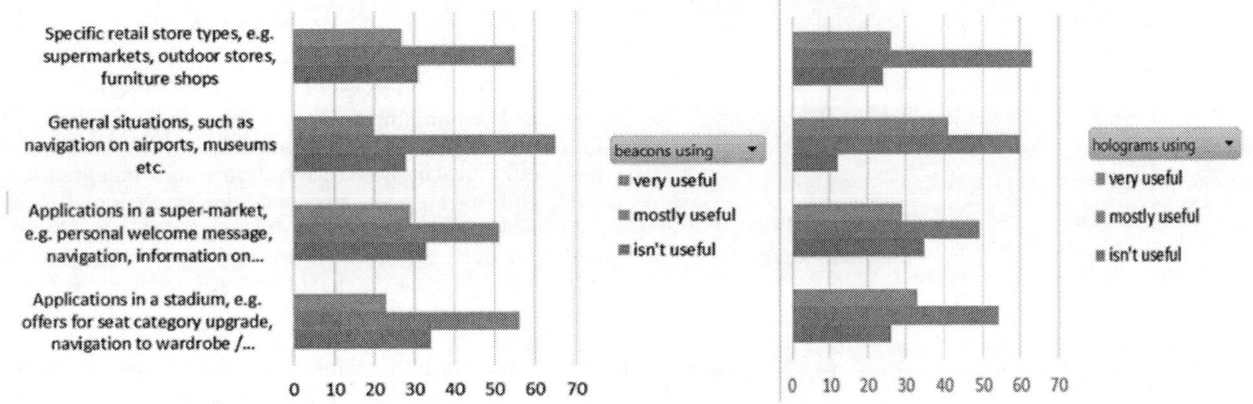

Figure 8. A survey about rediness of the user to use beacon-based services and holographic technology.

VI. Empirical Survey

The survey was conducted at the university. The total number of 115 students were offered the questionnaire. All of the participants were between the ages of 18 to 23 years old.

A. *A survey about the interest of end customers in beacon-based services, holographic technology, PECS, TTS and Speech Synthesis technologies.*

To investigate people's mindset towards the use of beacons, the use of holograms, drag-drop pictures, pictures to speech, TTS and Speech Synthesis an empirical study was conducted. The survey's purpose was to explore the interest of end customers in beacon-based services, holographic technology, PECS, TTS and Speech Synthesis technologies and the willingness to use them. As a base we use [34] but append some questions about new technologies.

With this end in view, we designed a questionnaire with the following tree sections. The participants were asked (Figure 7), whether they (1) own a smart-phone, (2) know Bluetooth, (3) know Bluetooth Low Energy, (4) know Holographic computer, (5) know Holographic technologies, (6) know beacons, (7) have used beacons before, (8) have used holograms before, (9) are familiar with PECS, (10) are familiar with TTS and speech recognizing technologies.

This helps to understand, whether consumers are aware of beacons. Then, they were given a short introduction of the beacon technology, holographic technology, PECS, TTS and speech recognizing technologies, as a preparation for the remaining questions. Participants were asked to assess the usefulness of typical applications, which were based on already existing scenarios by using beacon-based or holographic realizations (Figure 8): General situations, such as navigation on airports, coupons in stores, information on exhibits in museums, etc.; Specific retail store types, e.g., supermarkets, outdoor stores, furniture shops.; Applications in a super-market, e.g., personal welcome message, navigation to products on the shopping list, information on products, special offers, and electronic payment at the checkout.; Applications in a stadium, e.g., offers for seat category upgrade, navigation to wardrobe/restrooms, special offers for drinks and snacks.

Beacon-based technology and holographic technology are little known and the services based on them are not used widely yet, but the respondents declared willingness and readiness to use them.

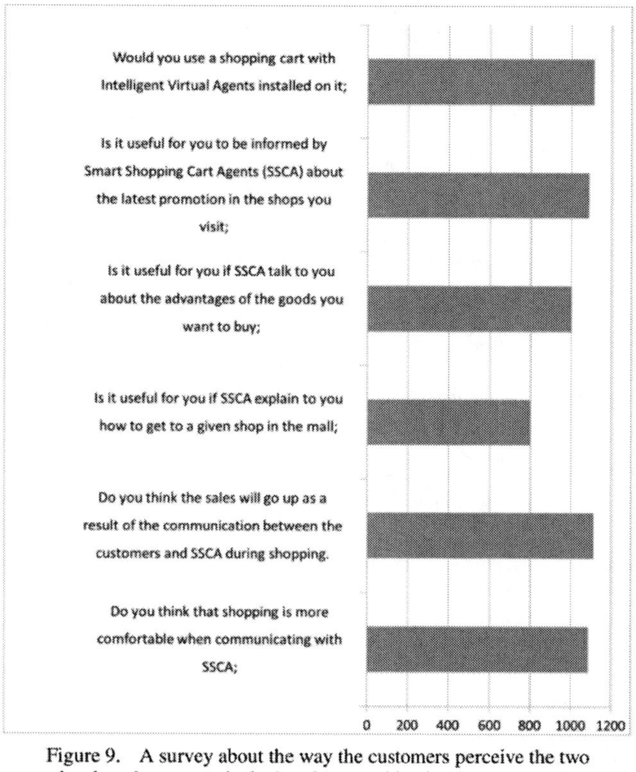

Figure 9. A survey about the way the customers perceive the two developed agents and whether they consider their purpose useful (values 1-10)

Five blind people aged 45-65 also took part in the survey. These respondents were not familiar with the described technologies and had not used them before. However, they do know and use in their daily routine Internet, Skype, smartphones, e-mail, all TTS programs and desktop reading programs. They showed great enthusiasm and willingness to get acquainted with beacon-based services and holographic services for navigation in buildings.

B. A survey about the way the customers perceive the two developed agents and whether they consider their purpose useful.

The capabilities of the two agents were demonstrated in front of the students. The idea of Smart Shopping and Smart Shopping Cart Agents was presented. Then, the students were asked to evaluate usefulness of the two agents, to compare their functionality and to consider the services of which agent prefer; to say their opinion about shopping with Shopping Cart Smart Agents. Some of the questions were: Would you use a shopping cart with Intelligent Virtual Agents installed on it; is it useful for you to be informed by Smart Shopping Cart Agents (SSCA) about the latest promotion in the shops you visit; is it useful for you if SSCA explain to you how to get to a given shop in the mall; do you think that shopping is more comfortable when communicating with SSCA; do you think the sales will go up as a result of the communication between the customers and SSCA during shopping.

It can be seen from Figure 9 that, the customers would use SSCA and they think the agents will be useful and their presence would make the shopping practice more comfortable. The utility goal-based learning agent that search for promotions and sales is the preferred one.

VII. CONCLUSION

The paper describes the design and implementation of an intelligent Smart Shopping Cart Learning Agents prototype and their environment. The system differs from other intelligent systems by the combination of machine learning techniques, beacon-based navigation and/or hologram-based navigation in the mall, the integration of Picture Exchange Communication System in it and by its language understanding and speech synthesis capabilities, drag-and-drop techniques and keyboard button combinations enabled access.

The task environment is partially observable, cooperative and a multi-agent environment. The shopping world is deterministic with some stochastic and uncertainty elements. The task environment is episodic and can be realized either as static or as semi-dynamic.

The utility goal-based agent uses a decision k-d tree to quickly find where (in which shop) the customer is located according to his/her coordinates. It getting to the new promotion in the shopping mall according to user's shopping list and inform them.

Reinforcement learning algorithm is used for the other Goal-based learning agent. The agent gets the shopping list from the customer and informs the customer about the sequence in which he/she can visit the shops to buy all needed goods.

The performance measure to which the shopping agents are aspired includes getting to the correct shop in the shopping mall; getting to the new promotion in the shopping mall according to user's shopping list; minimizing the path when going through the shops from the shopping list; maximizing customer comfort; maximizing purchases; and enabling people with different communication capabilities to navigate in big buildings and in particular to shop in big shopping centers.

The empirical survey conducted with a limited number of users showed their positive mindset for using such Smart Shopping Cart Learning Agents in indoor spaces. The utility goal-based learning agent that search and informs for promotions and sales is the preferred one. In the future work, it is intended to develop other commercial agents, such as those who will be familiar with users shopping habits.

ACKNOWLEDGMENT

The authors gratefully acknowledge the financial support provided within the Ministry of Education and Science of Bulgaria Research Fund Project FNI DN17/11.

REFERENCES

[1] A. Bondy and L. Frost, PECS - Picture Exchange Communication System. [Online] https://pecsusa.com/apps/ [retrieved: 03, 2019]

[2] Y. J. Chang, S. M. Peng, T. Y. Wang, S. F. Chen, Y. R. Chen, and H. C. Chen, "Autonomous indoor wayfinding for individuals with cognitive impairments," Journal of NeuroEngineering and Rehabilitation, 7(1), pp 1– 13, 2010

[3] Google Beacon Platform. [Online]. [retrieved: 03, 2019] https://www.youtube.com/watch?v=0QeY9FueMow

[4] National Autism Resources Inc.[Online]. [retrieved: 03, 2019] https://www.nationalautismresources.com/the-picture-exchange-communication-system-pecs/

[5] What is PECS. [Online]. [retrieved: 03, 2019]. https://pecs-unitedkingdom.com/pecs/

[6] Innoetics TTS Reader Female Bulgarian Voice IRINA. [Online]. https://www.innoetics.com/ [retrieved: 03, 2019]

[7] JAWS. [Online]. [retrieved: 03, 2019]. http://www.freedomscientific.com/Products/Blindness/JAWS

[8] Kuka robot. [Online]. [retrieved: 03, 2019]. https://cyberbotics.com/doc/guide/robots

[9] Microsoft HoloLens holographic computer. [Online]. hhttps://developer.microsoft.com/en-us/windows/mixed-reality/ [retrieved: 03, 2019]

[10] My Dream Companion project – YGA. [Online]. http://www.yga.org.tr/en/my-dream-companion [retrieved: 03, 2019]

[11] NVDA. [Online]. https://www.nvaccess.org/ [retr.: 03, 2019],

[12] R. S. Sutton and A. G. Barto, Reinforcement Learning: An Introduction, The MIT Press, Cambridge, Massachusetts, London, England, 2014. [Online]. [retrieved: 03, 2019]. http://incompleteideas.net/book/bookdraft2017nov5.pdf

[13] S. Russell and P. Norvig, "Artificial Intelligence A Modern Approach", Prentice Hall, Third Edition, 2010, ISBN-13 978-0-13-604259-4, ISBN-10 0-13-604259-7

[14] Estimote Beacons. [Online]. https://estimote.com/ [03, 2019],

[15] The Intel Open Source Computer Vision Library, vol. 2006: [Online]. https://software.intel.com, [retrieved: 03, 2019],

[16] Tomorrow's digital signage, today with 3d holographic kiosks, Intel IoT Digital kiosks, Solution brief, [Online], https://d1io3yog0oux5.cloudfront.net/_362a9c6b4a3713a10700da32acd8a3ad/provision/db/255/661/pdf/Intel+Provision+3D+Brief+2016.pdf, [retrieved 03, 2019]

[17] Vocalizer Android/Dariya/Bulgarian voice. [Online]. https://play.google.com/store/apps/details?id=es.codefactory.vocalizertts&hl=bg [retrieved:03,2019]

[18] P. H. Winston, "Artificial Intelligence," Addison-Wesley Publishing Company ISBN-13: 978-0201533774 ISBN-10

[19] A. Gosavi, "Reinforcement Learning: A Tutorial Survey and Recent Advances," INFORMS Journal on Computing 21(2), pp. 178-192, 2009

[20] V. Kulyukin, C. Gharpure, J. Nicholson, and G. Osborne, "Robot-assisted wayfinding for the visually impaired in structured indoor environments," Autonomous Robots, 21(1), pp. 29–41, 2006.

[21] L. Niua and Y. Song, "A schema for extraction of indoor pedestrian navigation grid network from floor plans," In The International Archives of the Photogrammetry, Remote Sensing and Spatial Information Sciences, volume XLI-B4, Prague, Czech Republic, pp. 325-330, 2016.

[22] N. Ç. Kılıboz and U. Güdükbay, "A hand gesture recognition technique for human–computer interaction," Journal of Visual Communication and Image Representation, Elsevier, pp 97-104,Volume 28, pp. 97-104, April 2015

[23] N. G. Shakev, S. A. Ahmed, A. V. Topalov, V. L. Popov, and K. B. Shiev, "Autonomous Flight Control and Precise Gestural Positioning of a Small Quadrotor, Learning Systems: From Theory to Practice," Springer, pp. 179-197, 2018. |

[24] Y. Y. Song and Y. Lu, "Decision tree methods: applications for classification and prediction," Shanghai Arch Psychiatry. 2015 Apr 25;27(2):130-5. doi: 10.11919/j.issn.1002-0829.215044, PMID: 26120265

[25] Y. Zhuang, J. Yang, Y. Li, L. Qi, and N. El-Sheimy, "Smartphone-based indoor localization with Bluetooth low energy beacons," Sensors, April 2016. 16(5), pp. 596, doi: 10.3390/s16050596

[26] D. Ahmetovic, et al. "Navcog: A navigational cognitive assistant for the blind," In International Conference on Human Computer Interaction with Mobile Devices and Services. ACM, pp. 90-99, 2016

[27] J. Cassell, et al. "MACK: Media lab Autonomous Conversational Kiosk," Imagina'02, Monte Carlo, 2002 vol. 2, 12–15. [Online] Available at: http://alumni.media.mit.edu/~tstocky/pubs/Cassell.Stocky Imagina02.pdf [retrieved: 03, 2019]

[28] E. Coupeté, et al. "New Challenges for Human-Robot Collaboration in an Industrial Context: Acceptability and Natural Collaboration," Fifth workshop "Towards a Framework for Joint Action", IEEE RO-MAN, pp. 1-4, 2016.

[29] S. R. Fletcher and P. Webb, "Industrial robot ethics: facing the challenges of human-robot collaboration in future manufacturing systems," A world with robots: international conference on robot ethics: ICRE 2015", 2017, pp. 159-169.

[30] C. Lord, M. Rutter, P. C. Dilavore, and S. Risi, "ADOS - Autism Diagnostic Observation Schedule," Western Psychological Services, 2002.

[31] L. McCauley and S. D'Mello, "MIKI: A speech enabled intelligent kiosk," IVA 2006, LNAI 4133, pp.132-144, 2006

[32] R. R. Torrado, P. Bontrager, J. Togelius, J. Liu, D. Perez-Liebana, "Deep Reinforcement Learning for General Video Game AI," IEEE Conference on Computatonal Intelligence and Games, CIG. 2018-August, 10.1109/CIG.2018.8490422

[33] A. Ch. Seyed, N. Vinod, and S. Kaushik, "IBeaconMap: Automated Indoor Space Representation for Beacon-Based Wayfinding," Human-Computer Interaction arXiv: 1802.05735v1 [cs.HC], USA, 2018

[34] A. Thamm, J. Anke, S. Haugk, and D. Radic, "Towards the Omni-Channel: Beacon-based Services in Retail", BIS 2016, Leipzig, Germany, July 6-8, pp. 181-192, 2016

[35] P. Viola and M. Jones, "Rapid object detection using a boosted cascade of simple features," CVPR,pp. I-511- I-518,2001

VoxelNET's Geo-Located Spatio Temporal Softbots

-including living, quiet and invisible data

Charlotte Sennersten, Craig Lindley and Ben Evans
CSIRO
Pullenvale, Australia
e-mail: charlotte.sennersten@csiro.au, craig.lindley@csiro.au, ben.evans@data61.csiro.au

Abstract— **Linnaeus and Darwin understood the need to classify 'living things' to determine the basis of their relationships and interrelationships. In an Internet-of-Things (IoT) world we need to do the same, to be able to identify and compute with objects by type. However, the IoT does not inherently deal with spatial or geometrical structure, and mass phenomena (e.g. air, water, rock) are not objects per se. This can exclude these 'non-object' things from the IoT, which can be a severe disadvantage in many application domains. The solution to this is voxelisation of mass phenomena in the world within an overall coherent three dimensional coordinate reference system. This allows 'non-things' to be coherently situated, classified and treated computationally in the same way as discrete things and individual objects. VoxelNET is a distributed digital architecture that supports this voxelisation model, providing a world of voxels containing various information at different geo locations that can be compared in terms of numerous and unlimited taxonomical categories, and over time. Performing computations across this highly distributed system of systems can greatly benefit from the use of distributed softbots or agents without the need for centralized computations or control. Hence the VoxelNET distributed architecture not only parses objects and materials into computable objects, but also includes spatially located and volumetric computational agents that can collectively achieve analytical outcomes in an inherently distributed way. Here this approach is exemplified by distributed VoxelNET agents collaborating to conduct 3D volumetric path finding through the VoxelNET space, using a distributed Dijkstra pathfinding algorithm. Stronger implementations of the agent concept can include supplementing the basic Dijkstra algorithm with more sophisticated competitive and/or collaborative behaviours on the agents/voxels involved.**

Keywords-Voxel Agents; Autonomy; Industry 4.0; Reasoning; Computation.

I. INTRODUCTION

Internet 4.0 is the currently emerging next stage in the evolution of the internet, expanding from client-server intercommunications to peer-to-peer systems, combining historical information based on where devices have been with information from diverse nearby sensors (eg. location sensors, smart home components) and using artificial intelligence analytics to create new knowledge and experiences [1]. In this evolution, the Internet will be available in all places and at all times in the background. Applied to industry, Internet 4.0 supports the concept of Industry 4.0, which has been defined as "the current trend of automation and data exchange in manufacturing technologies. It includes cyber-physical systems, the Internet of Things (IoT), cloud computing and cognitive computing. Industry 4.0 is commonly referred to as "The Fourth Industrial Revolution." [2]. The IoT extends internet connectivity to many kinds of devices and objects, especially in order to gather sensor data and/or parameterize and control the devices as part of larger scale systems and operations.

To digitise the world and comprehend it we need to classify knowledge in a digital system. The voxels in VoxelNET can be the basis for this systemization [3] and also support the use of various algorithms, such as Linear Classifiers, Decision Trees, and Nearest Neighbour [4]. Looking back at former scientists contributing, systematizing and taxonomising our (biological) world, Linnaeus published a system for classifying living things [5] and Darwin an evolutionary taxonomy (a branch of biological classification) with evolutionary change [6]. In a world of change we need to connect changes to understand cause and effect. The VoxelNET system is also at its base a taxonomical system, most fundamentally classifying things in the world by their location, but also supporting arbitrary further dimensions of classification. Also it is a distributed system, which makes collective computations highly amenable to agent-based computational processes, which are the focus of this paper.

Systems based upon Industry 4.0 technologies and methods constitute what Cardin [7] calls *Cyber-Physical Production Systems (CPPSs)*, defined as systems of systems of autonomous and cooperative elements connecting with each other in situation dependent ways, on and across all levels of production, from processes through machines up to production and logistics networks, enhancing decision-making processes in real-time, responding to unforeseen conditions and evolving over time. Cyber-physical systems in general monitor physical processes, using sensor data from the IoT layer to create and update a virtual copy of the physical world (a "digital twin"), and use the virtual twin together with analytical techniques to optimize operational decisions in real-time across the value chain. A digital twin can include site, object and agent spatial locations and structure, operations and process models, assets, plant, equipment, vehicle and staff representations, times and locations, etc.. Since CPPSs are systems of autonomous and cooperative elements, it is natural to look to artificial computational agents as a basis for computing within and across these systems.

This paper describes the VoxelNET [3] Industry 4.0 and CPPS platform and the way in which computational agents can be created and function using this platform, especially agents that are founded upon its inherent 4D structure (three dimensions of space plus time). Demonstrated VoxelNET applications include mine operations and Unmanned aerial vehicle Traffic Management (UTM), both of which have strong requirements for computational modelling and analysis of 3D space. A distributed, agent-based approach to path planning is presented, which addresses requirements within both of these application domains.

First in Section II 'The VoxelNET System' is introduced and its 'Functionality' and 'Architecture' are described. Section III describes 'The VoxelNET Agent Model' and how agents use the platform, and in Section IV 'The Voxel Agent Example', a distributed agent-based planning system is described to exemplify the system.

II. The VoxelNET System

The 4D VoxelNET system is so-called because it deals with locations, objects, and materials within an integrated 4D spatiotemporal framework of voxels, where a voxel is a volume element. The voxelisation of locations is made in the form of a 3D geodetic spatial coordinate reference system having default unit voxels of approximately one cubic meter over the surface of the Earth to any depth or altitude. One cubic meter location voxels can be dynamically aggregated or decomposed to create a location voxel coordinate system having one or more location voxels of any required size and with variable geodetic dimensions along each coordinate axis. The system also supports the definition of Euclidean local coordinate systems that have an origin within the geodetic spatial reference systems and rotations around geodetic axes. The voxelisation of object representations can amount to tessellated 3D models of whole objects or object parts having naturalistic shapes, which allows arbitrary models to have voxel properties and functions. The voxelisation of materials that are not already divided into objects spatially quantises the spatial extension of material otherwise typically described in mass terms (such as air, water, rock) into collections of discrete 3D spatial units. In this way VoxelNET can represent all 'open space' entities such as air, soil, rock, space and water that otherwise would not conform to typical IoT concepts into units that allow them to be integrated into the IoT. Hence both extended natural phenomena, objects and artefacts and their associated sensor data can be integrated within one architecture.

A. VoxelNET Functionality

VoxelNET spatial structure provides several generic functions that specific applications can be built upon, many of which are derived from OGC spatial standards for simple geometry types (see OGC: 06-103r4 Part 1 and Part 2, [8]). These include:

- Search by spatial criteria, such as object enclosure, proximity, intersection
- Synthesis of new shapes using mathematical operations defined upon input shapes, e.g. intersections, differences, unions
- Derivation of spatial relationships between shapes, such as distance, overlap, encapsulation

VoxelNET extends these geometrical operators and functions with functions built upon an underlying conceptual model including:

- Complex spatial object definitions expressed in terms of a variety of structures and relationships among simple geometry types
- Associations of shapes with material types and properties
- Association of complex shapes and associated materials with models for operations definitions, capabilities, performance and schedules, personnel, assets, processes and process segments, resources and resource relationships, equipment, workflow specifications, work definitions, job lists and schedules, test specifications and results
- Classes, types, instances and both class and instance properties
- Material transforms
- Modalities potentially associated with any numeric values, such as probabilities and ontological/epistemic status
- Aggregation of these elements as types and instances with higher level (or meta-level) conceptual constructs, such as domain paradigms/interpretative frameworks, data/information/knowledge bases, ontologies/taxonomies, knowledge bases and/or expert systems, agents, agent societies/communities, and computational ecosystems

The latter higher level (or meta-level) conceptual constructs may include specialised computational models in addition to the data, information and knowledge included within the underlying conceptual models. VoxelNET computing is achieved via several programming paradigms, of which agents are a high-level example. These paradigms include:

- *Scripted programs that sit outside of the voxel structure* and traverse it to achieve outcomes such as: i) finding voxels that meet some criteria (i.e.

data base querying, data filtering), ii) analysing voxel collections, iii) parsing and editing subsets of voxel space.

- *Triggers* associated with specific voxels (that are logically or conceptually *within*) a voxel, such that if their associated data changes, one or more defined computations are carried out. An example is, if a location voxel is mined, this can trigger the spawning of a material voxel. Since the voxel structure is hierarchical, and voxels can be members of a larger scale voxel or association, triggers can be inherited (potentially upwards or downwards).

- *Processes* associated with specific voxels (that are logically or conceptually *within* a voxel/structure), may run continuously, carrying out one or more defined computations. An example is, a voxel process interrogates a defined neighbourhood of voxels to check if any have been mined, and to derive a cost/value hypothesis from the mined states of its neighbours, their rock harness, grades, etc.

- *Finite state machines* (FSMs) are state transition engines that move a sequence of voxels from one state to another in response to changes in one or more of the voxels (i.e. inputs, or internally driven state changes). They fall between triggers and processes, since they are complex sequences, but driven by trigger events, rather than running continuously.

- *Agents* are more complex computational processes based upon any of a range of computational cognitive models. The most critical features include declarative knowledge modelling and goal-directed decision processing. *Social* agents are a specialisation of computational agents that can engage in collaborative or competitive behaviour (for example). A voxel or voxel association can be an agent if some part of its behaviour is controlled by a cognitive model, e.g. [9].

B. *VoxelNET Architecture*

The total vision for the VoxelNET system described above presents a highly complex computational environment that unpacks the concept of Industry 4.0 and intelligent cyberphysical production systems into the full range of high level elements and components needed for their realisation in the case of systems of significant size and complexity (e.g. a flexible manufacturing factory). Smaller scale systems may require a much more limited subset of these features. This leads to the following broad and overlapping classes of system architecture:

- **Stand-alone systems** that encapsulate modelling, monitoring, analytics and decision processes without the need to interact with other systems. Examples of this that have been demonstrated so far in the VoxelNET case include: a system for real time control of a UAV operating in underground mines, based upon a digital twin and third person view of the vehicle and its environment (see [10]); and a system for the analysis, feature detection and visualisation of heterogeneity in mineral deposits.
- A **cloud-based client/server/repository architecture** that has been demonstrated for real-time multi-user interaction with mineral resource drill hole, blast hole and block model data. In this case, the client/server messaging interface and underlying repository schema provide foundations for interoperability among client systems that may include third party software using proprietary data formats, provided that those formats can be translated into canonical VoxelNET schema constructs.
- A **fully distributed architecture**, with many application clients interacting with distributed servers/repositories via a mediating VoxelNET distribution server network. While not yet implemented, the standardised message syntax, semantics and underlying conceptual models required extend those used for client/server interaction in the cloud-based architecture.

Challenges in meeting this Industry 4.0 vision at a large scale include:

- **Avoiding over-engineering**. The system should try to focus on representations and functions that provide the most critical inputs to system understanding and decision processes, or else it may be difficult to place bounds upon how much needs to be sensed and represented (e.g. the context of a system is essentially endless).
- **Consistent syntactic and semantic mapping of data, information and knowledge** from multiple diverse sources to a uniform underlying conceptual model.
- The need to accommodate **changes in the structure and functionality** of physical and operational systems over time.
- **Achievement of trust and reliability** in the system.
- The need for **standardized terminology, types and classes** that may be expressed in ontologies and/or taxonomies. For example, object types or classes should not be open, but documented, where new types/classes can extend the

documentation. A particular range of phenomena may have more than one ontology/taxonomy associated with it, reflecting different perspectives, uses, etc.

The following sections of this paper describe the agent-based functions of the VoxelNET system, especially those based upon the 3D voxelisation of spatial structure.

III. THE VOXELNET AGENT MODEL

A. *Artificial Computational Agents*

VoxelNET is a highly distributed system concept, including the virtual and physical distribution in 3D space of artificial intelligence (AI) and autonomous decision making functions. This means that autonomous decision making that uses data, information and/or knowledge, or has output implications, beyond the bounds of individual server/repository nodes will need to interact with AI functions resident on other nodes. This lends itself to an agent-based AI model, where a software agent can also be referred to as a *softbot*, meaning a software robot [11]. This does not exclude softbots that constitute elements of the control architecture of physical robots.

There are many definitions and variants of agents in the research literature that are distinguished along numerous dimensions of variation (e.g. see [12], [13]). Some of these variations include: reactive versus deliberative/goal-driven, stand-alone versus collaborative, distributed versus centralised, mobile versus immobile, situated versus disembodied, hardware versus software, adaptive/learning versus un-adaptive, etc. Many architectures are hybrids of the distinctions made along these various dimensions. VoxelNET is compatible with any of these models, since they can exist as computational components in the server ecosystem or interfacing with generic VoxelNET functions accessible via the VoxelNET messaging layer.

It is a requirement of VoxelNET agents that they can be intelligent, although what constitutes intelligence in synthetic or natural agents can be greatly debated. Teahan [14] characterises an agent as acting intelligently when "what it does is appropriate for its circumstances and its goals, taking into account the short-term and long-term consequences of its actions, is flexible to changing environments and changing goal, learns from experience and it makes appropriate choices given its perceptual and computational limitations".

A benefit of this definition is that it is expressed in terms of functionality rather than mechanisms. Definitions based upon mechanisms are in general undesirable, since specific mechanisms do not necessarily guarantee intelligent outcomes, while a given level of intelligent functionality might be implemented by a different set of mechanisms.

B. *The VoxelNET Agent Model*

The VoxelNET system constitutes a data, information and knowledge ecology that is compatible with numerous computational, agent and intelligence paradigms, interacting via a foundational conceptual model and standardised message formats and protocols. It nevertheless has a more inherent agent paradigm based upon voxel structures, which is described in more detail in this section.

A voxel itself is able to function in the system as a self-contained inter-netted agent that can virtually perceive, receive and issue messages, compute, change its state and generate outputs. As noted above, any specific voxel may have associated triggers, processes, finite state machines, or agent models non-exclusively associated with it (i.e. one voxel may be associated with several computational components). This means that all voxels in VoxelNET can function as agents within the interlinked voxel world.

VoxelNET users are presented with a default navigational voxel structure for the Earth of approximately 1 m^3 voxels that extends over the mean surface and to altitudes from 20 km to a depth of minus 10 km (this range is dynamic and can be extended as required). This results in 10^{19} voxels, any or all of which can be an agent. Voxels can be aggregated or decomposed, and the resulting larger and smaller scale voxels can also be agents. The question then is, what can an individual voxel agent do and process? In principle, this could include a broad range of intelligent behaviours, including:

- perceiving, including recognize patterns
- learning (form correlations)
- learning (form concepts, i.e. abstractions)
- understanding (form predictive models)
- apply logic and reason
- comprehend ideas (use abstractions)
- plan
- solve problems
- make decisions
- retain data, information and knowledge
- use language to communicate (using the syntax and semantics of the VoxelNET messaging system)

VoxelNET agents may belong to one or more classes, although this is not elaborated in this paper. Instead, some general agent functions are presented, as well as a specific example of how voxel agents can interact to create a collective function.

General voxel-agent-functions include the capacity to send and receive messages addressed by specific voxel ID, by geodetic or local volume, or broadcast across the VoxelNET, with each voxel selecting to respond to messages by type or according to one or more specific criteria specified in the message. Message inputs can be sent to voxel triggers, finite state machines, processes and agents, according to message metadata and rules for processing each computation type held within the voxel. Specialised messages may carry programs, including implementations of agent decision processes, so that generic functions are primarily concerned with agent program input and management, rather than having extensive built-in behaviours.

It might be asked why a specific voxel should be an agent, rather than have external processes perform computations upon voxels? The reasons for this are:

i) That these two options are logically, and may be implementationally, equivalent. A computational agent in a closed computational environment (such as the single server/repository cloud-based version of the VoxelNET architecture) may be processed within a computational context that is external to the agent, but not external to the system. This may, for example, be an algorithmic loop that triggers or polls each agent to accept inputs, update its status, and generate outputs with each iteration of the loop. The more central question here is whether algorithms implementing agent state transitions are represented within the program structure of each agent, or exist as elements of an algorithm library that can be applied by the external process to a data structure that encapsulates the agent state. For a purely virtual agent system, the difference is one of packaging from the perspective of design and maintenance (analogous to the issue of procedural/structural versus object-oriented programming).

ii) An open computational environment (such as a fully distributed version of the VoxelNET architecture) is one in which agents may be created by different parties, using different languages, algorithms, etc. In this case, algorithms need to be implemented within agent components that can intercommunicate via standardised messaging formats, protocols and semantics, irrespectively of the languages and specific form of data structures and algorithms created by different parties that conform to standardised messages.

iii) Systems that include physical agents, such as robots, may include agents having widely varying internal implementation requirements and computational capacity and will generally require real time internal control, with potentially asynchronous and/or near-real time interaction with other agents as required within the ecosystem. This case is similar to case ii), but with additional requirements for encapsulating computational agents within physical bodies or structures arising from the needs of timeliness and the ability to operate in real time independently of external communication links.

Task types and performance details in different implementations may nevertheless be incorporated into task libraries, which can be accessed and downloaded into agents anywhere in VoxelNET, if a situation or message type arises for which a given agent does not already have an appropriate task definition.

IV. THE VOXEL AGENT EXAMPLE

An example of how voxels can function as agents is provided by considering an agent-based approach to path planning, based upon the Dijkstra algorithm [15]. VoxelNET can include physical robots and has been demonstrated as a platform for individual unmanned aerial vehicle (UAV) control in underground mines [10] and for control of systems of many UAVs in an urban environment. The voxel structure can be used to implement occupancy grids for autonomous vehicle navigation, and for the storage and representation of 3D mapping data [16], [17].

The path planning task has been demonstrated in two application scenarios for VoxelNET: i) UAV inspection and mapping in underground mines, and ii) UAV traffic management in urban environments. These were both single-point demonstrators of the path planning solution, while here we present a distributed approach to solve the same task. The high-level process is described by:

1. UAV sends StartPath message to starting voxel, using geo-located address and including flight start time, end time, priority, vehicle type, mission type, vehicle id, service class, etc.. The voxel state is changed to indicate that the voxel is part of this path planning process.
2. UAV sends End of Path message to geo-located address of end voxel, including flight start time, end time, priority, vehicle type, mission type, vehicle id, service class, etc. Voxel state is changed to indicate that the voxel is part of this path planning process.
3. Start and End voxel agents send the same message to each adjacent voxel not already involved in this path planning process, plus the path in progress, which path it is, the count of iterations and the count of path voxels.
4. If an adjacent voxel is available and is not already involved in this path planning process, steps 1 or 2 are repeated by this voxel, respectively, for the developing start and end path options from the perspective of the path developed so far. If an adjacent voxel is *not* available, its voxel state is changed to indicate that the voxel is part of this path planning process, but steps 1 and 2 are not iterated by this voxel for its adjacent voxels.
5. If a voxel in the starting path meets a voxel in an ending path, it will append the end path to the starting path and notify the originating voxel that a path has been found, with its parameters, including length.

6. The starting voxel agent can choose to accept the first path created, or wait to see if a shorter or more valued (optimal) path occurs.

This algorithm is potentially very inefficient, since, if not stopped at the first path found, it searches for all paths through a connected network. However, it lends itself to distributed computation and there is no need for any centralised representation of the total network – connected voxels are readily determined from the position of a given voxel and the structure of the coordinate system. This algorithm requires very simple agents, but more sophisticated agent capabilities could be built upon it, such as cooperative behaviours, in which voxels work together to negotiate which path a given request will have allocated to it, or competitive behaviours, such as pre-empting path calculations to effectively reserve paths or shorten pathfinding time.

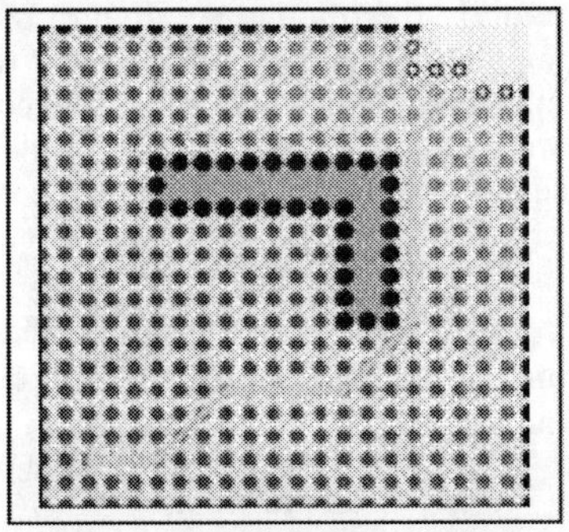

Figure 1. 2D Path planning problem.

A. *Implementation –Voxel Path Planning*

A path planning algorithm searching for the shortest path(s) [18] is often a top down 2 dimensional problem (see Figure 1), but here we are including the third dimension so the search space is volumetric.

Path length differences are illustrated in Figure 2; there can be many other paths adjacent to the shortest path, but they all involve at least 5 + 2 = 7 steps.

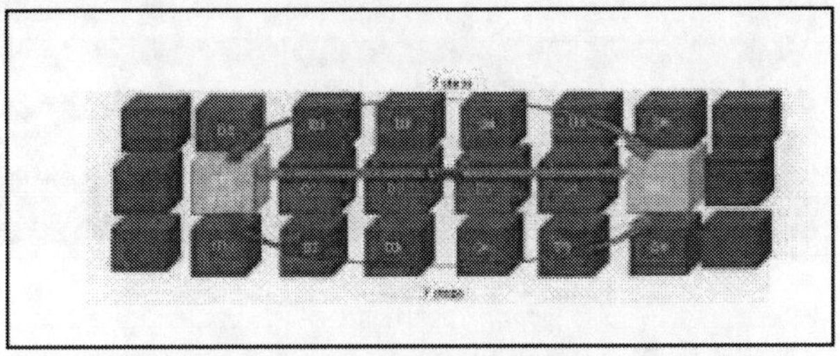

Figure 2. Example of path length calculation.

Here we adapt the well-known Dijkstra algorithm for finding paths between nodes in a graph, which may represent, for example, road or travel path networks. In this case the graph structure is the interconnected graph structure of a 3D, orthogonal voxel matrix. The algorithm exists in many variants. Dijkstra's original algorithm found the shortest path between two nodes. A more common variant fixes a single node as the "source" node and finds shortest paths from the source to all other nodes in the graph, producing a shortest-path tree.

The path finding solution shown in Figures 3 and 4 was implemented in C#. For the path finder to operate, a start voxel and an end voxel must be selected, and the pathfinding process begins simultaneously at these two voxels. Each voxel has a flag to identify whether it was approached from the start or end (referred to as the direction flag), whether it has been processed, and whether it is available.

Figure 3. Voxel Path Planning implementation in 2D (white is an obstacle, blue is traversed and green is the final path).

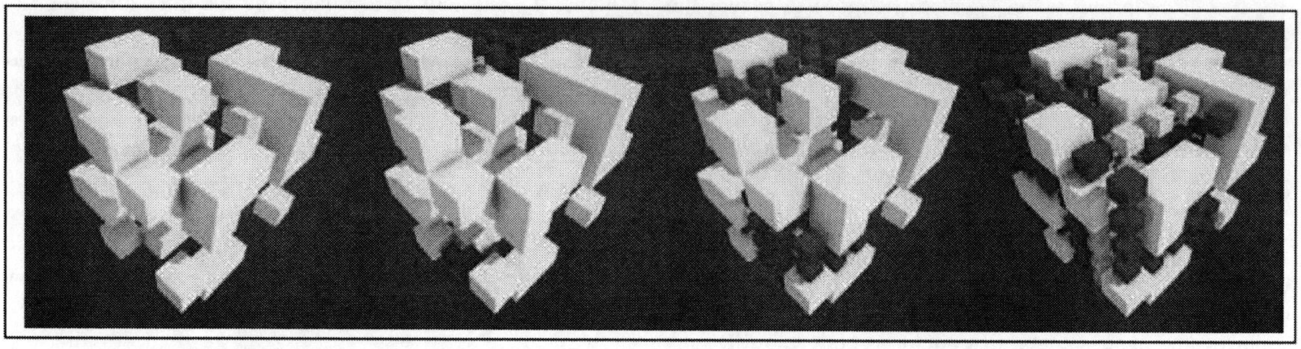

Figure 4. Voxel path planning implementation in 3D (white is an obstacle, blue is traversed and green is the final path).

Every adjacent voxel is evaluated and if it was not already evaluated and is available (meaning it is not obstructed), the voxel it was approached from is stored in its state and the evaluated flag is updated, as well as the direction flag, to identify whether it is in a path travelling from or to the end voxel. This voxel will propagate the evaluation to adjacent voxels and so on (implementing simple agent-agent interaction). If a voxel is already evaluated/processed and it has a different direction flag, it means that a path has been found connecting the start and end points. The voxel chain is traversed in a similar fashion to a linked list and each voxel is placed into a collection to make up the path, which is stored in an external object passed in at the start of the path finding process so that it can be retrieved externally or dealt with asynchronously (which was the case in the source code and should apply to a physically distributed system). The implementation finds the quickest path to compute (the path requiring the least number of iterations) but does not attempt to find the shortest or most optimal path. This functionality could be added with some small modifications.

V. Conclusion

This paper has described the VoxelNET distributed spatial data system and how the concept of agents can be applied within this system. A simple example of agent interaction has been implemented and described. Achieving path finding by the distributed agent approach allows voxels as agents to intercommunicate via voxel addresses as part of a logically connected voxel network, even though the information stored for specific voxels may be held on different computational and storage systems. Hence the voxel network is a single logical structure, implemented on potentially distributed processing architectures. The simple example presented does not do justice to the full, and even endless, range of sophistication possible in an agent-based system, but serves to illustrate the principals involved. The sophistication of agents within the overall VoxelNET can vary widely, by position, the types of data, information and knowledge that they can process, and in the complexity and adaptability of the agent cognitive architectures that they use. A more complex pathfinding example could involve agents that can compete to lure or drive away traffic, e.g. by including cost or payment data in addition to pure path data for traversable voxels. Pathfinding can then become an iterative Pareto optimisation process, where agents in potential paths can seek to increase their charges or payments to modify the optimal solution to meet their local goals of participation (e.g. to encourage more use of sparsely used path steps) or avoidance (e.g. to reduce demand and congestion on popular paths). Future work will include further investigation of these and related concepts.

Acknowledgment

We thank CSIRO Mineral Resources and Mining3 for supporting our VoxelNET research. VoxelNET™ is a patented technology.

References

[1] http://www.tnl.net/blog/2017/02/11/internet-4-0/ [retrieved: 15 January 2019].

[2] https://en.wikipedia.org/wiki/Industry_4.0 [retrieved: 15 January 2019].

[3] C. Sennersten, A. Davie and C. Lindley, "Voxelnet - An Agent Based System for Spatial Data Analytics", short paper, *Eighth International Conference on Advanced Cognitive Technologies and Applications (COGNITIVE 2016)*, March 20 - 24, Rome, Italy, 2016.

[4] https://medium.com/@sifium/machine-learning-types-of-classification-9497bd4f2e14 [retrieved: 15 January 2019].

[5] https://www.sciencelearn.org.nz/resources/1438-classification-system [retrieved: 15 January 2019].

[6] K. Padian, "Charles Darwin's Views of Classification in Theory and Practice", Syst. Biol. 48(2):352-364, 1999.

[7] O. Cardin, "Classification of cyber-physical production systems applications: Proposition of an analysis framework", Computers in Industry 104 (2019) 11–21, 2018.

[8] OGC: 06-103r4 Part 1 "Simple Feature Access - Part 1: Common Architecture" (https://www.iso.org/standard/40114.html, last accessed on 14 January 2019), 2004, and Part 2 "Simple Feature Access - Part 2: SQL Option" (https://www.iso.org/standard/40115.html, last accessed on 14 January 2019), 2004.

[9] D. Pentecost, C. Sennersten, C. A. Lindley, R. Ollington and B. Kang, "Predictive ACT-R (PACT-R): Using A Physics Engine and Simulation for Physical Prediction in a Cognitive Architecture", *Eighth International Conference on Advanced Cognitive Technologies and Applications (COGNITIVE 2016)*, March 20 - 24, Rome, Italy, 2016.

[10] C. Sennersten, C. Lindley, R. Lyu, A. Grace, B. Evans, D. L. Taylor, A. Davie, L. De Macedo Camargo, J. Craig, A. Hellicar, D. Biggins,

G. Timms, M. Coombe, S. Shariar Md, G. Smith, A. Morshed, A. Rahman, G. N. Salomão, 2015, "Unmanned Aerial Robots for Remotely Operated and Autonomous Surveying in Inaccessible Underground Mine Voids" *Third International Future Mining Conference*, Sydney, Australia, pp. 101-08, 4-6 November 2015.

[11] http://www.engyes.com/en/dic-content/softbot [retrieved: 15 January 2019].

[12] J. P. Müller. "Architectures and applications of intelligent agents: A survey." *Knowl. Eng. Rev.* 13, 4 (February 1999), 353-380. DOI=http://dx.doi.org/10.1017/S0269888998004020), 1999.

[13] D. L. Poole. and A. K. Machworth, "Artificial Intelligence: Foundations of Computational Agents", 2dn edn., CUP, isbn: 9781107195394, 2017.

[14] W. J. Teahan, "Artifical Intelligence –Agent Behaviour", bookboon, ISBN 978-87-7681-559-2, 2014.

[15] Dijkstra, E. W. (1959). "A note on two problems in connexion with graphs", *Numerische Mathematik*. **1**: 269–271. doi:10.1007/BF01386390, 1959.

[16] D. Maturana and S. Scherer, "VoxNet: A 3D Convolutional Neural Network for Real-Time Object Recognition", Conference Paper, IEEE/RSJ International Conference on Intelligent Robots and Systems, pp. 922-928, September, USA, 2015.

[17] Y. Zhou and O. Tuzel, "VoxelNet: End-to-End Learning for Point Cloud Based 3D Object Detection", USA, arXiv:1711.06396v1, 17 November 2017 (submitted).

[18] K. Mehlhorn and P. Sanders, "Chapter 10. Shortest Paths" (PDF). *Algorithms and Data Structures: The Basic Toolbox. Springer.* doi:10.1007/978-3-540-77978-0. ISBN 978-3-540-77977-3, *2008.*

Importance of Coordination and Cultural Diversity for an Efficient and Flexible Manufacturing System

Kashif Zia
Faculty of Computing and IT
Sohar University, Oman
Email: kzia@su.edu.om

Alois Ferscha
Institute of Pervasive Computing
Johannes Kepler University, Austria
Email: ferscha@pervasive.jku.at

Dari Trendafilov
Institute of Pervasive Computing
Johannes Kepler University, Austria
Email: dari.trendafilov@pervasive.jku.at

***Abstract*—Manufacturing systems of the future need to have flexible resources and flexible routing to produce extremely personalized products, even of lot size equal to one. In this paper, we have proposed a framework, which is designed to achieve this goal. Towards this, we have integrated an established cultural evolution model to achieve desired flexibility of resources and acceptable routing time. Promising results are evidenced through a simple proof-of-concept simulation.**

Keywords–Industry 4.0; resource flexibility; routing flexibility; personalized production; cultural dissemination; group coherence.

I. INTRODUCTION

The industrial manufacturing paradigm has already evolved from mass production to mass customization. Fueled by initiatives like Industry 4.0 [1], we foresee a further improvement in the coming years, namely the paradigm of personalized production. Personalized production targets an extremely flexible manufacturing system which could respond to predicted and unpredicted changes in the production environment.

According to [2], this flexibility should be a collection of three aspects, at least:

- Resource Flexibility: flexibility of machines/processing stations to make multiple parts.
- Routing Flexibility: flexibility to execute the same operation/function using multiple processing stations.
- Lot Size Flexibility: ability to produce a very small customized/personalized lot size in a non-batch mode.

Historically, many research efforts have focused on specific features of these aspects. Many scheduling [3] [4], resource optimization [2] [5], and constraint satisfaction [6] solutions have been presented. However, all these mechanisms either consider a mathematical abstraction or imitate a real-world situation as their manufacturing environment. The problem is that this results in a static configuration, and the solution proposed only works in these boundaries.

For modeling of a dynamical system, it is imperative to use a computational approach. For example, a more recent work uses an agent-based model while considering mobile processing stations as a mean to achieve flexibility in the manufacturing process [2]. The idea is to make resources available when and where these are required. Although their approach addresses the challenge of routing flexibility to an extent, the capabilities of resources still remain static.

In our research, we are mostly focusing on resource flexibility, which means that the processing units are able to dynamically change their *capabilities* and therefore a resource is able to perform several tasks. The goal is to keep resources stationary (and avoid expensive process of mobility) and arrange resources in groups of *complementing* capabilities. Ideally, a resource would designate itself for a capability that would optimize the manufacturing process in several dimensions, such as production rate, lead-time per order and reactivity index [2].

In this context, our mechanism exploits the cultural nature of the scenario; i.e. groups of *complementing* capabilities; and we are convinced that cultural diversity (complementation) has a lot of potentials to explore about. We argue that flexibility in resources, routing and personalizing closely relate to the evolution of culture, particularly cultural groups and diversification. This would provide an entirely new perspective for future research in this domain.

A culture is a multi-featured system evolving in time. One characteristic of culture is its coherence when seen from outside. Definitely, this coherence results due to a majority of people trying to acquire a similar behavior (often termed as a trait) in a certain context (often termed as a feature). Hence, a conceptual framework comprising of resources and products, driven by related features and traits can be formulated. A resource is a processing unit in the production line, whereas a product is obviously a product under production. Although a product can also be considered as a cultural entity, it is not the case for now. Only a resource is a cultural entity. The framework particularly focuses on limited coherence between cultural groups.

Resources are flexible, initially having some randomly chosen features and a randomly chosen trait against a feature. For example, a processing unit may have ability to perform one, two or more tasks T_1, T_2, ... with certain levels of precision P_1, P_2, ... Here, a tuple consisting of n values is a set describing capabilities of a resource. For example, the set $\{P_2, P_1, P_3\}$ can be interpreted as: this resource can perform task 1 with precision 2, task 2 with precision 1 and task 3 with precision 3. Furthermore, it cannot perform any other task.

Such a scheme is naturally compatible with the requirement of a flexible manufacturing system stated above, namely, flexibility in resources, routing and personalizing. Axelrod provides evidence in his seminal work [7] for such a simple configuration of cultural descriptions which can result in a locally coherent, but globally polarized culture as a consequence of localized interactions of participating entities.

However, in this paper, we argue that such a limitless coherence has no control over where the boundaries of the global polarization would occur, which turned out to be harmful to a system which usually seeks for the economy of resources and optimizations in several dimensions. That is the reason, we try to find conditions which end up in approximately acceptable structuring in terms of coherence (termed as limited coherence) vs. polarization. To achieve this, we have used and refined Axelrod's model of cultural dissemination [7].

Axelrod's model provides evidence of observation that the more time we provide for cultural dissemination, the cultural groups become increasingly coherent due to homophily. For scenarios, which require diversification of resources, we need to find a balance between coherence and diversification. This paper provides first insights into these aspects for a production shop floor. The paper presents an agent-based model, abstracting and simplifying the production process at a hypothetical shop floor.

The rest of the paper is structured as follows. In section II, a detailed description of the methods of modeling and simulation is given, followed by a discussion on initial findings in section III. We end the paper with an elaborate outlook of future work given in section IV.

II. METHODS

In the following, a detailed description of the models is given. Starting from desperation of Axelrod's model of cultural dissemination, next the motivation of the proposed model is given, followed by the details of the proposed method itself.

A. Axelrod's Model of Cultural Dissemination

Axelrod's model [7] thrived for cultural homogeneity [8], where adjacent cultures gets influence from each other. The model is based on cultural components defined by three factors; features, traits, and persons. Culture has many features, such as habits of eating, recreation, and leisure. These features may not be identical across different cultures. Each of these features has several traits, which may differ across cultures. A person is a placeholder of a culture described by one of f features and t traits. Axelrod proposed a model seeking for cultural homogeneity proclaiming that different cultures are destined to cohere together so that they appear as a cultural unity, but at the same time, there exists a clear-cut differentiation between cultures.

Axelrod model was able to demonstrate that the above two (rather contradictory) goals can be achieved by a simple interaction model (realized through N coordination games) between neighboring persons. Axelrod showed that N coordination games are necessary for a broader scale evolution of culture. Furthermore, groups' consistency across different aspects of societal norms makes a group culturally coherent and different from others. In the following, a hypothetical case study representing Axelrod's model of cultural diversification is presented.

In Figure 1, a grid of 10×10 cells is shown. Each cell is represented by a person or a culture depicted by color (one unique combination out of $f \times t$ possible combinations). Each cell's color has a meaning; for example, all green cells have the capability to perform task 1 with precision value 0, which is followed by precision values of task 2 (0, 1 or 2); last value is not path dependent and represented by z. A product has a unique sequence of the task to perform represented with an arrow shape (at the center of the space).

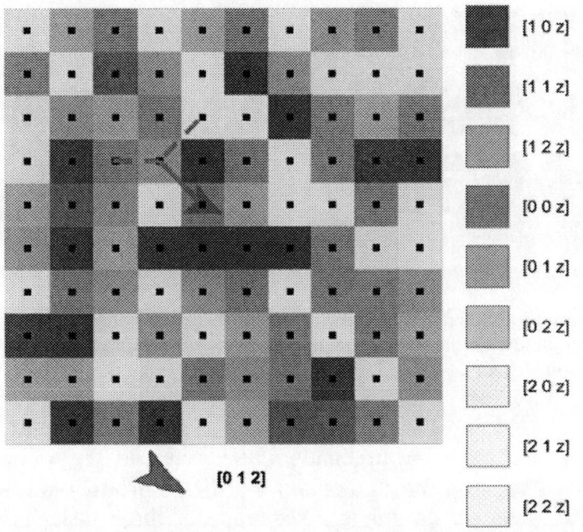

Figure 1. Initial distribution of a 10×10 grid constituted by blocks of culture; each block a tuple of 3, representing three features (green, blue, yellow) having three traits (3 shades of a color) each. Average $diversity\_index$ of random setting is around 0.660.

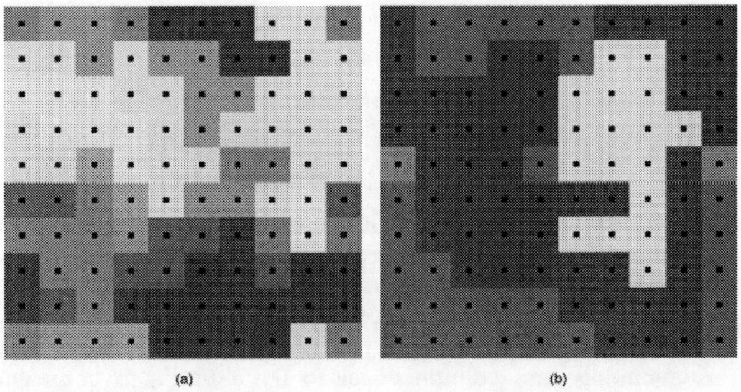

Figure 2. Axelrod's Model: Evolution of cultures shown in Figure 1. (a) at simulation iteration 6055 showing clusters of cultures starting to form. (b) at simulation iteration 12207 showing further consolidation of clusters of cultures. The evolution is destined to end up in very few cultures (1 or 2).

Axelrod model calculated similarity s between neighboring cultures. If s is not 1 (100%), with a probability p, the value of a $different$ column of a person is replaced by the corresponding value of the neighboring person. This simple mechanism is able to generate clusters of coherent cultures as shown in Figure 2. If we define **diversity_index** as the mean diversification of cultures of all persons when compared to their neighbors, the Axelrod model would converge into a single culture most of the time with $diversity\_index$ equal to 0. This is not desirable in the context in which we want to use this model. Therefore, the model was extended as detailed in the following.

B. The Motivation: Constrained, N-Coordination Games for Cultural Diversity

Before the description of the model, we formalize the scenario given in Figure 1 as a manufacturing process. Give that a processing unit is able to perform three possible tasks

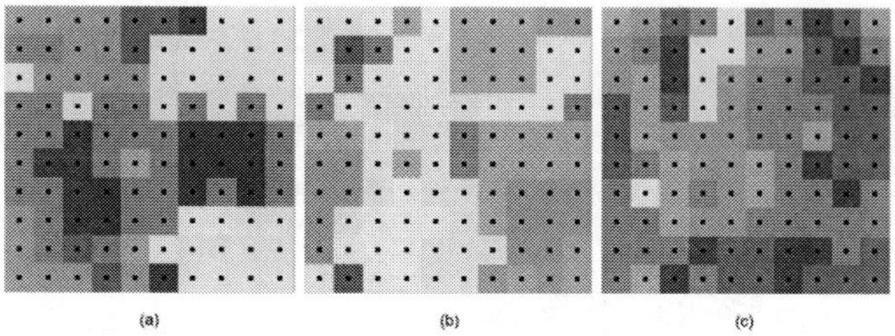

Figure 3. Extended Axelrod's Model: Cultural Diversity at iteration 50000. Three random outcomes shown in (a), (b) and (c) having a $diversity\_index$ of around 0.320.

with three possible precision values, we can see a clear capability matching through colors. Further, a product is introduced which need to complete a sequence of three tasks offered by different resources. We hypothesize that using the constraint, N coordination games, we can achieve cultural diversity, which is closer to what is desirable. This would directly impact products' traversing efforts in a positive way. A comparison of Figure 2 with Figure 3 shows less diversification from prior to the later. We hypothesize that this would help in reducing the traversing efforts of the products.

An Example Walkthrough: Referring to Figure 1 again, each resource (black agent at the center of a cell) is randomly populated with vector [x y z], where x, y, and z may have three possible values 0, 1 and 2. The product has to perform three tasks in a sequence. Task 1 with precision 0, task 2 with precision 1 and task 3 with precision 2. It starts at the shown position. First, it will perform task 1 with precision 0. That is right away available at the cell the product is situated. Next, it has to perform task 2 with precision 1. The nearest resource, which has first column equal to 0 (assuming a connection between task 1 and 2) and second column equal to 1 is the resource on immediate top-left; hence the product would move there. Next task is task 3 with precision 2. Assuming that it is an independent task, the product would try to find the nearest resource that has the third column equal to 2 (any color). This can be any resource (two valid possibilities are shown with dotted lines).

It seems that random configurations would be the best, but this cannot be the case in a structured environment, particularly in case of an assembly line type of manufacturing. The Axelrod model is too skewed towards coherence and would end up in too few cultures. Hence we propose to refine the Axelrod model in the following way.

C. The Proposed Diversity Dissemination Mechanism

Axelrod model sought for similarity s between neighboring cultures. If s is not 1 (100%), with a probability p, the value of a $different$ column of culture is replaced by the corresponding value of the neighboring culture. We extend this model by applying an extra constraint. That is, the replacement is only possible if s is also less than a threshold th, which is for now given a static value of 0.5. This is expected to increase overall *diversity_index* of the system. Before analyzing the impact of this refinement the mechanism of product traversing is explained.

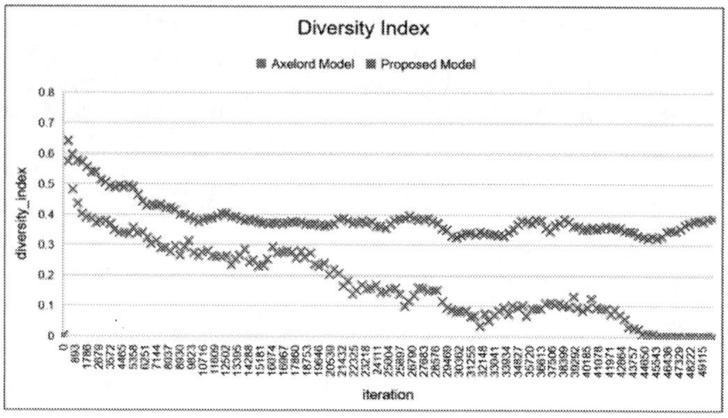

Figure 4. Comparison of time series of $diversity\_index$.

D. Traversing Mechanism

All products have a sequence of tasks to perform in the form [x, y, z]. A product first gets the value x, and maps it onto resources with an identical capability and residing close to its position. Let's denote the resource at r. After visiting r, the product seeks for the next nearest resource corresponding to y. It is assumed that y has a relationship with x. This means that, in terms of colors, this cell (and the resource residing on top of it) should have the same color. The last task z is independent and just show the range of flexibility that the system may have.

III. Analysis of Initial Findings

Definitely, the introduction of threshold th retains $diversity\_index$ in case of extension of Axelrod's model, as shown in Figure 4. This helps in task completion capability of the system due to the provisioning of a more diverse array of complementing capabilities. The graph shown in Figure 4 evidences this fact. The diversity_index of the proposed model is much higher than the Axelrod's model throughout the simulation and it never dies out no matter how long the system evolves, unlike Axelrod's model.This can be verified by analyzing the mobility of products in case of random configurations. In Figure 5, we can see five products which start from the center of the space. Products 100 and 101 needed to perform task 1, so they did it as the first step using the resource where product 102 is stationed now. Next, they move to the right and performed task 2. That means that both completed the first two task of their schedule successfully. The similar is true for the other three products. The system could acquire a mobility index equal to 2 on average for the first two tasks, which it did without any problem. As we mentioned already, a random configuration is most flexible and would always be best in its task completion capability. However, this configuration is unrealistic. In reality, we need to plan the placement of resources and put them in order.

In case of Axelrod's model, we have analyzed the results for $diversity\_index$ 0.5, 0.25 and 0.1. These three situations are represented in Figure 6. With increasing polarization and decreasing $diversity\_index$, the average mobility index drops. After running the simulation several times, it was observed that mobility index is 1.8 ($diversity\_index$ = 0.5), 1.4 ($diversity\_index$ = 0.25) and 0.03 ($diversity\_index$ = 0.10). As shown in Figure 6, this decrease is due to nonavailability of resources indicated by products turning into black color.

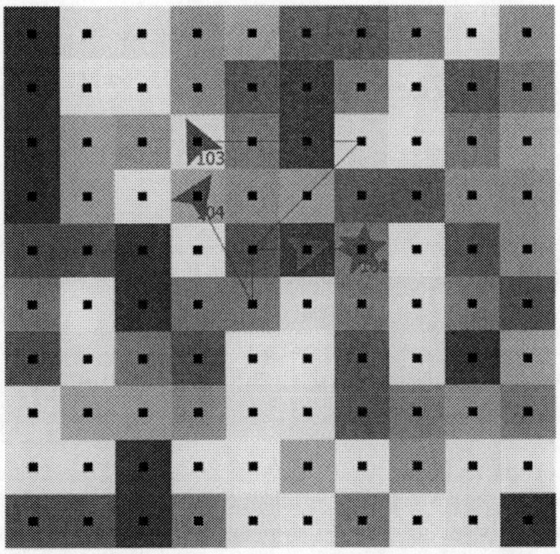

Figure 5. Traversing behavior in random configuration of resource capability.

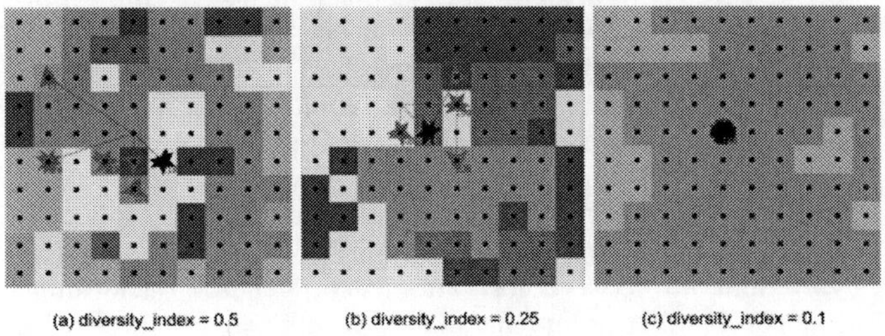

Figure 6. Traversing behavior in Axelord's Model.

Lastly, the extended models solve the above issue. We can see a smooth performance of tasks for all the products, which is evident from Figure 7. For even minimum possible diversity (0.33), in the majority of the cases, the mobility index achieved is 2 (the possible maximum).

IV. Conclusion and Future Work

Manufacturing systems of the future need to have flexible resources and routing to produce an extremely personalized product, even of lot size equal to one. What we have seen is that flexible manufacturing system can be realized without moving the resources (processing units) by enabling reconfiguration of capabilities of resources based on dissemination of culture concept proposed by Axelrod. However, the Axelrod model has a focus on the coherence of cultural groups, which most of the times end up in one or very few cultures. If we equate such an instance of a culture with a single capability of a resource, we are left with extremely limited resources and products cannot complete their production life cycle.

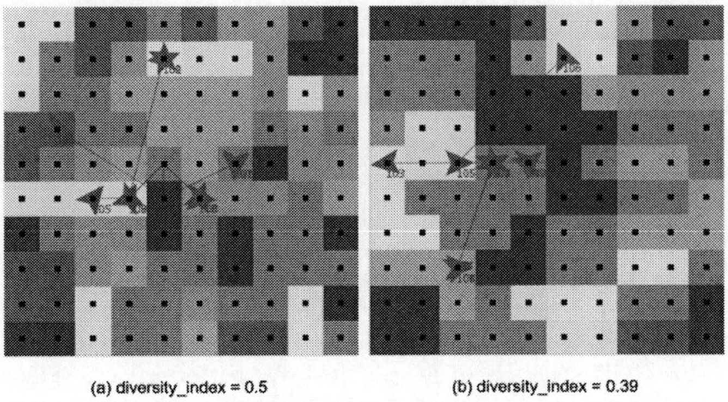

Figure 7. Traversing behavior in Extended Axelrod's Model.

Hence, we proposed to have a constrained cultural coherence mechanism by introducing a threshold. This tiny development has a significant impact on the increase in diversity of the culture along with related resources being in close vicinity to each other on average. This did not only ensure an increase in resource availability as a whole, but also managed to decrease the mobility of products in search of suitable resources.

However, the real contribution of the paper is the integration of manufacturing processes with cultural considerations, which naturally fits into the problem. In our view, this is a novel approach of real significance. However, the work reported in this paper is just a proof-of-concept. We need to have more thorough experiments to measure the efficiency of the model in challenging environments such as environments having inflow and outflow points, more in-depth capabilities and richer relationships between tasks.

In the next phase of the project, we will induct models of dynamics, which will include timing of tasks, conflict and deadlock resolution between products seeking identical resources, and more realistic analytics such as production rate, lead-time per order and reactivity index. Lastly, we would also include an autonomous learning system, which would help resources learn and change their configurations on the fly based on product types, requirements, and trajectories.

Acknowledgment

The authors would like to acknowledge support by FFG funded Pro^{2}Future under contract No. 6112792.

References

[1] J. Lee, B. Bagheri, and H.-A. Kao, "A cyber-physical systems architecture for industry 4.0-based manufacturing systems," Manufacturing Letters, vol. 3, 2015, pp. 18–23.

[2] R. Ogunsakin, N. Mehandjiev, and C. A. Marín, "Bee-inspired self-organizing flexible manufacturing system for mass personalization," in International Conference on Simulation of Adaptive Behavior. Springer, 2018, pp. 250–264.

[3] M. Wang, R. Y. Zhong, Q. Dai, and G. Q. Huang, "A mpn-based scheduling model for iot-enabled hybrid flow shop manufacturing," Advanced Engineering Informatics, vol. 30, no. 4, 2016, pp. 728–736.

[4] M. K. Marichelvam, T. Prabaharan, and X. S. Yang, "A discrete firefly algorithm for the multi-objective hybrid flowshop scheduling problems," IEEE transactions on evolutionary computation, vol. 18, no. 2, 2014, pp. 301–305.

[5] G. Beruvides, Artificial Cognitive Architecture with Self-Learning and Self-Optimization Capabilities: Case Studies in Micromachining Processes. Springer, 2018.

[6] J. Ezpeleta, J. M. Colom, and J. Martinez, "A petri net based deadlock prevention policy for flexible manufacturing systems," IEEE transactions on robotics and automation, vol. 11, no. 2, 1995, pp. 173–184.

[7] R. Axelrod, "The dissemination of culture: A model with local convergence and global polarization," Journal of conflict resolution, vol. 41, no. 2, 1997, pp. 203–226.

[8] J. Bednar, A. Bramson, A. Jones-Rooy, and S. Page, "Emergent cultural signatures and persistent diversity: A model of conformity and consistency," Rationality and Society, vol. 22, no. 4, 2010, pp. 407–444.

Neural Computation of Perceived Relative Size and Depth in Complex 2D Image Configurations

Birgitta Dresp-Langley
Centre National de la Recherche Scientifique (CNRS)
UMR 7357 ICube Lab Strasbourg University
Strasbourg, France
e-mail: birgitta.dresp@icube.unistra.fr

Adam Reeves
Department of Psychology
Northeastern University
Boston, USA
e-mail: a.reeves@northeastern.edu

***Abstract*—The neural networks of the human visual brain are capable of extracting 3D structure from specific 2D cues available in planar images. Many of the functional principles governing this ability are still not fully understood. Neural models backed by psychophysical data predict how local differences in either luminance contrast or physical size of local boundaries in 2D images may determine the perception of 3D structure, but do not generate predictions relative to the role of color in this process. To further clarify the potential contribution of color to 3D perceptual organization, we created 2D image configurations with multiple surface representations where the relative physical size of local boundaries between contrast regions was held constant. The only potential cues to 3D available in the images were specific local combinations of color and luminance contrast. Psychophysical experiments with human observers were run to test for selective local effects on the subjective relative depth and the subjective relative size of image regions. It was found that response probabilities for subjective depth and subjective size are systematically and consistently determined by local surface colors and their immediate backgrounds. The results show consistently varying perceptual judgments with a statistically significant correlation between subjective depth and subjective size. Moreover, there is a color specific effect on both dependent variables, and this effect depends on the polarity of the immediate surround of the reference surface rather than local center-surround contrast intensity. These findings are not predicted by any of the current neural models and suggest that the perceptual mechanisms generating 3D effects from 2D visual input selectively exploit specific color and background cues to enable the intrinsically coherent 3D perceptual organization of otherwise ambiguous 2D images with multiple surface representations.**

Keywords - colour; local contrast; background intensity; complex images; 2D image parts; subjective size; relative depth.

I. INTRODUCTION

Leonardo da Vinci [1] was the first to report on the importance of local luminance contrast as a perceptual cue to 3D in 2D images. Contemporary neural models and psychophysical data predict that contrast variations across image parts directly determine which parts of a planar image will be seen as "nearer" or "further away from" the human observer [1] - [10]. Previous studies on functional aspects of mechanisms for depth perception from neural computation of local image contrast properties have not yet fully explored all the complex interactions between color, luminance, and general background field intensities. In the absence of other spatial cues to depth, it appears that specific colors in combination with specific contrast intensities may produce more powerful 3D effects than others, as suggested by results on perceptual figure-ground organization, for example [10] [1] - [14]. Moreover, variations in brightness or luminance displayed across two or more different surface layers in complex 2D multiple-surface configurations may alter these perceptual effects significantly [7] [14] [15], or even reverse them [16] [17]. This study was designed to explore some of such possible interactions more systematically. Complex 2D image configurations with carefully controlled physical variations in local color, luminance, general background intensity, and constant spatial parameters were generated for this purpose. The local physical size of the test and reference surfaces submitted to perceptual judgments was not varied across comparisons. Center-surround surface combinations within image configurations were displayed on a high resolution monitor in a computer controlled psychophysical study with human subjects completing four Two-Alternative spatial Forced Choice (2AFC) judgment tasks. The subjects had to judge which of two comparison surfaces in the configurations appeared "bigger" (task 1) or "nearer" (task 3), and which of all the possible reference surfaces in a given configuration appeared "the biggest" (task 3) or "the nearest" (task 4) of all.

In Section 2, the materials and methods used to generate the image configurations for this study, some of the characteristics of the study population, and the experimental task procedures are explained. Section 3 summarizes the principal results and discusses their implications for our current understanding of perceptual 3D organization from 2D image input. Section 4 provides a conclusion in terms of the consistency and/or discrepancy of the findings with regard to current neural models of 3D perception from planar image input.

II. MATERIALS AND METHODS

Image configurations were computer generated and displayed on a high resolution color monitor (EIZO COLOR EDGE CG 275W, 2560x1440 pixel resolution) connected to a DELL computer equipped with a high performance graphics card (NVIDIA). Color and luminance calibration of the RGB channels of the monitor was performed using the appropriate Color Navigator self-calibration software, which was delivered with the screen and runs under Windows 7. RGB values here correspond to ADOBE RGB. All luminance levels were cross-checked with an external photometer (OPTICAL, Cambridge Research Systems). RGB coordinates, luminance parameters (cd/m^2), and color coordinates (X, Y, Z) of the different reference surfaces in the image configurations from this study are given in Table 1.

The size of each of the square surfaces in the center of each of the twelve local configurations in the images was 160x160 pixels and the size of each of the square surrounds was 400x400 pixels. The twelve local configurations were equally spaced, with 50 pixels between their surrounds, along the horizontal and vertical dimensions. They were displayed centrally on the dark and light general background of the 2560x1440 pixel screen. The size of a single pixel on the screen is 0.023 cm.

Grey, red, and blue-green center squares on their light and dark immediate surrounds were presented in pairs, as shown in Figure 1. Their position (left, right) in a pair was counterbalanced between trials and subjects. Presentation on light and dark general backgrounds was also counterbalanced between trials and subjects. The subject pool consisted of mostly undergraduate medical students, with normal or corrected-to-normal vision. All of them were naïve to the purpose of the experiment and run in individual sessions. They were comfortably seated in a semi-dark room, in front of the EIZO monitor at a viewing distance of about 1 meter. Each individual received the same standard instructions for the psychophysical tasks.

In the first task, the subject had to decide which of the two central squares in a paired configuration (*paired comparison*) appeared to be the "bigger" one of the two. In the second task, the subject had to pick the central square from all of the twelve configurations that appeared the "biggest" of all (*single pick*). In the third task, the subject was instructed to judge which of the two central squares in a paired configuration (*paired comparison*) appeared to be "nearer" to them, and in the fourth task he/she had to pick the central square from all of the twelve configurations that appeared the "nearest" of all (*single pick*) to the observer.

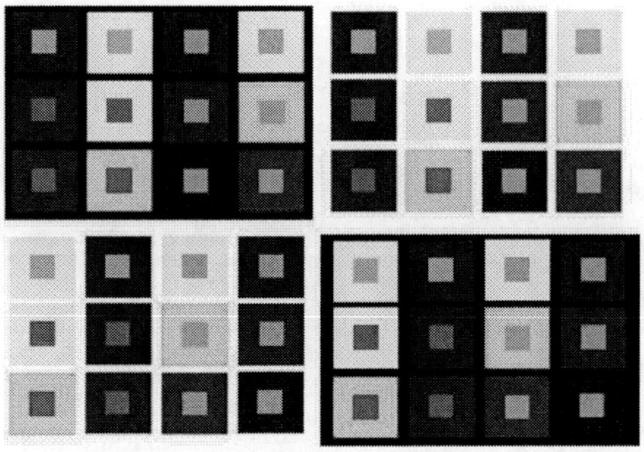

Figure 1. Center-surround surface configurations on dark and light general backgrounds.

The twelve local configurations shown in Figure 1 produce subjective differences in the relative size and depth of the centrally displayed squares. Grey, red, and blue-green center squares displayed on dark and light surrounds were paired for the relative psychophysical judgments. Trials were sequenced in counterbalanced sessions producing eight psychophysical judgments for each *paired comparison* and *single pick* task, general background condition, and subject. Therefore, a total of 80 data was generated for each of the four tasks and for each of the two general background conditions

The subjects who participated in this study were adult volunteers all naïve to the purpose of the study. We selected seven men and three women with normal or corrected-to-normal vision. The experiments were non-invasive and conducted in accordance with the Declaration of Helsinki (1964) and with full approval of the corresponding author's host institution's (CNRS) ethical standards committee. Informed consent was obtained from each of the participants.

TABLE I. COLOR AND LUMINANCE PARAMETERS

Reference Surface	Image Luminance (*L*) And Color Coordinates						
	R	*G*	*B*	*L* (*cd/m^2*)	*X*	*Y*	*Z*
Grey Center	190	190	190	58.6	49.8	52.3	57.0
Red Center	255	0	0	35.8	57.7	29.7	2.7
Blue Center	0	205	205	52.3	23.1	43.5	65.7
Dark-Grey Surround	25	25	25	2.0	0.6	0.6	0.6
Light-Grey Surround	240	240	240	95.3	83.2	87.5	95.3
Dark-Green Surround	0	50	0	2	0.5	1.7	0.2
Light-Green Surround	0	255	0	78.5	18.5	62.7	7.1
Dark-Blue Surround	0	0	70	0.5	1.1	0.4	5.8
Light-Blue Surround	10	10	220	5	13.7	5.52	71.6
Dark General Background	0	0	0	0.5	0	0	0
Light General Background	255	255	255	120.0	13.7	5.52	71.6

III. RESULTS AND DISCUSSION

A. Response probabilities for "bigger" and "nearer"

The response probabilities (*p*) from the two paired comparison tasks (task 1, task 3) were calculated for each of the twelve local center-surround configurations in the order in which they are displayed in the first of the four general display-panels shown in Figure 1. A *p* of 1 would correspond to the case where a local configuration of a given pair produces a total number of 80 observed/80 possible responses for "bigger" or for "nearer". In this case, the *p* associated with the other configuration from that pair would be 0. In the case a given pair produces random perceptual responses for "bigger" or for "nearer", the response probability associated with each of the two paired configurations would be 0.50. In a first analysis, the twelve configurations were sorted as a function of the magnitude of the response probabilities they produced for "bigger" and "nearer" and plotted in ascending order for each of the two "general background intensity" conditions. These plots are shown in Figure 2. The two graphs reveal consistent *p* distributions for "bigger" and nearer" ranging from 0.10 to 0.90 in each of the two general background conditions.

B. Correlation between response probability distributions from the paired comparison tasks

The response probability distributions from the paired comparison tasks were submitted to statistical correlation analyses (Pearson's product moment), returning statistically significant correlation coefficients (*P*), with 0.98 ($p<.001$) for "bigger" and "nearer" in the "dark general background" condition, and 0.99 ($p<.001$) for the probability distributions for "bigger" and "nearer" in the "light general background" condition. These analyses show that the center-surround configurations produced a wide range of significantly correlated perceptual differences in relative size and depth of their local center surfaces.

C. Response probabilities for "bigger" and "nearer" as a function of luminance contrast

In a second analysis, the configurations were sorted as a function of their local contrast intensity. The luminance contrasts (*LumC*) are expressed here in terms of Weber Ratios, which are calculated using

$$LumC = Lum_{center} - Lum_{surround} / Lum_{surround} \qquad (1)$$

The response probabilities for "bigger" and "nearer" were then plotted as a function of the twelve different Weber contrasts of the configurations and the two general background conditions, shown in Figure 2. Graphs in the top panel show significantly correlated magnitudes of *p* for "bigger" and "nearer" produced by the twelve configurations on the two general backgrounds, plotted in ascending order. The graphs in the middle panel show *p* distributions as a function of the luminance contrast intensity (Weber ratios) of the twelve configurations and the general background conditions. The graphs in the bottom panel show *p* as a function of the local color contrast of the configurations with positive (+) Weber contrasts, which produced greater magnitudes of p for "bigger" and "nearer" in the paired comparison tasks.

The data reveal that there is no simple function linking the *p* for relative size and depth to the luminance contrast of the local configurations. There is a systematic effect of the general background condition on all the *p*: the lighter general background produced systematically stronger response probabilities for "bigger" and "nearer". The configurations with the positive local contrast signs all produced greater magnitudes of *p* in comparison with their negative-contrast-sign pairs, however, the configurations with the strongest positive contrasts did not produce the highest response probabilities, neither for "bigger" (relative size), nor for "nearer" (relative depth) in the paired comparison tasks.

This is clarified further by the graphs shown in the panel at the bottom of Figure 2, where *p* for "bigger" and "nearer" are shown as a function of the local color contrast of the configurations which produced the stronger *p* magnitudes, and as a function of the general background condition. The highest *p* for "bigger" (relative size) and "nearer" (relative depth) are produced by the RED central squares on the dark-grey surround displayed on the light general background, and by the GREY central squares on the dark grey surrounds displayed on the general background. The BLUE central squares on dark surrounds produced noticeably lower p for "bigger" and "nearer" in comparison with the RED centers, yet, the blue on dark surrounds has a much stronger luminance contrast (25.5) than the red on dark surrounds (16.9). For the blue centers on dark surrounds we observe the strongest effect of general display background condition: the *p* for "bigger" and "nearer" are well above a certain positive probability threshold (>=0.75) for the blue-on-dark configurations displayed on a light general background, but approach the chance level (~0.50) in the condition where they were displayed on a dark general background.

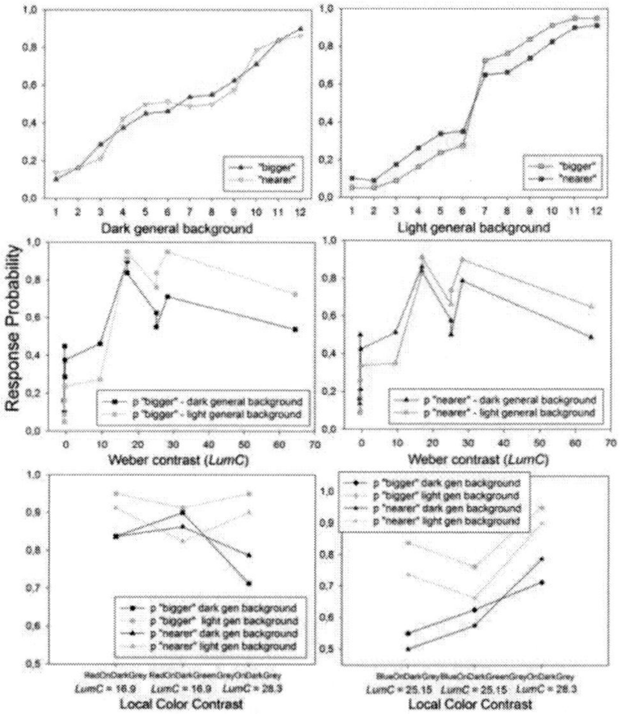

Figure 2. Response probability (p) distributions for relative size ("bigger of two") and relative depth ("nearer of two") judgments from the *paired comparison* tasks.

D. Response probabilities for "biggest of all" and "nearest of all " as a function of luminance contrast

In the final analysis, we plotted the *p* distributions from the two *single pick* tasks as a function of the contrast intensity of the twelve local configurations and the general display background condition. These results, shown in Figure 3, consistently indicate that the highest response probabilities for "biggest" and "nearest" are produced by RED centers on dark GREEN or GREY local surrounds. This result is consistent with earlier observations [9] and further highlights the hitherto not shown dependency of this selective color effect on physical parameters relative to the immediate and the general background intensities.

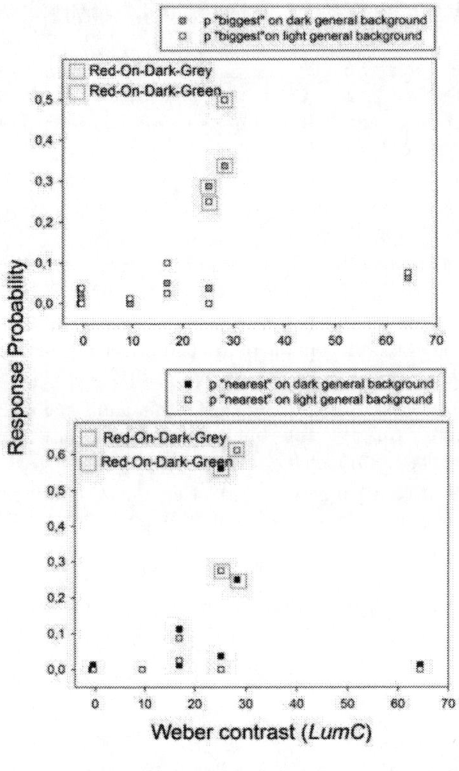

Figure 3. Response probability distributions for "biggest of all" and "nearest of all" as a function of local Weber contrasts (Weber Ratios) and general background condition from the *single pick* tasks.

IV. CONCLUSIONS

The results highlight complex interactions between color, local luminance contrast and global display background in the production of perceptual effects of subjective relative size and depth. Some of them, but not all, are predicted by current neural theories [6] [10] [15] [17] [18]. The subjective relative size of surface boundaries is significantly correlated with subjective depth, generating a perceptual 2D cue to 3D structure functionally equivalent to the "real", physically grounded, monocular depth cue. Although not explicitly predicted by any of the neural models, this observation supports a specific class of computational models of relative surface depth from ambiguous contrast input generated by 2D contrast surfaces and their boundaries [7] [11] [15] [17]. The perceptual judgments from this study support the idea that the human brain is capable of producing functional perceptual representations of figure and ground by using a multitude of different local and global cues in the 2D image. Ambiguous image input is dealt with by effectively exploiting whatever cue to structure is available in the display. Absence of a specific physically grounded depth cue may be compensated for by perceptually generated cues that allow the brain to compute coherent depth representations on the basis of global perceptual sensation rather than merely the direct or strictly local visual processing of an existing stimulus parameter such as a physical difference in the size of 2D surface boundaries, for example. Also, the way in which contrast is computed to achieve perceptual 3D structure reaches well beyond local processing. As shown here, the lighter general backgrounds of the configurations, resulting in image representations with more than two 2D surface layers, systematically produced stronger subjective depth effects, irrespective of the local color or contrast of the reference surfaces and their immediate surrounds. This has potentially important implications for the development of effective visual interface technology for image-guided systems designed to assist human operators in precision tasks [16]. The results from this study are consistent with previous findings that the color red is the most likely to produce depth effects in simple figure-ground displays with only two 2D surface representations [3] [9]. Red surface color on an achromatic background, for example, possesses a clear competitive advantage over other colors such as green [9] or blue [12] in the likelihood to be perceived as closer to the human observer. As shown here, when more than two surface layers are present in an image configuration, the advantage of the surface color red for perceptual organization appears to depend on the contrast polarities of all the image regions surrounding the reference surface, not on the local reference-surround luminance contrast. This result is new and may seem surprising, yet, it is fully consistent with experimental evidence from other studies showing that many different cues may cooperate adaptively and non-locally in figure–ground segregation from 2D cues [19]. Physiologically inspired model approaches which simulate how figure–ground segregation may be computed by neural mechanisms "beyond the classic receptive field", involving long-range feedback interactions between cells with increasingly larger receptive fields in higher visual cortical areas beyond V1, V2, or even V4 [15] [19] [20], are in principle suitable to account for the non-local processing of figure-ground. However, it is not clear how these models would account for selective color effects, as those shown here. It is possible that these effects may be linked to psychological effects of selective attention to specific colors and/or color cognition in a more general sense [21] [22]. These are still poorly understood and need to be investigated further.

ACKNOWLEDGMENT

The authors are grateful to Anne KELLY and Keith LANGLEY for helpful discussions.

REFERENCES

[1] L. Da Vinci, *Trattato della Pittura di Leonardo da Vinci*. Scritta da Raffaelle du Fresne, Langlois, Paris, 1651.

[2] G. E. Mount, H. W. Case, J. W. Sanderson, and R. Brenner, "Distance judgment of colored objects", *Journal of General Psychology*, vol. 55, pp. 207-214, 1956.

[3] H. Egusa, "On the color stereoscopic phenomenon", *Japanese Psychological Review*, vol. 20, pp. 369-386, 1977.

[4] M. Farnè "Brightness as an indicator to distance: relative brightness per se or contrast with the background?", *Perception*, vol. 6, pp. 287-293, 1977.

[5] H. Egusa, "Effects of brightness, hue, and saturation on the perceived depth between adjacent regions in the visual field.", *Perception*, vol. 12, pp. 167-175, 1983.

[6] S. Grossberg, "3D vision and figure-ground separation by visual cortex", *Perception and Psychophysics*, vol. 55, pp. 48-120, 1994.

[7] B. Dresp, "On illusory contours and their functional significance", *Current Psychology of Cognition*, vol. 16(4), pp. 489–518, 1997.

[8] B. Dresp, S. Durand, and S. Grossberg, "Depth perception from pairs of overlapping cues in pictorial displays", *Spatial Vision*, vol. 15, pp. 255–276, 2002.

[9] C. R. C. Guibal and B. Dresp, "Interaction of color and geometric cues in depth perception: When does "red" mean "near"?" *Psychological Research*, vol. 10, pp. 167-178, 2004.

[10] F. Qiu, T. Sugihara, and R. von der Heydt, "Figure-ground mechanisms provide structure for selective attention", *Nature Neuroscience*, vol. 11, pp. 1492-9 , 2007.

[11] B. Dresp and S. Fischer, "Asymmetrical contrast effects induced by luminance and colour configurations", *Perception & Psychophysics*, vol. 63, pp. 1262-1270, 2001.

[12] B. Dresp-Langley and A. Reeves, "Simultaneous brightness and apparent depth from true colors on grey: Chevreul revisited", *Seeing and Perceiving*, vol. 25, pp. 597-618, 2012.

[13] B. Dresp-Langley and A. Reeves, "Color and figure-ground: From signals to qualia", In S. Magnussen, M. Greenlee, J. Werner, A. Geremek (Eds.): *Perception beyond Gestalt: Progress in Vision Research*. Psychology Press, Abingdon (UK), pp. 159-71, 2014.

[14] B. Dresp-Langley and A. Reeves, "Effects of saturation and contrast polarity on the figure-ground organization of color on gray", *Frontiers in Psychology*, vol. 5, pp. 1136, 2014.

[15] S. Grossberg, "Cortical dynamics of figure-ground separation in response to 2D pictures and 3D scenes: How V2 combines border ownership, stereoscopic cues, and Gestalt grouping rules", *Frontiers in Psychology*, vol. 6, pp. 02054, 2015.

[16] B. Dresp-Langley, "Principles of perceptual grouping: implications for image-guided surgery", *Frontiers in Psychology*, vol. 6, pp. 1565, 2015.

[17] B. Dresp-Langley and S. Grossberg "Neural Computation of Surface Border Ownership and Relative Surface Depth from Ambiguous Contrast Inputs", *Frontiers in Psychology*, vol. 7, pp. 1102, 2016.

[18] R. von der Heydt, "Figure–ground and the emergence of proto-objects in the visual cortex", *Frontiers in Psychology*, vol. 6, pp. 1695, 2015.

[19] M. Dimicolli, "Figure-ground segregation: a fully non-local approach. Vision Research, vol. 126, pp.308-317, 2016.

[20] L. Spillmann, B. Dresp-Langley, and C. H. Tseng, "Beyond the classic receptive field: The effect of contextual stimuli", *Journal of Vision*, vol. 15, pp. 7, 2015.

[21] T. Xia, L. Song, T. Wang, L. Tan, and L. Mo, "Exploring the effect of red and blue on cognitive task performances", *Frontiers in Psychology*, vol.7, pp. 784, 2016.

[22] B. Dresp-Langley and A. Reeves, "Colour for behavioural success", *i-Perception*, vol. 9(2), pp. 1–23, 2018.

Resonance Thinking in Cartesian Systemic Emergence

Marta Franova, Yves Kodratoff
LRI, UMR8623 du CNRS & INRIA Saclay
Bât. 660, Orsay, France
e-mail: mf@lri.fr, yvekod@gmail.com

Abstract— **Cartesian Systemic Emergence (CSE) is concerned with strategic aspects relative to the conception of Symbiotic Recursive Pulsative Systems intended to solve real-world problems handling control and prevention in incomplete domains. This work is performed in order to prepare fundamentals for designing automated tools that help to perform this complex task. This paper presents the most important features of one particular way of thinking present in CSE. We call it 'Resonance Thinking'. Resonance Thinking takes care of generating and handling experiments during CSE. We explain that Resonance Thinking causes the complexity of CSE to be analogous to Ackermann's function computation complexity. The work presented is related to cognitive and computation models of human creative reasoning mechanisms. Our approach brings forward several challenging questions to Cognitive Science that will be given in the paper.**

Keywords-Cartesian Systemic Emergence; Symbiotic Recursive Pulsative Systems; Resonance Thinking; cognitive models; implementation of human reasoning mechanisms; design of experiments.

I. INTRODUCTION

In [11], we have described Cartesian Systemic Emergence (CSE) as a method that handles strategic aspects of construction and particular evolutive improvement of Symbiotic Recursive Pulsative Systems (SRPS). The construction and desired improvements have to guarantee control and prevention in the system. The need for this work came out during our research on automating program synthesis from formal specifications in incomplete domains. [7] [10]. For simplicity, we refer to it as Program Synthesis (PS).The constraints imposed on this PS research required us to develop a particular systems design methodology. CSE represents our way to tackle this task. We are thus developing theoretical models and criteria representing, among others, a background for capturing and understanding the complexity of cognitive tasks involved in CSE. Resonance Thinking (RT) introduced in this paper takes care of generating and handling experiments during CSE.

In [11], we describe several facets of CSE, namely tackling underspecified information, on-purpose invention instead of manipulating a specific search space, and formulating fruitful experiments during this invention. Resonance Thinking, as a symbiotic part of CSE, possesses also these facets and describes them in a more precise way, even though a formal description has still to be worked out. CSE can be used for creating a solution for complex real-world problems, mainly those that request some kind of security handling [19], [20].

Since the illustrations of Resonance Thinking in PS or other complex real-world problems would be very cumbersome, we shall re-use here the toy example presented in [11]. The purpose of this paper is four-fold:

- describe particularities of Resonance Thinking taking place in CSE;
- illustrate this method on a toy example nevertheless dealing with a problem that many innovative researchers may have to face;
- compare the complexity of Resonance Thinking to the computation process of Ackermann's function;
- mention the main problems and challenges addressed by Resonance Thinking to various fields of Cognitive Science.

The paper is organized as follows. Section II presents fundamental notions necessary for understanding CSE and Resonance Thinking. Section III recalls the notion of CSE. Section IV develops an illustration of Resonance Thinking. Finally, Section V presents several challenges that Resonance Thinking and CSE offer to Cognitive Science.

II. FUNDAMENTAL NOTIONS

The goal of CSE is to formalize strategic aspects of human creation of *informally* specified *symbiotic systems* in *incomplete domains* following our *pulsation* model. This formalization is performed in order to prepare fundamentals for designing automated tools that help to perform this complex task. In this section, we recall four terms by which this goal is expressed and that will be also used in our presentation of Resonance Thinking, namely

- informal specification,
- symbiosis,
- incompleteness, and
- pulsation.

We shall recall also the main features of our particular handling of the well-known Ackermann's function in the construction of our pulsation model, as given in [13]. These features will be used in our description of CSE's and Resonance Thinking's complexity.

Informal specification of a system that has to be constructed is a description of this system in terms that are not yet exactly defined and that, when considered out of a particular context, may even seem absurd. These terms, in which the specification is expressed, will evolve during the system construction. In other words, depending on some constraints and opportunities that will arise during the construction, the meaning of the terms used in the starting specification will evolve and will make a part of the solution. The initial ambiguity of terms is eliminated by the provided solution. We might say that the notions used in an informal specification are of evolutive and flexible character. Their evolution will also bring an exact specification of the context to be considered. In the framework of CSE, the notion of informal specification needs to be completed by the notions of formalized and formal specification. *Formalized specification* is an intermediary state in the progress from informal to formal specification. It consists in a collection of basic working definitions and basic tools that seem plausibly pointing out a successful completion process, even though some inventive steps may still be needed to complete the tools so as giving their final form to the working definitions. Formal specification then consists in the complete solution represented by the working system, the methodology of both functioning and system construction. These all are needed in order to be used in further evolutive improvement.

As far as *incompleteness* is concerned, from a practical point of view, we know that full reality is unknown. What we may know at a given time can be formalized by an incomplete system. From a decision point of view, it is well-known that incompleteness constitutes a large drawback [14]. Incompleteness, however, is not at all a drawback for the practical purpose of solving real-world problems that are asking for some kind of innovation. This means that, from a construction point of view, incompleteness brings a freedom for technological ingeniosity resulting in possible new technological inventions. Since an informal specification contains terms that are not exactly defined, a particular informal specification points to a context that can be represented by an incomplete environment. CSE can then be seen not only as a construction process for a system in its informally specified initial environment but also as a fruitful strategy for a progressive completion of this environment.

By *symbiosis* we understand a composition of several parts which is vitally separation-sensitive. By vital separation-sensitivity we mean that eliminating one part leads to the destruction or to a non-recoverable mutilation of the other parts and of the whole composition. This means that the widely used divide and conquer strategy is not at all suitable when creating and extending symbiotic systems. We can also say that analysis and synthesis are inappropriate tools when creating and observing symbiotic systems. Symbiosis is therefore different from synergy that is a mutually profitable composition of elements that are not destroyed nor mutilated by separation. From a pragmatic point of view, symbiosis of a system is embodied by the interdependence of all notions and parts of this system. We have illustrated this, in [9], on the example of Natural Numbers (NAT) defined by Peano's axioms. NAT can be seen as the simplest existing system incarnating the main features of SRPS.

Pulsation is a model for construction and evolutive improvement of incomplete systems that are concerned with the factors of control and prevention. In other words, pulsation provides a rigorous framework for the completion process of incomplete systems. This model is described in [13]. It relies on our particular handling of Ackermann's function. We shall recall now the features of its handling that will be referred to, later in the paper.

Let 'ack' be Ackermann's function defined, as in [18], by its standard definition, i.e.,

$$\mathrm{ack}(0,n) = n+1 \tag{1}$$

$$\mathrm{ack}(m+1,0) = \mathrm{ack}(m,1) \tag{2}$$

$$\mathrm{ack}(m+1,n+1) = \mathrm{ack}(m,\mathrm{ack}(m+1,n)). \tag{3}$$

Since ack is a non-primitive recursive function, by definition of non-primitive recursion, it is a particular composition of an infinite sequence of primitive recursive functions. In similarity to the infinite sequence which is used – in [13] – to construct Ackermann's function, the evolutive improvement (i.e., pulsation), relies on a construction of a potentially infinite sequence of systems that might, in an ideal world, be used to construct a global 'Ackermann's system' that contains all of these systems. In our work, by pulsation we thus understand a progressive construction of a potentially infinite sequence of incomplete theories T_0, T_1, …, T_n, T_{n+1}, … such that $T_i \subset T_{i+1}, T_i \neq T_{i+1}$ (for i = 0, 1, 2, …) and such that an infinite limit of this sequence represents an ideal, complete system. Pulsation does not reduce to one particular step in this sequence. This means that pulsative systems are formalized progressively and potentially indefinitely. Pulsation is a model that does not describe how the particular systems in this sequence are constructed. This is the role of Cartesian Systemic Emergence [11].

III. Cartesian Systemic Emergence

As said above, the goal of CSE is to formalize strategic aspects of human creation of informally specified symbiotic systems in incomplete domains. In this section, we recall two paradigms that play a fundamental role in CSE and that will be referred at in Section IV. The first paradigm can be formally represented by the formula

$$\forall \text{ Problem } \exists \text{ System solves(System,Problem)}. \tag{4}$$

The second problem can be represented by the formula

$$\exists \text{ System } \forall \text{ Problem solves(System,Problem)}. \tag{5}$$

There is one main difference between these two paradigms. Namely, in (4), each problem or a class of problems related to a system can have their own solution while in (5), a unique, universal solution is looked for. The first paradigm leads to a library of particular heuristics, while the second one results in a single universal method.

CSE is concerned with the pulsative construction of a system that verifies (5). As presented in [11], the main features of CSE are as follows:

- Works with an informally specified goal.
- Handles incompleteness.
- Takes into account symbiosis and pulsation.
- Generates experiments.
- Oscillates between the paradigms (4) and (5) in order to reach a solution described by (5).

CSE has to be considered in the framework of Cartesian Intuitionism and not in the framework of Newtonian Science. In [10], we explain in more details that the main keywords of Newtonian Science are

- exactness
- formal systems and tools justified in a logical way
- methods of demonstration reduced to some axioms and rules of inference
- decision and undecidability.

In contrast to this, as pointed out in the same paper, the main keywords of Cartesian Intuitionism are

- realization and ingeniosity
- systems and tools justified in an epistemological way
- methodology of construction taking into account also 'Cartesian Intuition' (i.e., a symbiotic composition)
- handling incompleteness in a constructive way.

This means that Cartesian Intuitionism has its own, we might say 'pragmatic', notion of rigor that allows, during the research and development stages, to rely on methods and tools that do not verify the modularity criteria of Newtonian Science. This non-conformity with logical criteria and a kind of 'rigorous freedom' is justified by the work with informal notions and incompleteness.

It happens that the process of construction of informally specified symbiotic systems is very difficult to describe exactly and in its full generality. Our CSE attempts to tackle the task of its description. In [11], we present a general, even though yet informal, scheme for CSE based on the method called Constructive Matching formula construction (*CM-formula construction*) which is used in PS (introduced in [6]) for problems of type (4). We shall refer here to it as CSE-scheme.

IV. Resonance Thinking

As said above, Resonance Thinking is a method for solving problems represented by paradigm (5). It takes care of generating and handling experiments in the process of CSE so that these experiences lead to new ideas hinting at suitable symbiotic solutions of 'mismatches' among experiences themselves as well as the desired solution expressed initially by an informal specification. It is inspired by our application of Descartes' rule XII ([3], p. 39), as well as by the main precepts of his method, in the present state of our construction of a particular SRPS for PS. In his rule XII, Descartes advises: "In sum, we must make use of all the help which intellect, imagination, sense-perception, and memory can supply in order to take a distinct intuition of simple propositions, combine according to the rules things that are searched for with those that we know, as well as to discover things that have to be related to others so that we neglect no fraction of human resources." Resonance Thinking describes our understanding of Descartes' "combining, according to the rules, things that are searched for with those that we know, as well as to discover things that have to be related to others" in the framework of Cartesian Intuitionism [10].

In order to take hold of the complexity of Resonance Thinking, it is necessary to keep in mind that CSE and Resonance Thinking are designed for a systems creation which has to provide control and prevention in the resulting system. Therefore, the criterion of security is strongly involved already in the system's creation. Such a particular security follows immediately from a careful simultaneous use of the following four precepts of Descartes' method [4], p. 120:

a) "Carefully to avoid precipitate conclusions and preconceptions.
b) Divide each of the difficulties into as many parts as possible and as may be required in order to resolve them better.
c) Suppose some order even among objects that have no natural order of precedence.
d) Make enumerations so complete and so comprehensive, so we can be sure of leaving nothing out."

Note, that these four rules represent also four fundamental (symbiotic) facets of CSE in this order:

a') Pulsative Thinking, i.e., taking care of security, control and prevention [13].
b') Metamorphic Thinking, i.e., taking care of resulting epistemological equivalence between paradigm (5) and particular CSE-handling paradigm (4).
c') Symbiotic Thinking, i.e., taking care of construction of a symbiotic system.
d') Resonance Thinking, i.e., taking care of generating and handling experiments.

A description of a one part in a symbiotic composition (such as the successor function 'Suc' in NAT) is not a simple task, as one can realize while trying to give an *exact* description of the successor function (Suc) in NAT. Indeed, an exact description of Suc would imperatively require explicit references to 0, NAT, the induction principle and Peano's axioms defining the addition and multiplication. Therefore, we do not intend yet to provide here a rigorous and complete description of Resonance Thinking, as we still need to describe in a future work, more in details, Metamorphic Thinking (MT) and Symbiotic Thinking (ST). On the other hand, CSE and Resonance Thinking handle informally specified notions (and thus incompleteness). This means that, it is only natural that procedures and notions of CSE come out through progressive evolution from informal specifications to formalized specifications and then to formal specifications. In this paper, we shall therefore limit ourselves to an illustration of the goal of Resonance Thinking and the basic procedures it relies upon.

We shall present Resonance thinking and its basic notions with the help of a toy example used, in [11], for description of CSE. In comparison to examples provided by PS framework, this example is simpler and could illustrate many other scientific fields than PS-research does. The example problem presented here concerns conveying a new original scientific knowledge in such a way that its essential content and creative potential are preserved by the next generations. This is not a trivial problem as already pointed out in the past [1] [4]. Our experience confirms that, for new knowledge that concerns creation and extension of symbiotic recursive systems, this problem remains relevant until now.

A. Specification of a toy example

In this section we present our example illustrating CSE and Resonance Thinking.

Let us suppose that René is a founder of a novel scientific theory with a high pulsative potential. Referring back to the bad founders' experience in the past, he needs to ask himself: "How to build some 'works' able to convey the full complexity of my new theory while simultaneously preventing a degradation of its pulsative potential?" In a more formal way, René must solve a problem informally specified as:

$$\exists\text{works } \forall\text{disciple conveys(René, works) \& conveys(works,disciple)} \Rightarrow \text{essential\_of(René) = essential\_of(disciple)} \quad (6)$$

Note that this problem has the same logical structure as the second paradigm presented in the form (5). Specification (6) is an informal specification. As said above, this means that the notions that appear in (6) are not defined in a rigorous way. They are only specified in an informal way in terms of some non-formal criteria (i.e., a kind of underspecified constraints). This means that a solution 'works' for (6) has to emerge simultaneously with suitable formalizations (thus, the final definitions) of notions that occur in (6). In the following, we shall denote by D_t the set of (initially underspecified) sentences specifying 'to convey' and by D_e the set of (initially underspecified) sentences specifying 'essential_of'. These sets evolve in the process of CSE and Resonance Thinking towards a more rigorous final form. For simplicity of presentation, we do not involve such an evolution in our notation.

In [11], we mention that, in order to solve (6), there is a particular switch to a framework of experiments described by the formula

$$\forall\text{disciple } \exists\text{works conveys(René, works) \& conveys(works,disciple)} \Rightarrow \text{essential\_of(René) = essential\_of(disciple)} \quad (7)$$

This formula represents paradigm (4). Above, we have explained that there is a difference between solving (4) and (5), and this obviously applies to their instances (6) and (7). In general, in order to be fruitful and justified, a switch from (5) to (4) has to rely on what we call Metamorphic Thinking. Roughly speaking, Metamorphic Thinking (MT) takes a care of a rigorous, epistemologically and pragmatically justified transformation of paradigm (5) into the context of paradigm (4). Our paper [11] gives its illustration. A more detailed description of MT is presently under development.

In other words, MT provides a switch from (6) to (7) that is useful in order to generate experiments leading, within the framework of (7), to some hints and inspiration for solving (6). These hints and inspirations represent temporary (see precept (a)) underspecified constraints that enlarge the already existing set of underspecified constraints. In order to generate such inspiring experiments, while considering (7), from the set of all disciples, we chose a finite number of disciples $d_0, d_1, \ldots, d_n$ that seem highly different so that each of them seems to need a different 'works'. Note that this step implicitly embodies the above precept (b). We shall call *representatives* these disciples. In other words, our experience shows us that challenging experiments are needed to obtain some inspirations contributing to a solution of (6) in the framework of paradigm (5). Note that we order these disciples in a numbered sequence just for the presentation purposes. This will be useful when describing recursive procedures that handle this finite set of disciples.

Very roughly speaking, in order to solve a problem represented by paradigm (5), it might seem possible to replace MT from paradigm (5) to (4) by a symbiotic composition of a set of solutions for carefully chosen representatives of universally quantified elements of this paradigm. A drawback of such a description lies in considering a lone symbiotic operation (i.e., one action), while Resonance Thinking, through precepts (a), (b), (c) and (d) requires performing a great number of interdependent symbiotic compositions, as will be described below.

Recall that the two operators 'conveys' and 'essential_of' are here specified informally only by some set of sentences that represent informal descriptions (i.e., underspecified constraints) relative to these notions. Thus, we shall replace these notions by their informal descriptions. Above, we have denoted by D_t the set of sentences specifying 'to convey' and by D_e the set of sentences specifying 'essence_of'. Therefore, (7) writes as

$$\forall\text{disciple } \exists\text{works } \{ D_t(\text{René, works}) \; \& \; D_t(\text{works,disciple}) \Rightarrow D_e(\text{René}) = D_e(\text{disciple}) \} \quad (8)$$

Let us consider (8) for each particular d_i, i.e.,

$$\exists\text{works } \{ D_t(\text{René, works}) \; \& \; D_t(\text{works}, d_i) \Rightarrow D_e(\text{René}) = D_e(d_i) \} \quad (9)$$

In [11], we show that a solution for (9) can be found for each d_i by following CSE-scheme and oscillating between paradigms (4) and (5). This solution consists of a concrete value w_i for 'works' and of less informal descriptors $D_{t,i}$ and $D_{e,i}$. We shall note $Sol_i = \{ w_i, D_{t,i}, D_{e,i} \}$. Due to a careful oscillation between paradigms (4) and (5) the descriptors $D_{t,i}$ and $D_{e,i}$, w_i refine 'works' and the operators 'to convey' and 'essential_of' in (6). These resulting refinements 'resonate' with the framework of paradigm (5). By their resonating we mean that, during the experimentation process, we feel that they might, probably after some 'judicious adaptations', be applied also to other instances of 'disciple'.

B. Resonance Thinking

Resonance Thinking relies heavily on what Merriam-Webster Dictionary considers as resonance: a quality that makes something personally meaningful or important to someone. Resonance Thinking thus involves the ability to create and explore personally meaningful or important relations in the process of generating and handling experiments.

We are going to describe it in the framework of René's example.

At this stage, we suppose that (9) for d_0 is already solved following the CSE-scheme. Sol_0 represents thus a 'temporary' solution for d_0. By 'temporary' we mean that this solution will still have to be approved or modified by Resonance Thinking. Procedurally, the part of generating experiences of Resonance Thinking is based on two procedures for which we cannot yet provide a detailed description (thus, making explicit also 'handling experiments' part of RT), as they rely also on other symbiotic facets of CSE not introduced yet (namely, MT and ST mentioned above). We shall therefore concentrate on explaining the role of these procedures. The first procedure will be called *topological symbiosis* (noted *ts*) and it is also a primitive operation for the second procedure. The second procedure is called *complementary topological symbiosis* (noted *cts*). Both these procedures require creativity in developing symbiotic systems. In this paper, we describe the way these procedures work: they are therefore to be handled, for the time being, by a creative human person. The following description of the role of *ts* and *cts* illustrate some of the challenges that *ts* and *cts* have to tackle.

1) On symbiosis in Resonance Thinking

We need to point out here two particular features of *ts*. The first one concerns the character of possible "mutilations" performed by *ts* and the second one concerns its goal.

In [8], we present an example of a pictorial symbiosis of two different women. One woman is young, the other is old. The resulting symbiosis is a face that can be seen simultaneously as a young and an old woman. The original two pictures of women have to be 'mutilated' so that the resulting symbiotic picture is convincing. For instance, an eye of old woman and an ear of young woman overlap in the symbiotic picture. As for the opposite ages of the women on the initial pictures, they are 'merged', since the symbiotic picture is at the same 'old' and 'young'.

In [9], we used the example of Peano's axioms that are (also) symbiotic since, by deleting one of its axioms, the reduced set of axioms leads also to other interpretation structures (such as, for instance, the set of Perfect Women in [8]). This example exhibits an explicit degradation due to the presence of a set of notions and constraints that obviously became underspecified when one of Peano's axioms is deleted. This shows that, at first glance, systemic symbiosis manifests itself not so much as 'merging' contradictory facets of the considered system (as 'merging' two opposites, namely young and old in the above mentioned pictorial symbiosis), but as constructing an emergent vitally separation-sensitive interdependence (i.e., symbiosis) of parts of the system. However, a detailed perception shows that this vitally separation-sensitive interdependence means 'merging' relationships that are usually contradictory, for instance, '*p* depends on *q*' and '*q* depends on *p*'.

2) On generating experiments in Resonance Thinking

We are going to describe *ts* and *cts* in the framework of René's example. At this stage, we suppose that (9) for d_0 is already solved following the CSE-scheme providing the solution Sol_0 for d_0. Sol_0 represents a 'temporary' solution for d_0. By 'temporary' we mean that this solution will still have to be approved or modified by RT. Similarly, for other disciples $d_1, \ldots, d_n$, we will obtain Sol_1, Sol_2 and so on. We assume here that the solutions are obtained in a particular 'linear' way, one after another. This 'linear' way looks as follows.

Once Sol_0 is constructed, a 'temporary' solution Sol_1 for d_1 is constructed ('temporary' in the same way as Sol_0 is a 'temporary' solution for d_0). Note that both these constructions may lead to new experiences and thus, *they modify the initial environment* by refining the informal notions of our definition (6) of our problem. For the sake of simplicity, we do not describe explicitly below this evolution of environment, though we take it into account by calling it a 'feedback' when we use it.

Now, suppose that we solved the problem for the first disciple. Before starting solving the problem for the next one, we try to take into account the informal notions present in (6). This try amounts to an attempt to 'merge' the solutions Sol_0 and Sol_1 using topological symbiosis *ts*, i.e., we try to achieve their symbiotic composition that resonates (as explained in Section 4.A) with the informal specification (6). We shall denote this process by $ts(Sol_0,Sol_1)$.

If solving $ts(S_0,S_1)$ fails, i.e., we cannot find relevant refinements, we keep in mind the feedback obtained while constructing Sol_0 and Sol_1, as well as the failure reasons of $ts(S_0,S_1)$. This failed step will have to be redone later while relying on some inspirations that may rise while finding the solutions for the next disciples. If this process fails, the problem will have to be considered as a challenge for one of the next pulsation steps.

If the process $ts(Sol_0,Sol_1)$ succeeds, both solutions are temporarily approved. Then, keeping in mind all the feedback obtained, a solution of (9) for d_2 is constructed. One might suppose that this process may continue linearly as suggested by its beginning, as we just have seen. However, recall that we work in an environment that requires control and prevention. Therefore, in this environment, we rely strongly on the above four precepts. This means that generating complementary experiments for topological symbiosis of solutions constructed is necessary. We call *complementary topological symbiosis* (noted *cts*) this procedure for generating new experiments.

Roughly speaking, *cts* is a particular generation process (defined with help of *ts*) for creating experiments. The goal of these complementary experiments is to provide inspirations for further refinement of underspecified notions and constraints. Similarly to the computation of ack (see [12]), in the process of generating experiments (via *ts*) for Sol_m and Sol_n, i.e., while 'computing' $cts(Sol_m,Sol_n)$, the operation $ts(Sol_i,Sol_j)$ for other solutions Sol_i and Sol_j is performed several times.

Let us denote by $ts_1(Sol_i,Sol_j)$ the solution of the first computation, by $ts_2(Sol_i,Sol_j)$ for the second computation, and so on. It is important to point out that $ts_p(Sol_i,Sol_j)$ and $ts_q(Sol_i,Sol_j)$ in this sequence of computations may carry two different feedbacks. Indeed, each inner step of *cts* (i.e., evaluating $cts(Sol_m,Sol_n)$), may bring new refinements, constraints as well as it may point out to missing knowledge or second-order notions and procedures. The procedures *ts* and *cts* have to insure that not only reasonable and achievable solutions are obtained but that a possibility of future evolutions are guaranteed while properly handling prevention and control.

Recall that *ts* and *cts* are, in our case, presently performed by a human mind. This means that human mind can rely on relevant creativity in order to decrease the number of repetitions. In consequence, even though *ts* and *cts* are not simple, CSE and Resonance Thinking are not overwhelming tasks for human performers. However, they may be overwhelming for a human observer even in this simplified form. This is why we believe that further research is necessary to give a reasonable formula for performing *cts* by machine.

V. DISCUSSION/RELATED WORK

Scientific creation, as a particular human invention [15], becomes a highly economically interesting topic when it can be turned into an implementable science. CSE does try to build an implementable theory of SRPS scientific creation. Since it is based on our relatively successful experience in creating a methodology for PS, the four fundamental facets of CSE bring several stimulating challenges to Cognitive Science (CS). Some of them have been presented in [11]. In this paper we would like to mention two more challenges. They concern frame problem [2] and conceptual blending [5].

Bermudez' work, as cited above, seems to imply that CS is somewhat wary of non-modular processing. One of the reasons is that non-modular processing very quickly meets frame problem-like difficulties. We have seen that, during Resonance Thinking, the human brain is rather at ease with the identifications needed to handle the frame-problem. Why it is so? Is it because there is a particular kind of internal representation human mind is able to construct? Alternately, is it because our mind includes mechanisms that are presently out of the scope of the current modular approach to our mind architecture [2]? Moreover, performing CSE includes a symbiosis of form, a meaning, a representation formalism, mechanisms and, importantly, reaching a human agreement via conceptual coherence [16] and real-world exploitation. Does it mean that a modular approach to mind architecture should be revised? Could it be possible that some kind of symbiotic approach might be better suited even though it is more complex?

Besides, we have tried to find some concepts of CS that resonate with CSE-thinking. We have found some similarities between Resonance Thinking and Conceptual Blending (CB) as presented in [5]. On a high-level of abstraction, RT and CB seem similar, since they are both concerned with construction of meaning and they both involve 'merging'. Of course, they also show some differences at this high-level because RT is consciously performed, while CB is considered as taking place outside consciousness and is not available to introspection (as in [5], p. 33). We believe that this unconscious feature of CB disappears if people work in domains where rigor, justification and reproducibility of results are essential. Incidentally, let us point out that Fauconnier and Turner's illustrations, in [5], do not fulfill these stipulations.

At a lower-level, RT seems to us more complex than CB. Let us mention several features of RT that contrast CB.

- CB is highly nondeterministic while, in RT, the solution is specified in advance, even-though informally. Thus, RT performs what could be called a 'goal-oriented symbiosis'. While handling the generated experiments, RT focuses on what resonates as contributing to a universal solution, as in René's example, 'works' in (6).
- RT involves solving underspecified constraints due to the presence of incompleteness and an informal specification.
- RT not only handles a given data input (experiments) but it also generates complementary data (experiments).
- CB usually works with two mental spaces. RT, via topological symbiosis, works with three inputs (two experiments and one goal) and the solutions obtained are temporary until other experiments confirm the output.
- Fauconnier and Turner [5], in relation with CB, claim that researchers are unaware of how they are thinking. RT is a description of our way of thinking relevant to creation of SRPS.
- CB is performed on mental spaces, i.e., small conceptual pockets constructed for purposes of local understanding and action ([5], p. 40). In RT, there are no small conceptual packets since global understanding is required even in considerations that may seem local.
- In the case of CB, the effects of some unconscious imaginative work are captured by consciousness, but the operations that produce it are not ([5], p. 58). As said above, RT (and CSE) is a description of our way of thinking that is relevant to SRPS creation. This means that we are consciously aware of the informal specifications of the operations performed by our mind. Presently, our goal is not to apprehend all the conscious details of the operations performed by RT and CSE. Our present goal is to specify what enters into the 'game' of RT (and CSE) and what the 'winning strategies' are in order to conceive all the rules of 'the full game' of CSE. In other words, presently, we aim to develop a 'prosthesis' that can be implemented and used during CSE. We are convinced that apprehending human operations first by relevant informal specifications is half way to a reasonable implementable solution.

We can also compare 'mismatch-based learning' presented in [21] to our 'mismatch-based creativity' in the following sense. Any proof performed in an incomplete domain always faces a possibility of leading to a failure. This means that we are bound to provide means of recovery from these temporary failures or, alternatively, strategies making use of the failure itself – which is a way to recover from such a failure by including the failure cases inside the domain. An example of the last kind of recovery has been provided by Grossberg who, in [21], introduces a procedure including 'mismatch-based learning' cases in order to enable a rapid adaptation to changing bodily parameters relative to the posterior parietal cortex. Our approach, however, relies on a creative recovery more than a learning one, as explained above.

VI. CONCLUSION

It is largely accepted that inspiration seems to take place anytime, such as while walking (e.g., Poincaré's case), showering or during a pause playing the violin (e.g., Einstein's case). It is usually also accepted that some sort of unconscious incubation precedes this inspiration. Since we differentiate 'unconscious' and 'non-verbal', this does not take place during RT. Furthermore, contrary to Popper's opinion [17] that "there is no such a thing as a logical method of having new ideas, or a logical reconstruction of this process," RT is a systemic method for generating new and relevant ideas. Of course, its 'logical reconstruction' is not trivial, as is illustrated by this paper. CSE, CSE-scheme, RT, Symbiotic Thinking and Metamorphic Thinking nevertheless seem to be a good start for a 'Cartesian reconstruction' of this process. Thus, we believe that, even in its presently incomplete version, CSE brings forward thinking mechanisms that are essential for exploration, creation of possibilities, anticipation, resonance, blending, on-purpose creating of informally specified tools, invention, discovery, and so on.

We are aware that our description of the cognitive tasks involved in CSE does not provide a clear idea whether it is possible (or reasonable) to find a way to break down the cognitive tasks that are performed into more determinate tasks. We describe what humans do or what they have to do without specifying how these tasks are performed by our brain. We thus believe that research on these topics in the field of CSE in particular and its comparison with scientific creativity in general (i.e., a comparison with scientists' creative thinking in several scientific domains) might bring new conceptual and procedural switches not only in Computer and Cognitive Sciences, but also in other human activities.

ACKNOWLEDGMENT

We thank Michèle Sebag and Yannis Manoussakis for their moral support.

REFERENCES

[1] F. Bacon, Novum Organum, P.U.F, 1986.

[2] J. L. Bermúdez, Cognitive Science, An Introduction to the Science of the Mind, Cambridge University Press, 2014.

[3] R. Descartes, "Rules for the Direction of the Mind," in R. Descartes, translated by J. Cottingham, R.Stoothoff, D. and Murdoch, Philosophical Writings of Descartes, vol. 1, Cambridge University Press, 2006, pp. 9-76.

[4] R. Descartes, "Discourse on the Method," in R. Descartes, translated by J. Cottingham, R.Stoothoff and D. Murdoch, Philosophical Writings of Descartes, vol. 1, Cambridge University Press, 2006, pp. 111-151.

[5] G. Fauconnier, M. Turner, The Way We Think, Conceptual Blending And The Mind's Hidden Complexities, Basic Books, 2003.

[6] M. Franova, "CM-strategy: A Methodology for Inductive Theorem Proving or Constructive Well-Generalized Proofs," in A. K. Joshi, (ed), Proceedings of the Ninth International Joint Conference on Artificial Intelligence, 1985, 1214-1220.

[7] M. Franova, "An Implementation of Program Synthesis from Formal Specifications," in Y. Kodratoff, (ed.), Proceedings of the 8th European Conference on Artificial Intelligence, Pitman, 1988, pp. 559-564.

[8] M. Franova, "The Role of Recursion in and for Scientific Creativity," in R. Trappl (ed.), Cybernetics and Systems 2010, Proc. of the Twentieth European Meeting on Cybernetics and System research, Austrian Society for Cybernetic Studies, 2010, pp. 573-578.

[9] M. Franova, "A Cartesian Methodology for an Autonomous Program Synthesis System," in M.Jäntti, G. Weckman (eds)., proc. of ICONS 2014, The Ninth International Conference on Systems, ISBN, 978-1-61208-319-3, 2014, pp. 22-27.

[10] M. Franova, "Cartesian versus Newtonian Paradigms for Recursive Program Synthesis," International Journal on Advances in Systems and Measurements, vol. 7, no 3&4, 2014, pp. 209-222.

[11] M. Franova and Y. Kodratoff, "Cartesian Systemic Emergence - Tackling Underspecified Notions in Incomplete Domains," in O. Chernavskaya, K. Miwa (eds.), Proc. of COGNITIVE 2018, The Tenth International Conference on Advanced Cognitive Technologies and Applications, ISBN, 978-1-61208-609-5, 2018, pp. 1-6.

[12] M. Franova, Trace of computation for ack(3,2), https://sites.google.com/site/martafranovacnrs/trace-of-computation-for-ack-3-2, retrieved 03/2019.

[13] M. Franova and Y. Kodratoff, "Cartesian Systemic Pulsation: A Model for Evolutive Improvement of Incomplete Symbiotic Recursive Systems," Internat. Journal On Advances in Intelligent Systems, vol 11, no 1&2, 2018, pp. 35-45.

[14] K. Gödel, "Some metamathematical results on completeness and consistency, On formally undecidable propositions of Principia Mathematica and related systems I, and On completeness and consistency," in J. van Heijenoort, From Frege to Godel, A source book in mathematical logic, 1879-1931, Harvard University Press, 1967, pp. 592-618.

[15] J. Hadamard, An Essay on the Psychology of Invention in the Mathematical Field, Read Books, 2007.

[16] G. L. Murphy and D.L. Medin, "The Role Theories in Conceptual Coherence," Psychological Review 92(3), 1985, pp. 289-316.

[17] K. Popper, The logic of scientific discovery, Harper, 1968.

[18] A. Yasuhara, Recursive Function Theory and Logic, Academic Press, New York, 1971.

[19] H. Mantel and A. Schairer, "Exploiting Generic Aspects of Security Models in Formal Developments", in Mechanizing Mathematical Reasoning, Lecture Notes in Computer Science Volume 2605, 2005, pp. 452-475.

[20] D. Hutter, H. Mantel, I. Schaefer and A. Schairer, "Security of multi-agent systems: A case study on comparison shopping", ournal of Applied Logic, Volume 5, Issue 2, 2007, pp. 303-332.

[21] S. Grossberg, Cortical and subcortical predictive dynamics and learning during perception, cognition, emotion and action. Phil. Trans. R. Soc. B 364, 2009, pp. 1223–1234.

Multimodal Interactions Viewed as Dual Process on Multi-Dimensional Memory Frames under Weak Synchronization

Muneo Kitajima

Information and
Management Systems Engineering
Nagaoka University of Technology
1603-1 Kamitomioka,
Nagaoka, Niigata 940-2188, JAPAN
Email: mkitajima
@kjs.nagaokaut.ac.jp

Jérôme Dinet

Psychology and Neuroscience Laboratory
University of Lorraine
54021 Nancy Cedex, France
Email: jerome.dinet
@univ-lorraine.fr

Makoto Toyota

T-Method
Chiba Japan
Email: pubmtoyota@me.com

***Abstract*—Behavior of users interacting with multimodal interfaces looks complex because the degrees of freedom of sensory input and motor output is large. This paper suggests that this complexity can be alleviated by applying the Simon's ant metaphor to the multimodal interaction situations, i.e., "What users do is simple. 1) they use perceptual input to generate a mirror image of the real world surrounding the self to be shared in conscious and unconscious processes, 2) they select next actions by consciously planning ahead and unconsciously tuning motor movements for the event to happen, and after performing the action, they unconsciously modify the participated neural network and consciously reflect on the result of action, and 3) they perform 1 and 2 in synchronous with the ever-changing external environment, which this paper calls "weak synchronization." A cognitive architecture, Model Human Processor with Realtime Constraints (MHP/RT) and its associated memory structure, Multi-Dimensional Memory Frames, developed by the authors is briefly introduced considering the situation of users interacting with multimodal environment. Then, the above three items are derived as the essential principles for organizing user's behavior in multimodal interaction environment. Future work on designing mixed reality multimodal interaction environment is introduced that has its basis on the perspectives for multimodal interactions this paper claims.**

Keywords–Dual process; Multimodal interaction, Two Minds, Multi-dimensional memory frames; Weak synchronization; Time scale of human action.

I. Introduction

Multimodal interaction provides multiple communication channels between users and automated systems. Speeches, finger movements, hand movements, eye movements, and so on, can be used for transmitting messages from users to systems. Synthesized voices, sounds, vibrations, texts and graphics rendered on visual display can be used for sending messages from systems to users. What happens at the multimodal interface between users and systems *looks vey complex* because the degrees of freedom of both sides is large. Multimodal interaction using virtual reality technologies to realize immersive environments is an emerging and continuously evolving domain, in which development of a theoretical framework to reduce the inherent complexity is required for advancing principled design of multimodal interaction [1].

This paper suggests an approach for alleviating this complexity by applying the metaphor of Simon's ant to the situation where users are engaging in multimodal interaction to use automated systems. Simon describes in the book entitled "The Sciences of Artificial" [2, pp.51–53] as follows:

> *An ant [A man], viewed as a behaving system, is quite simple. The apparent complexity of its behavior over time is largely a reflection of the complexity of the environment in which it finds itself.*

In these sentences, he described a situation where an ant produced a very complex path across the terrain of a beach while making decisions on which direction to go at each moment when it encounters an obstacle. A person observing only the path itself might be inclined to ascribe a great deal of intelligence of ant. However, it turned out that the complexity of the path is really produced by the complexity of the terrain over which the ant was navigating. The ant only selected the optimal operator from doable simple alternatives for the specific situation where it was needed to reduce the distance from the current location to its nest. The specific trajectory was the result of successive decisions of selecting locally optimal simple operators.

Simon [2] claims that decision making in problem solving situations, which looks complex and intractable, is in reality governed by two principles, i.e., *satsficing principle* and *bounded rationality*. The role of these behavioral principles for understanding a variety of decision making behaviors in problem solving situations is the same as that of the Newtonian equation of motion for predicting configurations of the planets of the solar system at specific times in the future. They should provide a firm basis for considering behaviors of decision makers; any models for explaining and predicting behaviors of decision makers in specific situations have to be constructed on them.

Users interacting with multimodal interfaces are placed in the situation where they have to select next actions and execute them by acting to the external environment through their body parts, e.g., limbs, eye balls, and so on, via motor neurons as serial processing, and receive signals from not only the external systems but also themselves (i.e., seeing their finger movements and hearing their voices) through the five senses, i.e., taste, sight, touch, smell, and sound, via sensory neurons as parallel processing. The received signals traverse the networks of intermediate neurons to select next actions. This is a circular

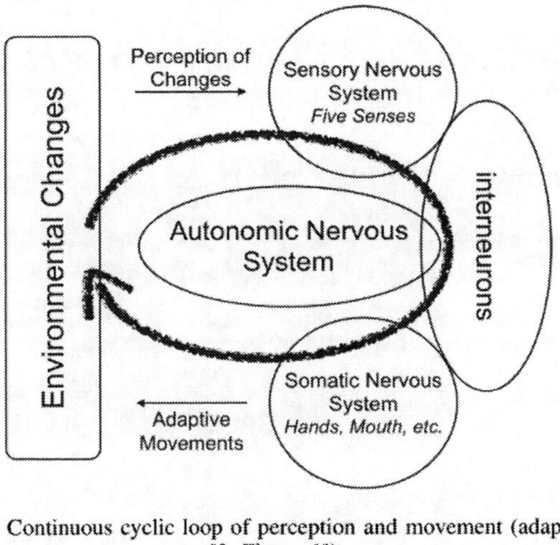

Figure 1. Continuous cyclic loop of perception and movement (adapted from [3, Figure 1]).

process as shown by Figure 1. After s/he perceives the results of movements of his/her body parts, as well as the changes of the external environment, a next Perceptual–Motor cycle occurs. Interneurons in-between the sensory neurons and motor neurons convert the input patterns to the output patterns – these constitute a Perceptual–Cognitive–Motor (PCM) process. Memories associated with the respective activities of sensory, motor, and intermediate neurons continuously accumulate and change as the PCM cycle runs. In multimodal interaction situations, the PCM cycle equipped with the memories associated with the respective processes runs in synchronous with the ever-changing multimodal environment, otherwise the user and the system are not able to establish "interaction." Given the very basic architecture of PCM cycle shown by Figure 1 and its associated memories, how synchronization between a user and a multimodal system could be established? This paper suggests a form of synchronization, "weak synchronization", should serve as the operational principle for the PCM architecture, as the satisficinig principle and bounded rationality do for decision making in a problem space.

This paper is organized as follows. Section II introduces a theory of action selection and memory that the authors have developed [4][5][6], which essentially elaborates the basic idea of endless cycle of PCM as depicted in Figure 1, and defines a cognitive architecture that would be most suitable for understanding people interacting with ever-changing environment. Section II-A introduces the Model Human Processor with Realtime Constraints (MHP/RT) that defines the PCM cycle, and Section II-B shows the memory system that accompanies with MHP/RT. Section III starts with explanations how MHP/RT interacts with multimodal environment, then, derives an operation principle "weak synchronization" as a critical means for a user as modeled by MHP/RT to interact smoothly with multimodal environment. Finally, Section IV provides a summary of the paper with future work focusing on how the insight of this paper could be used to better understand users interacting with multimodal environment.

II. Theory of Action Selection and Memory

Starting from the basic cycle of PCM processes depicted by Figure 1, Kitajima and Toyota [5][6] have constructed a comprehensive theory of action selection and memory, MHP/RT, that should provide a basis for constructing any models for users interacting with multimodal environment. The theory integrates the fundamental characteristics of human beings interacting with ever-changing environments. This section introduces briefly MHP/RT that defines the PCM processes and its associated memory, Multidimensional Memory Frames, that is used and modified while MHP/RT works.

A. MHP/RT

MHP/RT is an extension of Model Human Processor (MHP) developed by Card, Moran and Newell in 1983 [7]. MHP is a cognitive architecture to simulate users interacting with *then-available* information devices, such as The Star workstation, officially named Xerox 8010 Information System. MHP/RT aims at simulating users who interact with richer in contents and more dynamic modern information environment, such as multimodal interaction environment. MHP/RT has to deal with more information-rich situations than MHP was supposed to do.

MHP/RT implements at a higher level the following three facts concerning processing with an assumption. The facts are as follows:

1) The fundamental processing mechanism of brain is Parallel Distributed Processing (PDP) [8],
2) Human behavior emerges as the results of competition of the dual processes of System 2, a slow *conscious* process for deliberate reasoning with feedback control, and System 1, fast *unconscious* process for intuitive reaction with feedforward control for connecting perception and motor, called Two Minds [9][10], and
3) Behavior is organized under happiness goals [11], e.g., target happiness, competitive happiness, cooperative happiness, etc.

The assumption is that the endless PCM cycle continues from his or her birth to death in the ecological system, consisting of a person and his/her environments, as a periodic circulation system, called autopoiesis [12]. The system is truly dynamic and evolves in the irreversible time dimension.

In summary, MHP/RT essentially defines a specification for an organic version of PDP by incorporating Two Minds and happiness goals in the original version of PDP. The term, "Organic Parallel Distributed Processing (O-PDP)", was first introduced by [13]. O-PDP develops cross-networks of neurons in the brain as it accumulates experience of interactions in the environment. The neural network development process is circular, which means that any experience at a particular moment should reflect somehow the experience of the past interactions that have been recorded in the shape of current neural networks. In this way, an O-PDP system is organized evolutionally, and realized as a neural network system, including the brain, the spinal nerves, and the peripheral nerves to construct an O-PDP system.

MHP/RT, illustrated in the left portion of Figure 2, describes the cyclic PCM processes. It consists of four major autonomous systems: Perceptual Information Processing for perception, Autonomous Automatic Behavior Control Processing (System 1) and Conscious Information Processing (System 2) for cognition, and Behavioral Action Processing for motor

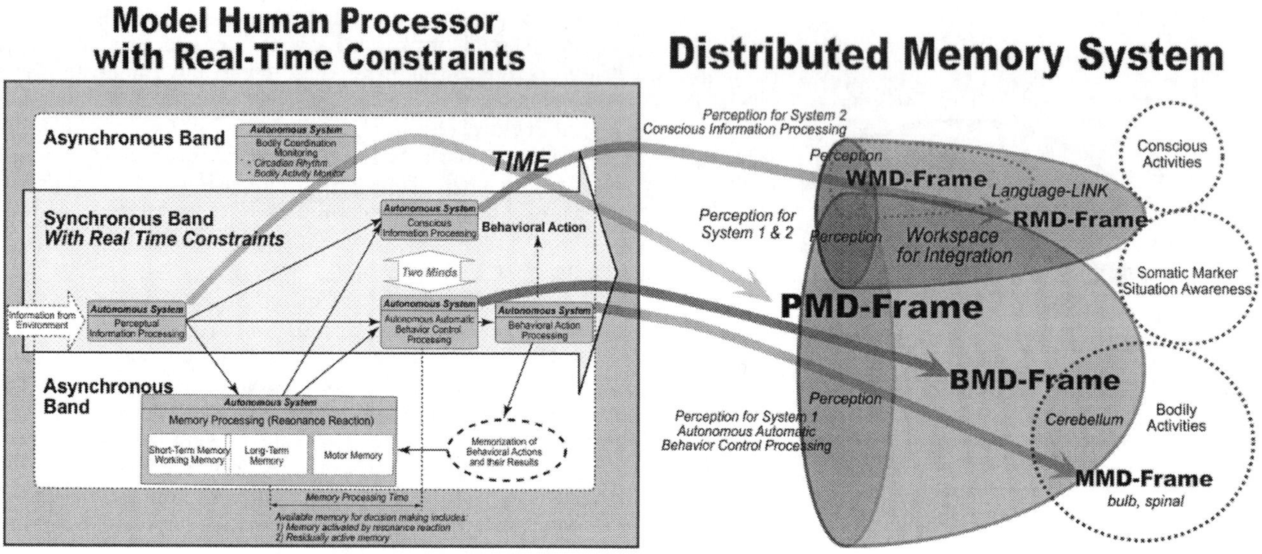

Figure 2. MHP/RT ([6, Figure 3]) and the distributed memory system.

movement. These processes work in synchronous with the ever-changing external environment, which effectively imposes real time constraints on the PCM processes. In addition, these processes connect with Memory Processing autonomous system to make use of stored contents in memories via resonance reaction, which happens not synchronously but asynchronously with the environmental changes.

The cyclic PCM processes are implemented in O-PDP as hierarchically organized bands having their respective characteristic times for operations, i.e., Biological, Cognitive, Rational, and Social bands defined as Newell's time scale of human action (Figure 3). Respective bands have their characteristic times. A number of phenomena that occur in a certain single band would be related with each other and therefore they could have linear relationships. On the other hand, they should have non-linear relationships with those phenomena that happen in a different band. For example, conscious activities in Rational Band, System 2, cannot have linear relationship with unconscious activities in Biological Band, System 1, but have non-linear relationships.

The existence of gaps between bands indicates that a phenomenon in one band evolves quasi-independently with another in a different band. However, one side would have some effect on the other in order to organize the activities of the O-PDP system coherently in the environment. System 1 runs quasi-independently with System 2 with occasional exchanges over the gap, e.g., conscious process, System 2, intervenes unconscious process, System 1, before unconscious feedforward process would derail. In many cases in our daily life, application of irrational cognitive bias could be avoided by deliberate thinking by System 2. This is a kind of synchronization between System 2 and System 1 when action selection is done by MHP/RT. This interaction is shown in the left portion of Figure 2 as "Two Minds" that connects Autonomous Automatic Behavior Control Processing (System 1) and Conscious Information Processing (System 2). As described, synchronization is an important mechanism to make the behavior of O-PDP system stable. This issue will be further discussed later in Section III-C.

MHP/RT is a *real* brain model comprising of System 1's unconscious processes and System 2's conscious processes at the same level as shown in Figure 2, in which both System 1 and System 2 receive input from the Perceptual Information Processing autonomous system in one way, and from the Memory Processing autonomous system in another way. System 1 and System 2 work autonomously without any superordinate-subordinate hierarchical relationships but interact with each other when necessary [6].

This feature of MHP/RT should be contrasted with the goal-oriented cognitive architectures such as ACT-R [14][15] in which the conscious processes are considered as the processes to control people's behavior and the unconscious processes are considered subordinate to the conscious or intentional processes [6]. What ACT-R tries to do is to show how System 2 can be implemented on top of System 1. The procedural memory system is very similar to System 1, and then ACT-R models tend to consist of a set of production rules that give rise to the slower, deliberative planning behaviors seen in System 2. This is a very different conceptualization for autonomously behaving creatures in the ever-changing environment from that given in this paper. However, ACT-R models are totally adequate for simulating stable human activities with weak time constraint in which deliberate decision making would work effectively, but might be hard for the situations with strong time constraint where the environmental condition changes chaotically and deliberate decision making implemented on System 2 might not work as effective. Multimodal interaction is one of those human activities that goal-oriented cognitive architectures would not be suitable.

B. Multidimensional Memory Frames

As illustrated in the right portion of Figure 2, each autonomous system for carrying out PCM processes in the synchronous band of MHP/RT is associated with its corresponding memory, which is implemented as a distributed memory

Time Sale of Human Action

Scale (sec)	Time Units	System	World (Theory)
10^7	months		
10^6	weeks		Social Band
10^5	days		
10^4	hours	Task	
10^3	10 min	Task	Rational Band
10^2	minutes	Task	
10^1	10 sec	Unit Task	
10^0	1 sec	Operations	Cognitive Band
10^{-1}	100 ms	Deliberate Act	
10^{-2}	10 ms	Neural Circuit	
10^{-3}	1 ms	Neuron	Biological Band
10^{-4}	100 μs	Organelle	

Figure 3. Newell's time scale of human action (adapted from [16]).

system. The contents of memory is structured as specified by the Structured Meme Theory [17]. A brief explanation of the respective multi-dimensional memory frames is as follows [18]:

- **PMD (Perceptual Multi-Dimensional)-frame** constitutes perceptual memory as a relational matrix structure. It collects information from external objects followed by separating it into a variety of perceptual information, and re-collects the same information in the other situations, accumulating the information from the objects via a variety of different processes. PMD-frame incrementally grows as it creates memory from the input information and matches it against the past memory in parallel.
- **MMD (Motion Multi-Dimensional)-frame** constitutes behavioral memory as a matrix structure. The behavioral action processing starts when unconscious autonomous behavior shows after one's birth. It gathers a variety of perceptual information as well to connect muscles with nerves using spinals as a reflection point. In accordance with one's physical growth, it widens the range of activities the behavioral action processing can cover autonomously.
- **BMD (Behavior Multi-Dimensional)-frame** is the memory structure associated with the autonomous automatic behavior control processing. It combines a set of MMD-frames into a manipulable unit.
- **RMD (Relation Multi-Dimensional)-frame** is the memory structure associated with the conscious information processing. It combines a set of BMD-frames into a manipulable unit.
- **WMD (Word Multi-Dimensional)-frame** is the memory structure for language. It is constructed on a very simple one-dimensional array.

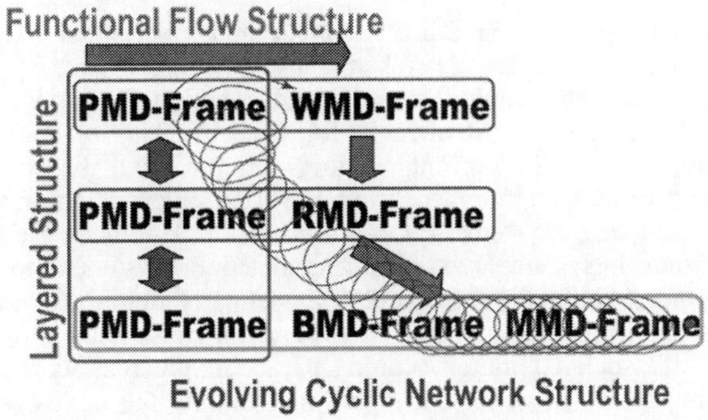

Figure 4. Multi-dimensional memory frames characterized by functional flow structure, layered structure, and evolving cyclic network structure [19, Figure 4]

Figure 4 provides a topological representation of the distributed memory system depicted in the right portion of Figure 2. It can be viewed from three perspectives:

1) The distributed memory is structurally organized in three layers. The top layer is controlled by words, consisting of simple one-dimensional array of symbols, logically constructed language, grammars that specify language use, etc. The middle layer resides on the behavioral eco-network for the individual to generate consciousness. In this layer, one acquires the meaning of behavior in the social ecology. The bottom layer creates unconsciously controlled behavioral eco-networks for the individual. This is a cyclic network starting from PMD, towards MMD via BMD, and returning to PMD. The results of activities of motor neurons, that reflect the activation of MMD, are perceived by sensory neurons to cause activation of PMD, which constitutes a closed network of PMD, BMD, and MMD.
2) Activation in the memory network spreads according to the Functional Flow Structure in the order of PMD, WMD, RMD, BMD, and MMD. An activated portion of RMD corresponds to consciousness. The flow can stay at the same layer for a while. For example, a certain word activates a set of words, and then, they activate another set of words. Consciousness formed at RMD at some moment shifts to another consciousness. No action can be associated for these System 2 activities.
3) The memories are cyclic and evolve in a cumulative and irreversible way, characterized by Evolving Cyclic Network Structure. The activated state of MMD is reflected on the activities of motor neurons, followed by updated input via sensory neurons to cause activation of PMD. PMD is shared by the three layers and serves as a common source of activation. Repetitive use of specific combinations of memory frames would strengthen the connections between them, and evolve.

It is important to note that memory serves as a mechanism to establish synchronization. A rough sketch concerning how synchronization between the external world and the internal world, i.e., successive PCM processes, could be done can be drawn by combining MHP/RT and Distributed Memory System in Figure 2. When sensory neurons are activated by external stimuli, Perceptual Information Processing fires relevant portions of memory followed by firing of connected networks in the current memory structure, and the activated portions of memory are available for Conscious Information Processing (System 2) and Autonomous Automatic Behavior Control (System 1) via resonance reaction for some amount of time, then, finally the output of System 1 is input to Behavioral Action Processing to carry out behavior by sending signals to the associated motor neurons to act in the real world. The movement of one's body part will initiate the next cycle of PCM processes. What is going on in the external world and what the self is behaving are internalized through perception, and the perceived world goes through a PCM process by activating relevant portions of memory and utilizing it via resonance mechanism. In this way, memory processes play an important role to bridge the gap between the perceived external world and the internal world of PCM cycles to have them go coherently, i.e., keeping them synchronized.

III. Cognitive and Behavioral Principle in Multimodal Interactions

The cyclic connection is critical to understand the relationship between behavior and memory. The three features shown in Figure 4 enable pipelining the processes. However, it has to be scheduled in such a way that the PCM processes work smoothly as the external environments change at their pace. This section derives cognitive and behavioral principles in multimodal interactions that should organize the pipelining processes. They would provide a firm perspective to understand otherwise complex multimodal interaction processes.

A. Four Processing Modes: Conscious/Unconscious Processes Before/After an Event

Experience associated with a person's activities is characterized by a series of events, each of which is recognized by a person consciously. When one looks at the cognitive architecture MHP/RT from *a particular event* that occurred at the absolute time T in order to answer the question what it is doing for the event, MHP/RT's behavior looks as if it works in one of *four modes* [6][20] at one time before and after the event at T as shown by Figure 5.

Two of the four modes concern the processes carried out *before* the event:

- System 2 Before Mode: In the time range of $T-\beta \leq t < T-\beta'$, where $\beta' \sim$ 500msec and β ranges a few seconds to hours, and even to months, MHP/RT uses memory, WMD and/or RMD, for *consciously* preparing for what would happen in the future.
- System 1 Before Mode: In the time range of $T-\beta' \leq t < T$, it *unconsciously* coordinate motor activities to the interacting environment. This mode uses PMD, BMD, and MMD.

The other two modes concern the processes carried out *after* the event:

- System 1 After Mode: In the time range of $T < t \leq T+\alpha'$, where $\alpha' \sim$ 500msec, MHP/RT *unconsciously* tunes the connections between sensory inputs and motor outputs for better performance for the same event in the future. This mode updates the connections at the bottom layer of Figure 4.
- System 2 After Mode: In the time range of $T+\alpha' < t \leq T+\alpha$, it *consciously* recognizes what has happened, and then, modifies memory concerning the event, where α ranges a few seconds to minutes, and even to hours. This mode modifies the connections at the middle layer of Figure 4. Note that, since language (knowledge concerning words) is not directly related with multimodal interaction, the top layer of Figure 4 remains intact in the situations this paper deals with.

It is important to note, however, that an experience represented as a series of consciously identified events by a person has to be regarded as the results of unrecognized unconscious activities: metaphorically speaking, consciousness in System 2 is one of tips of icebergs that appear above the sea level, and the tips are interrelated with each other via the unseen relationships established below the sea level in System 1. A system of icebergs develops in the natural condition of seawater (temperature, tidal currents, etc.) and atmosphere, which may not be trivial for all people. Apparently, congruent configurations of the tips of two iceberg systems at a certain moment do not assure that they are entirely congruent. They may evolve differently as time goes by even if the surrounding environment is identical.

In summary, this subsection suggests that an understanding of the phenomena, that users are interacting with multimodal environment, could be obtained by regarding the phenomena as a series of conscious events, which could be further decomposed into four processing modes of MHP/RT concerning each event.

B. Representing Multimodal Interaction Event by Using the Four Processing Modes

Any event in multimodal interaction can be viewed from a user as an event that has happened in the time range of $[T-\beta,\ T+\alpha]$, and this should be an appropriate representation for the system event that occurs at T, accompanied with the portions of multi-dimensional memory frames that have participated in the processes in the time range of $[T-\beta,\ T+\alpha]$. It would be useful to consider a situation where a multimodal interface is expected to have the user integrate positive past experiences that are activated by provision of appropriate external cues at T from the system. The integrated memory formed in System 2 After Mode for the particular system event that happened at T would be activated in the future in System 2 Before Mode while preparing for the identical system events to happen repeatedly. The event appears recursively in the PCM processes, and is likely to extend the relevant time range longer, i..e., β and α would become larger. The larger β becomes, the farther the person can foresee. The larger α becomes, the wider the person can elaborate on the event. These should make the person smarter in living.

It is important to notice the fact that consciousness concerning the event comes to play in System 2 After Mode after the event at $T+\alpha'$ implies that consciousness lags at least by the amount of time, α', behind the real world. More specifically, the user is consciously blind during the period of $[T-\beta',\ T+\alpha']$ but would integrate consciously the blind period into conscious activities during the time

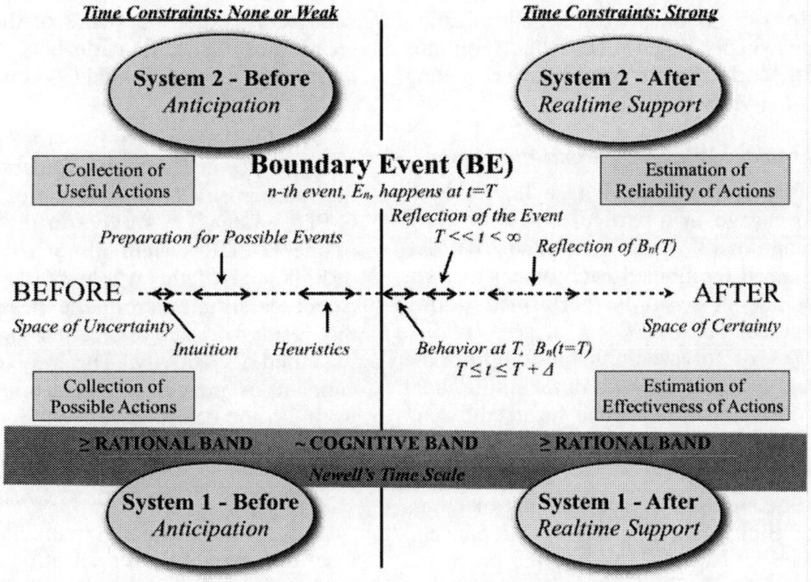

Figure 5. How the Four Processing Modes work (adapted from [20])

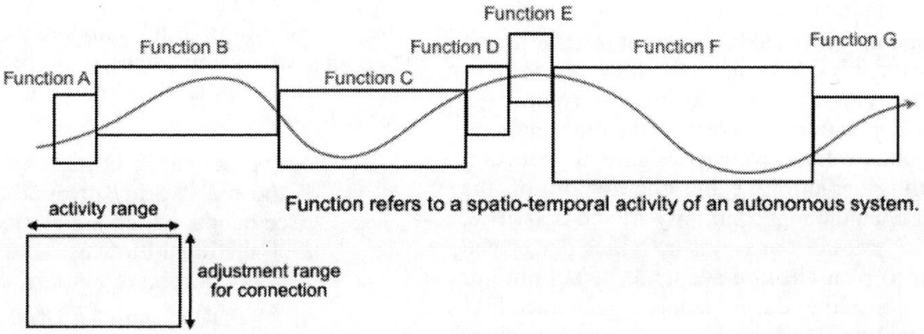

Figure 6. Successive functions are connected within the adjustable band in the spatio-time dimension.

range of $[T-\beta,\ T+\alpha]$. Therefore, consciously retrievable multimodal interaction experience has to be considered as memory structure concerning the event at T in the extended time range of $[T-\beta,\ T+\alpha]$ with consciously *inaccessible* but integrated memory region corresponding to the consciously blind time range of $[T-\beta',\ T+\alpha']$.

C. Weak Synchronization

Normally, the term "synchronization" refers to co-occurrence of two events on two distinct streams at the same time. In the case of multimodal interaction, the one side is a multimodal system and the other side is a user. It is said this way: a system and a user is synchronized if every system event at $T_{\rm sys}$ occurs as a user event at $T_{\rm user}$ with some amount of time allowance of Δ, $|T_{\rm user}-T_{\rm sys}|<\Delta$, where the actual values of Δ depend on the nature of interactions.

An example is as follows: a system sounds auditory cues, then, it shows text messages on a secondary display for 10 seconds with the expectation that its user hears the sound, comprehends it as the indication of something important to be shown on the secondary display for about 10 seconds, and moves his/her eyeballs to the target within, say, $2 \sim 3$ seconds. In this way, the system event and its corresponding user event are combined together to form a synchronized event at the overt information exchange level.

However, as depicted in Figure 5, a person's activity related with an event has to be considered from the four processing modes, which ranges relatively long time before and after the actual time the event happens. Therefore, "synchronization" has to be considered alternatively as the phenomena a person's activities during the time range of $[T-\beta, T+\alpha]$, which are linked with the specific recognizable system event at time T through a sequence of processes carried out in either of the four processing modes: all the processes have some link with the system event at T. When this is satisfied, the event is considered synchronized with a person's activities, which is called *weak synchronization* [21].

A smooth flow of the four processing modes can break when a person has to adjust his/her activity while s/he is in System 1 Before Mode in such a way that his/her movement goes in synchronous with the current environment. When this happens, the condition for weak synchronization is not satisfied but s/he has to make efforts to establish weak synchronization by adjusting his/her movement. When s/he reflects on this event in System 2 After Mode, he/she would have a feeling associated with anticipation-violated [21].

D. How MHP/RT Works under Weak Synchronization

In order for an O-PDP system, which is a higher level concept of MHP/RT, to engage in a particular system event at T during the time range of $[T - \beta, T + \alpha]$, the MHP/RT processes have to be chained (combined each other) to form a procedure, which include those to be performed during the respective time ranges of $[T - \beta, T - \beta')$, $[T - \beta', T)$, $(T, T + \alpha']$, $(T + \alpha', T + \alpha]$ for accomplishing appropriate functions in the ecological system composed of the multimodal system and the user. A mechanism is needed for establishing chains between functions that exist quasi-independently and discretely.

An O-PDP system is composed of autonomous elements in a band-structure, i.e., Biological, Cognitive, Rational, and Social Bands as suggested by Newell [16], and the processes carried out in the respective bands are combined each other to form a function. For example, in the Rational Band, a person could perform a series of inferences by logical deduction. Each inference is regarded as an element to obtain a logical result starting from an initial premise.

Autonomous elements are weakly synchronized with the external world, and the way how actually they work indirectly reflects the circularity of the existing environment – autopoiesis [12], and fluctuations inherent in the environment. This situation is schematically shown by Figure 6. Function C is connected with Function D using the region of the overlapping edge for maintaining continuity of the activities. Function C could be a series of conscious activities performed in the Rational Band to plan ahead a sequence of actions for controlling the car by consulting the contents of RMD (see Figure 4) followed by Function D, which could be an unconscious activity for tuning the planned activities for the particular road conditions by using the bottom layer of the memory structure, PMD, BMD and MMD, for which activations come from the middle layer following the Functional Flow Structure depicted in Figure 4. Function C is carried out in System 2 Before Mode in the time range of $[T - \beta, T - \beta')$ and Function D in System 1 Before Mode in the time range of $[T - \beta', T)$.

Note that elements in Biological, Cognitive, Rational, and Social Bands work autonomously. Conscious processes carried out in the upper bands run in parallel with unconscious processes performed in the lower band within the time range of $\leq$ 500msec. In Figure 6, Function C is a segment of an entire series of working of conscious elements that happens to establish connections with Function B, a segment from another conscious elements that was carried out before Function C, and with Function D, which is part of unconscious activities carried out by using the cycle of PMD, BMD, and MMD. The red curved line symbolically shows a trajectory of network firing in the O-PDP system, that is structured as Figure 4 by indicating the regions to connect to elements in different bands or those used for different processing modes. Various combinations of functional chains between parallel processes can occur, causing path proliferation of the network. This is possible because there exists *time relativity* among a variety of functions due to network circularity and fluctuation in processing in the behavioral ecology network of the O-PDP system. When the recall rates of specific paths become higher, proliferation along these paths are suppressed to centralize the activations on these paths thereafter.

An O-PDP system is created as a developed form of naturally formed energy circulation. Weak synchronization is the mechanism, or the principle, for a cognitive architecture, O-PDP system, to survive in the environment. Each element of the O-PDP system plays a certain role in achieving the overall goal of the whole O-PDP system. However, its role is not determined from the beginning but it exists only as the result of each element's own efforts to survive since it started its activity. The way of synchronization between elements is incidentally determined, and the synchronization itself is not deterministic but incomplete and flexible weak synchronization.

IV. Conclusion and Future Work

Whatever multimodal interaction environments users are in, what they would do for selecting next actions is simple: users just perform the dual-process of unconscious and conscious processes for every consciously recognizable event in certain time ranges before and after the event. Then, why is reasonable stability maintained in the uncertain procedure dependent on the autonomous reaction of the O-PDP system? In the situation of multimodal interaction, "stability" connotes the situations where the interactions between the system and the user continues smoothly without any breakdowns. The reasons are as follows:

- Perceptual input is used to generate a mirror image of the real world surrounding the self and shared in three bands, which are related with each other through the Functional Flow Structure and the Evolving Cyclic Network Structure (Figure 4).
- An O-PDP system is formed in the nonlinear hierarchically structured bands [16] to select next actions by applying four processes described in Section III-A as a means to survive in the ever-changing environment (Figure 5).
- Time constraints from the external environment is satisfied by fluctuations in the characteristic times of autonomous activities in respective bands through the mechanism of weak synchronization (Figure 6).

The first two items in the above list show the important characteristics derived from the architectural definition of O-PDP system, and the last item, weak synchronization, defines the principle for coordinating O-PDP in the ever-changing real environment. These three items jointly define the cognitive and behavioral principles necessary to understand users interacting with multimodal environment.

A. Future Work

The actual values of β and α, which define the time range of weak synchronization, can vary depending on the particular event at T, the contents of memory of the user, and the amount of time the user is allowed to allocate for the event. However, they can be estimated by simulating user behavior by MHP/RT. The purpose of simulation is to derive initial hypotheses concerning distinguishable users' behaviors caused by qualitatively different workings of MHP/RT, and the structure and contents of memory in the multimodal interaction environment. The hypotheses will be field-tested by having *selected users* representing the different segments in terms of characteristic behaviors in the particular multimodal interaction environment carry out the interactions. This approach, called *Cognitive-Chrono Ethnography (CCE)*, has been successfully applied to a variety of fields [4][5][22][23].

On the theoretical basis of the principles this paper described, some case studies are on-going to understand users' activities in multimodal interactions. Two of them are briefly described as future work that will come next to this work.

1) Designing Memorable Events: People live in the environment filled with artifacts, part of which is real and the rest is virtual. An initial theoretical simulations have been conducted to understand how the PCM processes along with the memory process result in memorable experiences [24]. Preliminary experiments were conducted to see how omnidirectional movies in virtual reality augmented with audio-guide made the experience memorable by timely *weak* synchronization and integration of multi-modal information. The contents of audio-guide for giving explanations to the visual contents to come after a few seconds have to be consciously processed by the usr in System 2 Before Mode. Some visual cues may be used to have the user unconsciously moves his/her eyeballs to the visual contents just having been given explanations, which is done in System 1 Before Mode. If this process happens while the memory is active, there is a good chance of strengthening the memory in System 2 After Mode, to cause the event memorable.

2) Designing Immersive Events: Immersive virtual environments are distinct from other types of multimedia learning environments. Initial theoretical considerations were reported that focused on the conditions necessary to produce "immersive experience" for the user [21]. Immersive feeling eliciting condition for an artificial environment to have the user feel immersive-ness is 1) it must be new to him/her, i.e., the range of memory activation is limited, 2) s/he is able to carry out actions with an anticipation activated by the artificial environment without any breakdown in performing motor-level actions System 2 Before Mode followed by no serious adjustment requited in System 1 Before Mode), 3) s/he is able to consciously recognize an event associated with the series of just-finished actions, and 4) s/he is able to reflect on the event to integrate it with the recognized feeling associated with the event (in System 2 After Mode). The study will continue in the context of developing a multimodal interface to help young pedestrians acquire necessary skills for safe navigation in dangerous traffic environments.

References

[1] J. L. Rubio-Tamayo, M. Gertrudix Barrio, and F. García García, "Environments and virtual reality: Systematic review and advances in communication, interaction and simulation," Multimodal Technologies and Interaction, vol. 1, no. 4, 2017.

[2] H. A. Simon, The Sciences of the Artificial, 3rd ed. Cambridge, MA: The MIT Press, 1996.

[3] M. Kitajima and M. Toyota, "Hierarchical Structure of Human Action Selections – An Update of Newell's Time Scale of Human Action," in Procedia Computer Science, BICA 2014. 5th Annual International Conference on Biologically Inspired Cognitive Architectures, vol. 41, 2014, pp. 321–325.

[4] ——, "Simulating navigation behaviour based on the architecture model Model Human Processor with Real-Time Constraints (MHP/RT)," Behaviour & Information Technology, vol. 31, no. 1, 2012, pp. 41–58.

[5] M. Kitajima, Memory and Action Selection in Human-Machine Interaction. Wiley-ISTE, 2016.

[6] M. Kitajima and M. Toyota, "Decision-making and action selection in Two Minds: An analysis based on Model Human Processor with Realtime Constraints (MHP/RT)," Biologically Inspired Cognitive Architectures, vol. 5, 2013, pp. 82–93.

[7] S. K. Card, T. P. Moran, and A. Newell, The Psychology of Human-Computer Interaction. Hillsdale, NJ: Lawrence Erlbaum Associates, 1983.

[8] J. L. McClelland and D. E. Rumelhart, Parallel Distributed Processing: Explorations in the Microstructure of Cognition : Psychological and Biological Models. The MIT Press, 6 1986.

[9] D. Kahneman, "A perspective on judgment and choice," American Psychologist, vol. 58, no. 9, 2003, pp. 697–720.

[10] ——, Thinking, Fast and Slow. New York, NY: Farrar, Straus and Giroux, 2011.

[11] D. Morris, The nature of happiness. London: Little Books Ltd., 2006.

[12] H. Maturana and F. Varela, Autopoiesis and Cognition (Boston Studies in the Philosophy and History of Science), softcover reprint of the original 1st ed. 1980 ed. D. Reidel Publishing Company, 8 1991.

[13] M. Kitajima and M. Toyota, "Two Minds and Emotion," in COGNITIVE 2015 : The Seventh International Conference on Advanced Cognitive Technologies and Applications, 2015, pp. 8–16.

[14] J. R. Anderson and C. Lebiere, The Atomic Components of Thought. Mahwah, NJ: Lawrence Erlbaum Associates, 1998.

[15] J. R. Anderson, How can the Human Mind Occur in the Physical Universe? New York, NY: Oxford University Press, 2007.

[16] A. Newell, Unified Theories of Cognition (The William James Lectures, 1987). Cambridge, MA: Harvard University Press, 1990, page 122, Fig. 3-3.

[17] M. Toyota, M. Kitajima, and H. Shimada, "Structured Meme Theory: How is informational inheritance maintained?" in Proceedings of the 30th Annual Conference of the Cognitive Science Society, B. C. Love, K. McRae, and V. M. Sloutsky, Eds. Austin, TX: Cognitive Science Society, 2008, p. 2288.

[18] M. Kitajima and M. Toyota, "Distributed Memory System Architecture based on the Analyses of Human Brain Memory," in Proceedings of the 35th Annual Conference of the Cognitive Science Society, M. Knauff, M. Pauen, N. Sebanz, and I. Wachsmuth, Eds. Austin, TX: Cognitive Science Society, 2013, p. 4002.

[19] ——, "Topological Considerations of Memory Structure," in Procedia Computer Science, BICA 2014. 5th Annual International Conference on Biologically Inspired Cognitive Architectures, vol. 41, 2014, pp. 45–50.

[20] ——, "Four Processing Modes of *in situ* Human Behavior," in Biologically Inspired Cognitive Architectures 2011 - Proceedings of the Second Annual Meeting of the BICA Society, A. V. Samsonovich and K. R. Jóhannsdóttir, Eds. Amsterdam, The Netherlands: IOS Press, 2011, pp. 194–199.

[21] J. Dinet and M. Kitajima, "Immersive interfaces for engagement and learning: Cognitive implications," in Proceedings of the 2015 Virtual Reality International Conference, ser. VRIC '18. New York, NY, USA: ACM, 2018, pp. 18/04:1–18/04:8. [Online]. Available: https://doi.org/10.1145/3234253.3234301

[22] M. Kitajima, H. Tahira, S. Takahashi, and T. Midorikawa, "Understanding tourist's *in situ* behavior: a Cognitive Chrono-Ethnography study of visitors to a hot spring resort," Journal of Quality Assurance in Hospitality and Tourism, vol. 12, 2012, pp. 247–270.

[23] M. Kitajima and M. Toyota, "Cognitive Chrono-Ethnography: A Methodology for Understanding Users for Designing Interactions Based on User Simulation with Cognitive Architectures," in Biologically Inspired Cognitive Architectures 2012 - Proceedings of the Third Annual Meeting of the BICA Society, 2012, pp. 193–198.

[24] M. Kitajima, S. Shimizu, and K. T. Nakahira, "Creating memorable experiences in virtual reality: Theory of its processes and preliminary eye-tracking study using omnidirectional movies with audio-guide," in 2017 3rd IEEE International Conference on Cybernetics (CYBCONF), June 2017, pp. 1–8.

A Framework for Tutoring Computational Thinking: Learning Environment and Task Analysis

Kazuhisa Miwa

Graduate School of Information Science
Nagoya University
Nagoya, Japan 464-8601
e-mail: miwa@is.nagoya-ua.jp

Kazuaki Kojima

Learning Technology Lab.
Teikyo University
Utsunomiya, Japan 320-8551
e-mail: kojima@lt-lab.teikyo-u.ac.jp

Abstract—**Computational thinking refers to thinking like a computer scientist. In this paper, we posit an approach of class design to train general university students in computational thinking. In our class practice, we let participants build a rule-based model to solve the following problem: There is a robot in a room with a banana and a box. Build a model with the knowledge to be given to the robot in order to make the robot get the banana. Computational thinking has four functions: decomposition, pattern recognition, abstraction, and algorithm (procedure). We discuss the participants' engagement to solve this problem and the four functions of computational thinking.**

Keywords - Computational Thinking; Cognitive Modeling; Tutoring

I. INTRODUCTION

Computational thinking refers to thinking like a computer scientist. In fact, computational thinking has great influence not only in the natural sciences of physics, chemistry, biology, but also in psychology, economics, literature, and psychiatry. The stage of the activity of computer scientists is now spreading in broad area.

Computational thinking is not reserved only for experts in these areas, but rather is applicable for anyone who engages in problem solving. In this respect, various efforts to implement computational thinking training in education should be emphasized. Above all, many attempts to develop computational thinking in the context of problem-solving education have been made in K-12 education [1][2].

In this paper, we posit an approach to including computational thinking training into the curriculum for general university students. In fact, in her paper on computational thinking, Jeannette M. Wing insists that professors of computer science should teach university freshmen subjects such as " a way to think like a computer scientist " in the department of computer science but also to other areas of study [3].

We have developed a framework called " Learning by Building Cognitive Models " in which general university students build rule-based cognitive models [4]-[7]. We developed a production system architecture for education, DoCoPro (Production system for anytime and anywhere), as learning environment for that purpose [8][9].

The first learning effect obtained there is the promotion of theory-based thought, which tries to understand the data in relation to the theory. For many university students, it is easy to explain data descriptively, but difficult to interpret data on a theoretical basis. As such, there is a gap between the data and the theory. A model is built by refining the theory, while predicting the data. That is, a model has the function of bridging theory and data. Based on this perspective, building a model to explain the data will promote activities to theoretically interpret the data [10].

The second learning effect is the refinement of the mental model and the improvement of mental simulation [11]. When behavior is observed, it is difficult to infer the mental model behind it. In our approach, when the result of calculation including error was observed, it was requested to identify the mental model behind it, i.e., the bug model. In doing so, participants were required to create a cognitive model that simulates the behavior (the result of the calculation including the error). By creating a cognitive model, participants can more clearly understand bugs that cause errors in cognitive procedures. In addition, using the mental model, simulating error generation becomes possible [12].

These efforts support that Learning by Building Cognitive Models can be used as a learning framework for fostering computational thinking. Based on this insight, this paper examines the following:

- In DoCoPro as learning environment, we propose an available learning task for fostering computational thinking.
- We examine that the proposed learning task is useful for fostering computational thinking based on the task analysis.

In Section 2, we indicate four core functions of computational thinking. In Section 3, we introduce a task and learning environment to test our approach. In Section 4, we discuss how computational thinking is specified in the task referring to the definition of computational thinking in this paper. Section 5 is our conclusions.

II. FOUR ELLEMENTS OF COMPUTATIONAL THINKING

Jeannette M. Wing posits that thinking like a computer scientist means more than just being able to program a computer, which requires multiple levels of abstract thought [3]. Computational thinking has several definitions; however, computational thinking is consistently said to have the following four functions [13].

1) Decomposition
   Disassemble complex problems so they can be solved.
2) Pattern Recognition
   To see periodicity and law.
3) Abstraction
   Cut out branches and leaves and extract only important elements.
4) Algorithm (Procedure)
   Step by step, to clarify the problem-solving procedure.

We test if participants engage in cognitive activities with the four functions in our class practice.

III. TASK AND LEARNING ENVIRONMENT

We assessed whether participants engaged in cognitive activities using the four functions in our class practice.

In our class practice, we requested that participants build a rule-based model to solve the following problem. There is a robot in a room with a banana and a box (Figure 1). Build a model with the knowledge to be given to the robot to retrieve the banana (Figure 2). In order to retrieve the banana, move the robot to the same place as the banana. The robot can move to a high place by standing on the box. The robot can also move the box.

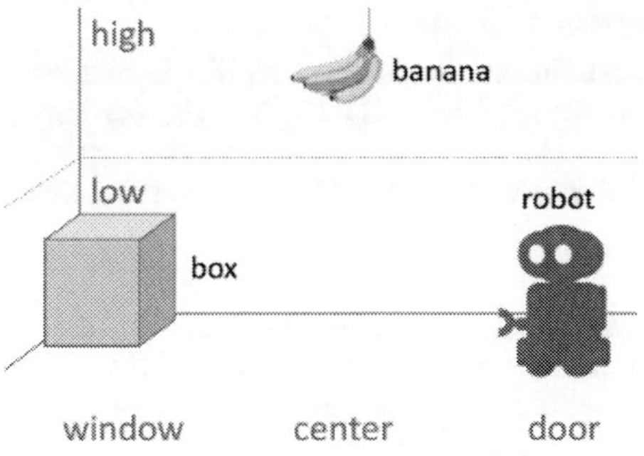

Figure 1. Initial state (stage (a))

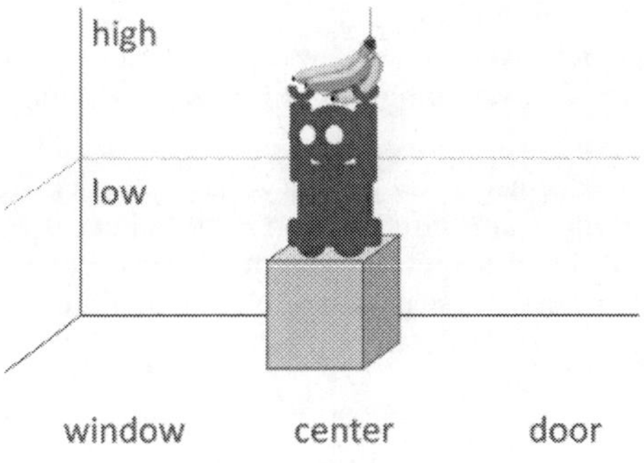

Figure 2. Goal state (stage (b))

DoCoPro was used as learning environment for building models. Below is a screenshot of DoCoPro (Figure 3). Representations of the states observed during the problem-solving processes are shown in the working memory in the left frame. The students created their models by editing rules in the editor in the right frames and simulating and evaluating problem-solving processes by executing the models with the controller in the upper frame.

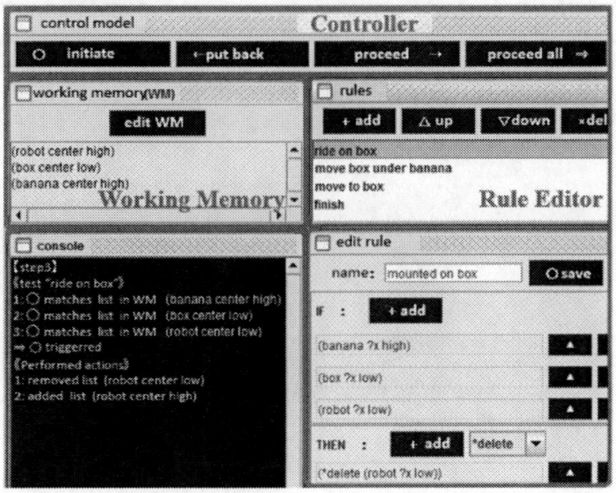

Figure 3. An example screenshot of DoCoPro as learning environment

The participants confirm that the robot can grasp the banana properly from this initial condition according to the model that they create.

Subsequently, the participants address the following problems in the next learning stage. The participants are presented with the scenario (as four new initial stages (c) to (f)) presented in Figure 4. If the conditions and operations are successfully set, the model can reach the goal state and stop even from any of the four newly presented initial states, or the model will be improved for reaching the goal.

IV. TASK ANALYSIS

Next, we discuss the participants' engagement in solving this problem and the four functions of computational thinking.

A. Decomposition

In order for the robot to acquire the banana, the participants are required to break down and assess the problem. To reach the target state (Figure 2) from the initial state (Figure 1), this problem is typically decomposed into the following four sub-problems.

- The robot moves toward the box.
- The robot moves the box under the banana.
- The robot stands on the box.
- The robot retrieves the banana.

B. Pattern recognition

See the initial stages (a) and (d). The initial knowledge for each situation is as follows.

Rule for (a):

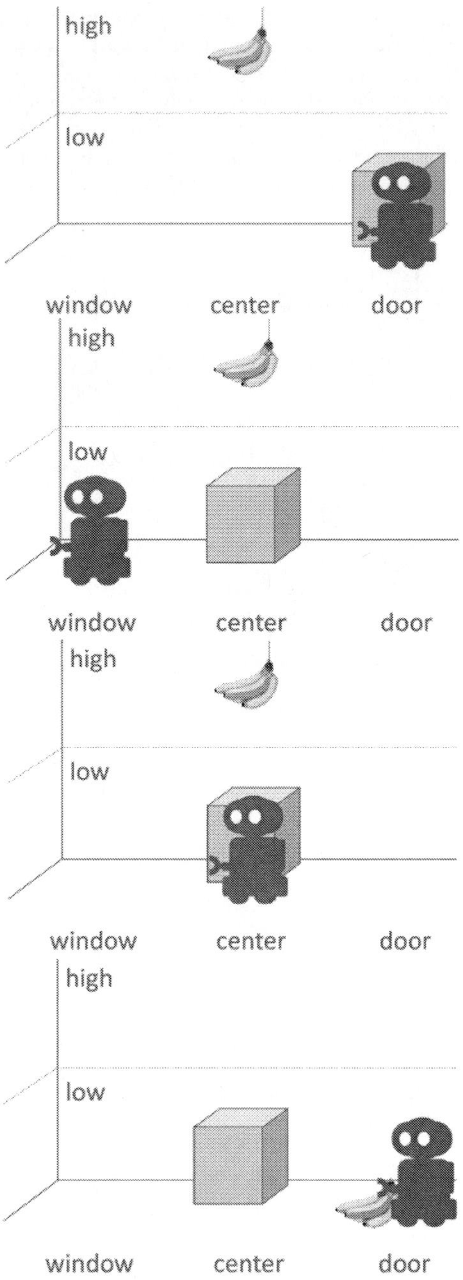

Figure 4. Four initial stages for model expansion: (c), (d), (e), and (f)

```
IF
Position of robot is RIGHT
Position of box is CENTER
THEN
Move robot to CENTER
```

Rule for (d):

```
IF
Position of robot is LEFT
Position of box is CENTER
THEN
Move robot to CENTER
```

If the participants can find the commonality of this knowledge, the following rule is drawn:

Rule for (a) and (d):

```
IF
Positions of robot and box are different
THEN
Move robot to the position of box
```

C. Abstraction

The level of abstraction is represented in the if-clause of each rule. For example, the above rule for (a) and (d) is too abstract because it fires at the condition of the initial state (f), even though it should not because the robot does not need to go up on the box because the banana is on the floor. On the other hand, the above rules for (a) and (d) are too specific.

The adequate rule is as follows:

```
IF
Positions of robot and box are different
Banana hangs from the ceiling
THEN
Move robot to the position of box
```

D. Automation

The crucial nature of our practice is that models are built as computer programs in DoCoPro. The participants can test if the model behaves as expected. The participants can improve the model while observing the behaviors of the model.

V. CONCLUSION

In this paper, we examined our learning framework to foster computational thinking for university students. We have established an educational production system architecture, DoCoPro, as learning environment. Our task analysis based on the four functions of computational thinking implies that our framework expect to work well for the educational setting.

The primary objective of this paper is to establish the foundation of our approach by formalizing the functions of computational thinking and analyzing the training task used in our approach. Additionally, we have begun to make an initial challenge for examining the utility of our framework through class practices.

We performed a preliminary class practice for evaluating our learning framework. The results indicated that the rules described in the pretests omitted many conditions in the pretests, whereas the presence of the conditions improved in the posttest. More detailed results were found in Kojima and Miwa, 2018 [14].

ACKNOWLEDGEMENT

This work was supported by JSPS KAKENHI Grant Number 18H05320 and 15H02717.

VI. APPENDIX

Our production system, DoCoPro, is a specific notation of stages and rules. The following is the specific description of the two stages (a) and (b) seen in Figures 1 and 2.

Initial State (a) in Figure 1:

```
(Robot DOOR LOW)
(Box WINDOW LOW)
(Banana CENTER HIGH)
```

Goal State (b) in Figure 2:

```
(Robot CENTER HIGH)
(Box CENTER LOW)
(Banana CENTER HIGH)
```

The following is an example complete set of rules for solving the task. When the set of rules is applied to the initial stage (a): the robot moves to the box located in the window side by rule 1, the robot moves to the center of the room with the box by rule 2, the robot goes up to the box by rule 3, and the robot grasps the banana by rule 4. Through the above process, the goal state (b) is reached.

```
- name: Robot moves
  if:
  - (Robot ?x LOW)
  - (Box ?y LOW)
  - (Banana ?z HIGH)
  - (*test-not-equal ?x ?y)
  then:
  - (*delete (Robot ?x LOW))
  - (*deposit (Robot ?y LOW))
- name: Move box
  if:
  - (Robot ?x LOW)
  - (?z ?x LOW)
  - (Banana ?y HIGH)
  - (*test-not-equal ?x ?y)
  then:
  - (*delete (Robot ?x LOW))
  - (*deposit (Robot ?y LOW))
  - (*delete (?z ?x LOW))
  - (*deposit (?z ?y LOW))
- name: Ride on box
  if:
  - (Robot ?x LOW)
  - (Box ?x LOW)
  - (Banana ?x HIGH)
  then:
  - (*delete (Robot ?x LOW))
  - (*deposit (Robot ?x HIGH))
- name: Getting banana
  if:
  - (Robot ?y ?z)
  - (Banana ?y ?z)
  - (Hand EMPTY)
  then:
  - (*delete (Hand EMPTY))
  - (*deposit (Hand Banana))
```

REFERENCES

[1] A. Yadav, C. Mayfield, N. Zhou, S. Hambrusch, and J. T. Korb, "Computational thinking in elementary and secondary teacher education," Trans. Comput. Educ., vol. 14, no. 1, Mar. 2014, pp. 5:1–5:16. [Online]. Available: http://doi.acm.org/10.1145/2576872

[2] S. Grover and R. Pea, "Computational thinking in k-12: A review of the state of the field," Educational Researcher, vol. 42, no. 1, 2013, pp. 38–43.

[3] J. M. Wing, "Computational thinking," Communications of the ACM, vol. 49, no. 3, 2006, pp. 33–35.

[4] K. Miwa, "A cognitive simulator for learning the nature of human problem solving," Journal of Japanese Society for Artificial Intelligence, vol. 23, no. 6, 2008, pp. 374–383.

[5] K. Miwa, J. Morita, R. Nakaike, and H. Terai, "Learning through intermediate problems in creating cognitive models." Interactive Learning Environments, vol. 22, 2014, pp. 326–350.

[6] K. Miwa and K. Terai, H.and Shibayama, "Understanding procedural knowledge for solving arithmetic task by externalization," in Proceedings of ITS 2016, ser. LNCS, vol. 9684, 2016, pp. 3–12.

[7] K. Miwa and H. Terai, "Learning by building cognitive models that reflect cognitive information processing: A preliminary class exercise," in Proceedings of the ninth International Conference on Advanced Cognitive Technologies and Applications (Cognitive 2017), 2017, pp. 50–53.

[8] R. Nakaike, K. Miwa, J. Morita, and H. Terai, "Development and evaluation of a web-based production system for learning anywhere," in Proceedings of 17th international conference on computers in education, 2009, pp. 127–131.

[9] K. Miwa, R. Nakaike, J. Morita, and H. Terai, "Development of production system for anywhere and class practice," in Proceedings of the 14th International Conference of Artificial Intelligence in Education, 2009, pp. 91–99.

[10] H. Saito, K. Miwa, N. Kanzaki, H. Terai, K. Kojima, R. Nakaike, and J. Morita, "Educational practice for interpretation of experimental data based on a theory," in Proceedings of 21th international conference on computers in education, 2013, pp. 234–239.

[11] K. Miwa, J. Morita, H. Terai, N. Kanzaki, K. Kojima, R. Nakaike, and H. Saito, "Use of a cognitive simulator to enhance students' mental simulation activities," in Proceedings of ITS 2014, ser. LNCS, vol. 8474, 2014, pp. 398–403.

[12] K. Miwa, N. Kanzaki, H. Terai, K. Kojima, R. Nakaike, J. Morita, and H. Saito, "Learning mental models on human cognitive processing by creating cognitive models," in Proceedings of AIED 2015, ser. LNCS, vol. 9112, 2015, pp. 287–296.

[13] J. Krauss and K. Prottsman, Computational Thinking and Coding for Every Student The Teacher's Getting-Started Guide. CORWIN: A SAGE Company, 2017.

[14] K. Kojima and K. Miwa, "Preliminary study on fostering computational thinking by constructing a cognitive model," in Workshop Proceedings: 26th International Conference on Computers in Education, 2018, pp. 272–277.

Delivering Comprehensive Knowledge of the World to the Computer:

How to make the computer understand meaning

Victor Raskin
Linguistics & CERIAS
Purdue University
West Lafayette, Indiana, USA
Email: vraskin@purdue.edu

Julia Taylor Rayz
Computer and Information Technology
Purdue University
West Lafayette, Indiana, USA
Email: jtaylor1@purdue.edu

Abstract—**Ontological Semantic Technology is a mature theory that we have developed for 30 and 14 years, respectively to the co-authors, and it has been demonstrated to represent the meaning of text well. Designed first as an engineering ontology for natural language computer applications, it became a paradigm for theoretical, as well as computational semantics. This paper claims that it is also a legitimate approach to a much larger cognitive task of representing the human knowledge of the world in the computer, without which text understanding is unattainable.**

Keywords-ontology; ontological semantics; semantic theory; representing computer knowledge of the world

I. Introduction: Representing Meaning

The main purpose of this position paper is to demonstrate how a comprehensive ontology, extended from forming the basis and substance of natural language semantics, can and must be extended to the basis and substance of human knowledge that is computerized in applications. The former task was established in Ontological Semantics developed in the late 1980s through 1990s.

In a parallel and unrelated development, the same decades saw the growing presence of non-linguistic natural language processing that became dominant. It makes sense now, for a number of reasons, that computational semantics, the linguistic field, and natural language processing, the non-linguistic "techie" field, would combine their efforts in the near future. This paper, coming out of the former field addresses researchers in both areas: it shows the computational semanticists how the approach reaches into the cognitive area of modeling human knowledge of reality for the computer; and it informs the 'techies' of the existing and developing effort outside of machine learning, neural networks, deep learning, word embedments, and such.

Section II traces the genesis and trajectory of ontological semantic, thus establishing its basic tenets. Section III deals briefly with the other approach, commenting only on what matters for this paper. Section IV explains how the ontological semantics paradigm progressed from the basis of limited computational semantic application to that of semantic theory in general, Section 5 introduces the ontological plane as that substance in which semantic symbols are interpreted in. Immediately, Section VI shows how the approach can, then, handle the modeling of comprehensive human knowledge for the computer. Section VII is the brief conclusion.

II. Mission of Ontological Semantics

Ontological Semantics originated in the late 1980s and was developed in the 1990s as a way to represent meaning in computational linguistic applications. The procedure closely followed human understanding of natural language, which was largely compositional. Native speakers intuitively assemble sentences out of the words they know; these meaning interact in established way, and then the sentence means whatever the speaker or writer needs to express.

It was informed by two intuitions about meaning that were new and not very popular. First, there was Raskin's idea that language meaning was organized into scripts/frames rather than being confined to separate words. The same idea was being developed by several people at the time and was probably initiated much earlier in psychology (see [1]-[3]). It was applied and somewhat developed for the first linguistic theory of humor [4].

Second, in the context of the briefly resurrected machine translation, Nirenburg and Raskin, in the 1980s, put forward the idea of interlingua as a mediating system between a source language and a target language. This appeared to be much smarter than the transfer systems translating only between a pair of languages in one direction at a time. It made perfect sense for the interlingua to be usable in any pair of languages, and for that, it had to be a semantic representation.

Machine translation was the process of translating text in a natural (source) language into its meaning representation and then from that representation to another natural (target) language. Immediately, the major issue hampering the development of linguistic semantic for centuries raised its head: What was the medium of the semantic interlingua? Increasingly, various private and government groups were talking about ontologies, meaning primarily inventories of terms. The purpose of these systems was largely the standardization of terminology, and most, if not all items, were nominals. The funding came first from NSF and later, massively, from NSA. [5] somewhat timidly, referred to our interlingua as an ontology, and it took.

Ontological Semantic ontology, in its numerous incarnations, contains properties and concepts, and in that it is somewhat similar to other ontologies in the semantic web.

However, as any ontologist would know, ontologies are not compared by the number of concepts or even the number of properties that they support, it is how the concepts and properties are used for the reasoning capabilities that should be compared. In this sense, Ontological Semantic is very different from a well-known CyC or various ontologies of description logics.

An initial massive acquisition of ontology took place at the Computing Research Laboratory at New Mexico State University which was inherited by Nirenburg from Yorick Wilks, a somewhat apprehensive friend of Ontological Semantics, and Raskin became a regular PI-level consultant there. The collaboration took place in 1994-2002 and was supported by a variety of grants, mostly from NSA.

By 2001, the rich experience, historical but mostly ideational, was summarized in the monograph distributed generously online and published later [6]. The book's title, "Ontological Semantics," gave the name to the 1990s approach and resources, though sometimes they have been referred to, reviewed, followed, and criticized as "Mikrokosmos," which was the title of a central grant and conformed to the CRL tradition of Greek names for computers and other items—hence, the k's in the spelling.

Figure 1 shows the architecture of a later developed Ontological Semantic Technology (OST) system, as it interprets every sentence ontologically. The ontology contains concepts, which are mostly events and objects, linked with named properties, all connected hierarchically on the ISA property. The ontology is language independent, which means that it is the same for all languages, the concepts are labeled in English; the labels are not English words in that they are not polysemous, have no synonyms, and are not understood by the computer; they just name the unique nodes (which also have IDs) and their links and are convenient to use for the presumably English-reading acquirers. The specific language information is acquired in the language-specific lexicon supported by morphological and syntactic knowledge (phonology is added for specific applications).

While the ontology is language-independent, the lexicons are language-specific. It is worth noting, however, that while word-for-word translation is somewhat useless, an empirical evidence suggests that sense-for-sense translation makes the development of another lexicon an easy 6-person-month project by a bilingual undergraduate.

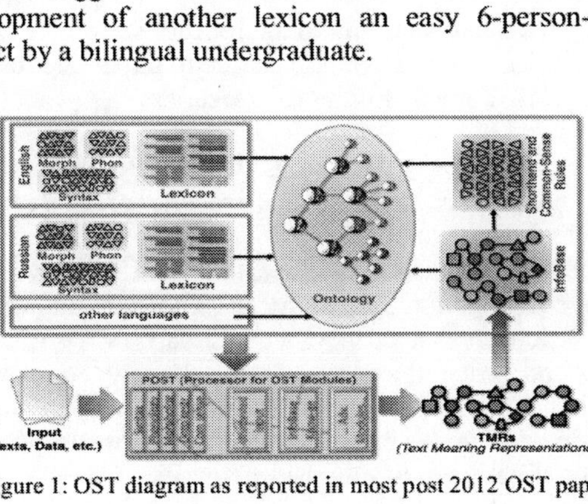

Figure 1: OST diagram as reported in most post 2012 OST papers

The resources are acquired semi-automatically supported by an online resource that shapes and automatically fills out the entries. The human user is asked only to exercise judgment about meaning. In ontological acquisition, the human determines, very importantly, where to find it in the ontology, possibly under a different label, and in case of failure, where to add it as "child," or leaf, of an existing concept. The difficult decisions, such as opening high-level leaves or making changes and pursuing them consistently, are made by Master Ontologists, of whom the current co-authors are two (of possible three or four altogether).

An obvious argument here is if it was easily done, why is there only several Master Ontologists. The answer is opportunistic and fashion-related: with the machine learning producing promising results, the race for using ML methods attracted and pulled in the majority of researchers whose careers required publications (with popular methods). It is only now that the field slowly realized that deep learning and machine learning are not an answer to all questions, and going back to and incorporating the so-called-first-wave of AI might be a good idea [7-8].

Various versions of Ontological Semantics exist today, some can be accessed online. Figure 2 illustrates a few top ontology layers of the current version of Purdue online resource, available at engineering.purdue.edu/~ost, implemented by several of Rayz's undergraduate students. Each node can be clicked to show the sub-hierarchy, if any, of which it is on top.

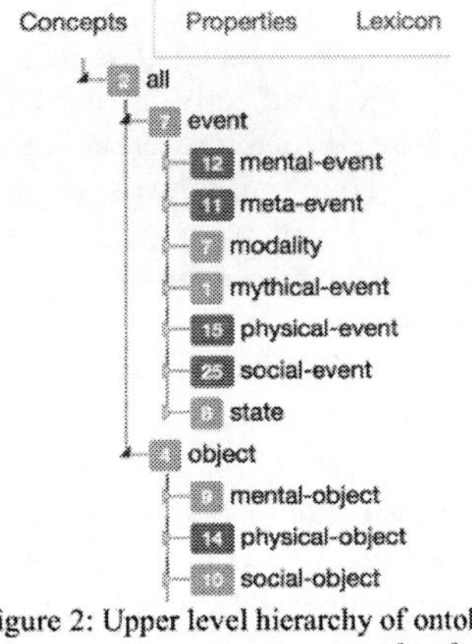

Figure 2: Upper level hierarchy of ontological concepts, Purdue OST webtool

The lexicon is acquired by native speakers, and the training is limited to a session or two for the basic acquisition. Most nouns and verbs are anchored in a concept, and the concept frame prompts the acquirer to the related words in their slots. Thus, the verb *enter* will want to identify a typical agent, theme, instrument, etc. A typical adjective will be anchored in a property, and those are defined in terms of domains and ranges, that is, the object or events they define and what values they receive. All that information is contained in the resource, and the acquirer is prompted for it automatically.

A simple English sentence *John is driving to the store for groceries* will be transformed onto this simplified format (Figure 3), where all items are ontological:

go
agent John
instrument car
Destination store
item-for sale groceries

Figure 3: Conceptual representation of a TMR

This schema is a Text Meaning Representation (TMR), and the purpose of obtaining TMRs for all sentences was basically achieved in principle and for limited applications by the late 1990s. In 1997, NSA published an RFP that called upon all applicants to follow the ontological semantic format. They all said they would but…

III. Vectors as Meaning

By the time Raskin distributed locally the mimeographed edition of his "Concise History of Linguistic Semantic" in 1973 [9], he included the one then known example of a statistical approach to linguistics. A. Shaykevich [10] obtained a copy of the published concordance of Shakespeare's complete works where every line was numbered throughout his legacy and every adjective was listed with the line numbers where it occurred, He then calculated pairs of adjectives cooccurring much more than statistically; he assigned them links that were reversely proportionate to these ratios, so that, on a graph, they were closer to each other. The result was spectacular: they were whole areas of semantically linked adjectives. Encouraged, he took the show on the road, and Raskin was one of many session chairs who tried to get him to finish the paper on time. That was a rare bird then: linguists pretty much ignored the statistical methods and did not accept their papers at linguistic conferences. So they developed outside of and aggressively without linguistics, done not by trained linguists but by statisticians, programmers, "techies."

By the early 1990s, at least partially energized by Rumelhart's ideas of the 1980s, the statisticians broke the dam, and within a decade, they came to completely dominate the field of natural language processing. Originally presented as the alternative to rule-based approaches, solidly rooted in linguistics, the first wave of machine learning, rapidly growing through computer science and engineering graduate programs, came up with packs of inventive algorithms that quickly and reliably identified outliers in a large sample of data, and they did it without any effort on linguistic resources like lexicons.

The approach first claimed boldly that it was not interested and did not aspire to represent what the text meant. This was no longer the task or purpose of natural language processing. Starting with machine learning, it evolved into neural networks, word embeddings, and deep learning. The purpose of each undertaking is to obtain vectors that are somehow presented as meanings.

We fully realize that the goals of old-school computational semantics is very different from all these approaches, the technical and formal virtuosity of their best work is admirable, and finding the attempts to semanticalize their scope somewhat hopeful. Thus, the word2vec [11, 12], being the first of word embedding papers, have rediscovered Firth, the last structuralist to try and define semantics "distributionally," that is non-semantically. Famously at the time but then forgotten until now, Firth [13] described the ability of the word *night* to be combined with *dark* as part of its meaning, and, of course, vice versa. This can be extended to saying that the meaning of dark is its ability to be combined with all the words it is combined with. This will blur several different meanings of dark together (*dark mood, dark comedy*) and describe it non-substantively. In fact—and it was not seen then—it is not significantly different from Wittgenstein's defeatist statement that language is use ([14]—see also Section V below). Interestingly, within several years of word embedding promising results, papers staring to appear showing that word embeddings do not correspond to human knowledge and reasoning (see papers in Cognitive Science conferences starting with 2016). Ideally, we wonder if phenomena discovered and defined substantively ontologically can then be identified on large data with the best of automatic methods.

IV. Extension I: From Applied to Theoretical Semantics

Let us forget about vectors substituting for meaning and return to representing what sentences in natural language mean for the users.

The TMR on Figure 3 represents, like any one TMR, a number of sentences that are paraphrases (shown below), and those are numeral in any natural language (in the 1960s, Mel'cuk calculated that a regular Russian sentence stating that it was hard for Smith to translate the text because there were many technical terms in it could be paraphrased in over a million ways). In this case, the paraphrases include sentences like (i-iii) and many more.

(i) John is driving to the grocery store
(ii) John is driving to a store to buy groceries
(iii) John is driving for groceries

There are many other things that are closely related and are assumed by the speakers: that groceries are in a store, that the store must be open in order for John to achieve the goal, that the store is reasonably close, that John will have to park the car before going to the store, etc. These are often referred to as inferences, and they are all part of what humans understand when they process the largely compositional meaning of a sentence consisting of certain words. The same idea can and often is expressed differently, while keeping or perhaps slightly modifying the inferences.

What is clear is that explicit semantics assigning a TMR to a sentence fails to express clearly and accurately what a sentence actually means because meaning is largely implicit. The recall experiments of the 1970s [15] demonstrate that, a week after being exposed to a verbal event, the subjects remembered the exact wording differently while all reproducing the gist of the event accurately without differentiating much among the inferences.

This is primarily how and why it dawned on us, in the late 2000s, that Ontological Semantics is not limited to computer applications and to computational semantics in them: it is, in fact, the theoretical basis of semantics in general—it is the only reliable way to handle meaning. We call the new applied approach Ontological Semantic Technology (OST: [16]-[18]), developed and extended for a while to a couple of high-tech start-ups. We were still developing semantic applications and resources for them but, theoretically, we were enlarging the scope to scripts and other complex semantic phenomena, often deliberately limiting the scope of the approach to specific applications, past and current. In both theoretical and applied undertakings, we are often extending the scope to verbal humor, a structured form of discourse, leading to promising scalable applications in computational humor [19].

V. Meaning Substance

One persistent problem with semantics, both as a linguistic subdiscipline and a branch of philosophy and mathematics but especially the first one, is the elusive nature of its substance. Meaning is real but what is it? It is something humans know, share, and convey but the messy and informal mechanism of paraphrase is the only manifestation of that understanding.

Bloomfield [20] is often referred to as having excluded semantics from linguistics even though his monograph has a chapter entitled "Meaning." He was the one who claimed counterintuitively that in order to understand the meaning of the English word *pie*, not only to we have to know all of its ingredients and how they were baked together but also the state of each of its molecules at all times. He saw the meaning of Jill's request to Jack to get her an apple from a tree as a replacement for the extralinguistic substance of stimulus and response: Jill sees an apple, she is hungry but instead of responding to that directly by picking it she replaces that with a linguistic stimulus.

Yngve [21] reiterated his similar desire to replace semantic substance with that of scientific observation and, capitalizing on a good friendship over decades, invited Raskin to join him there. Raskin had to decline because it was clear to him that no matter how well his behavior is observed and recorded, there is no way to know what is being said or written: the substance of observation is much too coarse.

In semiotics [22], semantics was introduced as a component where the items were interpreted. The examples included interpreting some variables were interpreted as named contacts. This is how semantics is used formally in logic except that it is not used there much. The substance of the interpretations never needed elucidation, so there was none.

At the very late beginning of linguistic semantics in the 1860s, the discipline happily and innocently substituted purview for substance. It included multiple facts, from an assortment of languages, about words changing their meanings historically. Those meanings, both past and present, were outlined very approximately, usually with one reference to a class term, such as clothes for Latin *vestis*, later English *vest*, a garment.

When, next, semantics started studying the nature of meaning, the purview got limited to Frege's distinction between, roughly, meaning and reference, neither of which were well-defined. The most significant effort toward discovering the substance of semantics had to do with the field's 20-30-year romance with semantic features within the componential analysis approach of the 1930-1950s. The exciting mathematical idea that 21 binary features can describe over a million items has rather quickly lost its attraction when it turned out that, in semantic reality, many features have a very limited scope, such as 'never-married' describes the meaning of *bachelor* and its awkward female counterparts *spinster* and *old maid*. Also confusing to critics was the labeling issue: because they were named with English words, Kats and Fodor's [23] semantic markers were dismissed by Lewis [24] as Markerese for no apparent reason.

Within sentential semantics, formalism, rules replaced any serious concern with substance, and foundational considerations have been abandoned or relayed to mathematical logic, which is where the formalism originated from. Somewhat in that tradition, Barwise and Perry [25] attempted to replace the two truth values only as the range of extension of a proposition with facts, that is what the proposition was about. This would have revived perhaps the intension/extension debate, with benefits to various semantics, but the authors could not withstand the ferocious attacks from philosophers about how fact was defined.

Yet meaning is definitely about something other than the words used to express it. Sentences state something about items mentioned in them. Marked in a natural language, this content is independent from it. Living in bilingual environments, we are both perfectly aware of that, and the fact that everything is double-coded barely interferes with our non-linguistic perception of reality. When interpreting between languages, we do not replace words with their translation but rather reconstruct the reality from the sentence in the source language and then express it in the target language (in the process, incidentally, some words are replaced by their translations).

When one learns about a new piece, area, or domain of reality one needs to identify the major agents and events they participate in. We have gone over that ontologically whenever our ontology needed an extension. A major text in the field provided an index where we started. We extended the then current ontology into banking and into information security, and it took under 6 person/months of doctoral labor at the cost of under $20K. The users were implementing a very specific well-defined job, and the domain reality was definitely not a linguistic object (incidentally, both acquirers were, of course, English speakers but with different native tongues; one of them later singlehandedly extended the single ontological node, FEELING, into all other feelings from psychology, and in much more detail, into the field of humor research—see [26]. Similarly, an ontology was expanded to a domain of phishing detection, with a similar effort, producing successful results in phishing detection [27].

VI. Extension 2: Ontology as Human Reality

The disparate considerations in the previous section seem to indicate that people can think of various pieces of reality as separate from the languages in which they describe them. We propose then to see the ontology as the extralinguistic structure of reality and the medium of semantic substance. This is already how we have used it prior to this claim. What is different now is that we present our ontology as the description and representation of human reality in the computer. Quite simply, what the computer knows about the world depends on its ontology, both explicit and implicit, and we are interested in doing that explicitly. The concept and role of ontology is thus extended from an application-focused tool that works well within it to the theoretical basis of all meaning studies and, finally, to the structure of the world in the computer.

This is not very easy to understand because people easily confuse the accumulation of large data in the computer storage with what the computer knows. IBM Watson is a good example. The promotion materials and journalists easily describe it as knowing an awful lot but the serious founders carefully explained in the NPR Nova program before the introduction of the system on "Jeopardy" back in 2011 that it was devoid of any intelligence. What Watson could do in 2011, with amazing technical speed and dexterity, was accessing everything from its enormous storage which has the same words as the query and manufacturing a response on this basis. It had no idea what the question was about nor what its memorized quotes say.

A more recent example is Amazon's Alexa. As of March 2019, Alexa is perfectly capable of telling a user about the weather (in whatever scale the user specified in the setting), it can also convert from one temperature scale to another. What it cannot do, however, is tell the weather in the scale that a user asked in his/her question. In other words, information retrieval works very well, but any additional manipulation of the retrieved information presents a challenge.

Ontological competence underlies inferences. The more intelligent the person is the more inferences are available to it. Unlike the computational inference engines of yore (read: 1980s), people do not generate inferences combinatorially: besides being guided by ontological links, they have an ability to cut through to the relevant ones only, and we need to understand this capacity better and to emulate it in the computer, and statistics will not help us here.

Alexa, Siri, and other personal assistant software are usually listed in the media as successes in artificial intelligence. It can control many smart home devices, including a smart thermostat when explicitly asked to do so. However, it cannot answer the question, *Why am I cold*?—with something like, *Do you want me to raise the setting inside*? At the same time, Alexa constantly evolves: new pieces of knowledge are added, some of them bizarre. It can translate some days of the week into Russian, but not all. It knows who Anna Akhmatova is, likely surprising its customers including most in post-Soviet Russia, who are much better familiar with Beyoncé. The question is, how are these disparate pieces are selected to be added? Is there a selection process? How does one determine what is useful and what is not?

With ontology, the process of extension and filling the gaps is guided, and the ontology is improved and corrected with every new text that is processed and new TMRs generated. We achieve here a new theoretical level of completeness: a theory is complete if it has handled everything well so far, and it is indefinitely extendable. Much of human knowledge is infinite, and its adequacy is temporary.

The improvement record in Ontological Semantic Technology is constant, systematic, and reducing in volume. A small group of experts has to be maintained to take care of it, though it will be increasingly automated. One may try and argue that trying to fill the gaps ontologically is as haphazard as what is being done with Alexa. The difference is the links in the ontology, which lead to all possible inferences directly or transitively.

The most important difference between the ontology as we do it and any other formalism is isomorphism between every single TMR and a reality fact (pace Barwise and Perry) that takes place or may take place or not take place in the world, including the extensions to myths, fantasies, and counterfactuals. The ontological items, when done right, relate to each other exactly as in real life: whatever happens (or does not) in the world is reflected ontologically. And the ontology as the computer knowledge of the world is constantly checked, corrected, and upgraded in computational linguistic applications on demand.

VII. Conclusion

We have guided the reader briefly through a different and difficult terrain. Contrary to the dominant view that semantics is unknowable and the knowledge of meaning should be replaced by machine learning methods and their extensions, we propose a view that it is accessible. This view provides explanation for every decision it makes, and produces reasoning scenarios that are needed for the "third wave" of AI. Then, we take you to a *terra incognita* of the semantic substance: what it is that the meaning is interpreted and presented as. The answer is, of course, the conceptual hierarchy with many properties, the comprehensive ontology. After that, it is almost easy to claim that this ontology represents our knowledge of the world. And because it is a formal object it can be introduced into the computer so that it also knows the world.

REFERENCES

[1] F. C. Bartlett, Remembering. Cambridge: Cambridge University Press, 1932. Reprinted by Cambridge University Press, 1977.

[2] M. Minsky, A framework for representing knowledge, in The Psychology of Computer Vision, P. H. Winston, Ed. New York: McGraw Hill, pp. 211-277, 1975.

[3] R. C. Schank and R. Abelson, Scripts, Plans, Goals, and Understanding. New York: Wiley, 1977.

[4] V. Raskin. Semantic Mechanisms of Humor. Dotdrecht-Boston-Lancaster: D. Reidel.

[5] L. Carlson and S. Nirenburg, World Modeling for NLP. Technical Report CMU-CMT-90-121, Center for Machine Translation, Carnegie Mellon University, Pittsburgh, PA, 1988. A short version appeared in Proceedings of the Third Conference on Applied Natural Language Processing, Trento, Italy. April.

[6] S. Nirenburg and V. Raskin, Ontological Semantics. Cambridge, MA: MIT Press, 2004.

[7] A. Prabhakar, Powerful but Limited: A DARPA Perspective on AI, https://sites.nationalacademies.org/cs/groups/pgasite/documents/webpage/pga_177035.pdf.

[8] J. Launchbury, A DARPA Perspective on Artificial Intelligence, Machine Learning, 2017.

[9] V. Raskin, A Concise History of Linguistic Semantics. Tel Aviv: Tel Aviv University, mimeographed, 1973. Reprinted at Purdue University, 3rd ed., 1983.

[10] A. Ya. Shaykevich, Vydelenie klassov slov i paradigm posredstvom distributivno-statisticheskogo metoda (na materale komediy Shekspira) /Identification of classes of words and of paradigms with the distributive-statistical method (on the material of Shakespeare's comedies), Prikladnaya Lingvistika, Vol. 18, pp. 96-134, Moscow, 1976.

[11] T. Mikolov, K. Chen, G. Corrado, and J. Dean, Efficient Estimation of Word Represenetation in Vector Space, ICLR Workshop, 2013.

[12] T. Mikolov, I. Sutskever, K. Chen, G. Carrado and J. Dean, Distributed Representations of Words and Phrases and their Compositionality, NIPS 2013.

[13] J. R. Firth, Modes of meaning, in his Papers in Linguistics, London: Oxford University Press, 1964.

[14] L. Wittgenstein, Philosophical Investigations, Oxford: Blackwell, 1953.

[15] W. Chafe, Language and memory, Language 49:2, pp. 261-281, 1973.

[16] J. M. Taylor, C. F. Hempelmann, and V. Raskin. On an automatic acquisition toolbox for ontologies and lexicons in ontological semantics, Proceedings of the International Conference on Artificial Intelligences, Las Vegas, NE, pp. 863-869, 2010.

[17] J. M. Taylor, V. Raskin, and C. F. Hempelmann, From disambiguation failures to common-sense knowledge acquistion: A day in the life of an ontological semantic system, Proceedings of Web Intelligence Conference, Lyon, France, 2011.

[18] J. M. Taylor, V. Raskin, and C. F. Hempelmann, Towards computational guessing of unknown word meanings: The ontological semantic approach, Proceedings of the Cognitive Science Conference, Boston, MS, 2011.

[19] V. Raskin, C. F. Hempelmann, and J. M. Taylor, How to understand and assess a theory: The evolution of the SSTH into the GTVH and now into the OSTH, Journal of Literary theory, 2009 (as marked but came out in 2010).

[20] L. Bloomfield, Language. New York: Holt, 1933.

[21] V. Yngve and Z. Wasik, Hard-Science Linguistics, New York: Continuum, 2006.

[22] Ch. Morris, Signs, Language, and Behavior. Chicago: University of Chicago Press, 1946.

[23] J. J. Katz and J. A. Fodor, The structure of a semantic theory, Language, 39: 1, pp. 170-210, 1963. Reprinted in The Structure of Language: Readings in the Philosophy of Language, J. A. Fodor and J. J. Katz, Eds. Englrwood Cliffs, NJ: Prentice-Hall, pp. 479-518, 1964.

[24] D. Lewis, General semantics, in Semantics of Natural Language, D. Davidson and G. Harman, Eds. Dordrecht-Boston, D. Reidel, pp. 169-218, 1973.

[25] J. Barwise and J. Perry, Situations and Attitudes. Cambridge, MA: MIT Press, 1983.

[26] K. E. Triezenberg, The Ontology of Humor, Unpublished Ph.D. Dissertation, Program in Linguistics, Purdue University, West Lafayette, IN, 2006.

[27] G. Park and J. Rayz, Ontological Detection of Phishign Emails, IEEE-SMC 2018.

Cognitive Products: System Architecture and Operational Principles

Dari Trendafilov*‡, Kashif Zia†*, Alois Ferscha*‡, Ali Abbas*‡,
Behrooz Azadi‡, Johannes Selymes‡, Michael Haslgrübler*‡
*Institute of Pervasive Computing
Johannes Kepler University
Linz, Austria
†Faculty of Computing and Information Technology
Sohar University
Sohar, Oman
‡Pro²Future GmBH
Linz, Austria

***Abstract*—Future commercial products and product assemblies could greatly benefit from recent developments in machine learning, providing the foundation of cognitive products equipped with sensors and actuators and embedded into tangible objects operating in the real world. This paper identifies key challenges in the related fields and provides motivation for further advancements particularly in the domain of resource-constrained distributed and embedded Artificial Intelligence. Enabling cognitive capabilities, such as perception, reasoning, learning and planning, could result in higher reliability, adaptivity and improved performance, however it would require an increased involvement of non-technical disciplines like cognitive neuroscience. We propose a generic top-level cognitive architecture providing a reference to various research areas involved in this multifaceted field. Conceptual prototypes of two cognitive products, targeting real-world industrial environments, are presented and discussed.**

Keywords–cognitive systems; ambient intelligence; embedded systems; distributed intelligence; cognitive components.

I. INTRODUCTION

Humans have developed skills to survive in a complex world by evolving adequate information processing mechanisms well suited to deal with ill-structured problems involving a high degree of uncertainty. The human brain, however, cannot compete with machines on tasks requiring massive computational resources. Machines are faster, more accurate and stronger than humans. However, humans outperform machines in many tasks, which require flexible, reliable and adaptive control. Since these abilities are currently beyond the reach of state-of-the-art Artificial Intelligence (AI), much of the inspiration for implementing future intelligent machines needs to be taken from cognitive sciences that study computational models of human perception, attention and motor control. The ultimate goal is to turn machines into ones that can reason using substantial amount of appropriately represented knowledge, learn from its past experiences in order to continuously improve performance, be aware of its own capabilities, reflect on its own behavior and respond robustly to surprise [1]. Such a high level intelligence should be complemented by low level cognitive abilities provided by reactive models. This would enable a major leap in the quality of interaction and cooperation with humans.

Therefore, the aim of ongoing research in this field is to develop efficient computational mechanisms for artificial cognitive systems, which consolidate and benefit from findings about the structure and functional organization of natural cognitive systems, while taking into consideration the differences in their characteristics. For example, sensorimotor loops of humans and machines differ significantly in sensing accuracy, actuation precision and internal processing latency, implying different cognitive abilities. Therefore, while following the basic principles of human cognition, certain deviations in the realization of Artificial Intelligence systems can be expected.

Cognitive products are created from a combination of mechatronic systems equipped with artificial sensors and actuators and advanced software algorithms. They integrate cognitive functionality, such as perceiving the environment, learning and reasoning from knowledge models. This field is still in its infancy, however the time is ripe for laying down the foundations of basic system architecture and operational principles, which are key challenges for the research community towards developing future cognitive products.

The main contribution of this paper is the introduction of a generic system architecture and the description of the key operational principles of future products with cognitive capabilities. For illustrative purposes, we provide two conceptual examples of tools incorporating generic cognitive components and building on the notion of embedded AI. Furthermore, we raise key open research questions, which need to be addressed in order to enable the integration of advanced AI into a broad range of future commercial products.

Integrating cognitive capabilities such as perception, learning, reasoning, planning and action into future robots, manufacturing systems, autonomous vehicles, etc. requires the orchestrated effort of various scientific fields, i.e., Cognitive and Neuroscience, Control and Information Theory, Artificial Intelligence and Engineering. In recent years, disciplines concerned with cognitive systems have cross-pollinated each other in various ways. The interdisciplinary research in this area includes two major subfields, Cognitive Science, which develops 'human-like' computational models of cognition, perception and action, inspired by recent advances in neuroscience and sensorimotor control, and AI, which explores algorithms realizing cognitive capabilities building on advanced methods of machine learning and Bayesian reasoning.

In Section 2, we briefly review the related scientific fields. Section 3 introduces the concept of cognitive products and identifies the key challenges to be addressed by the AI community in order to enable human-like cognitive functions in machines. Section 4 presents a top-level generic architecture for cognitive products and describes its key elements. In Section 5, we introduce two concept devices, building on a set of generic cognitive features. Section 6 sums up key aspects of cognitive products and production systems of the future.

II. Background

Cognitive neuroscience and Artificial Intelligence have a long relationship, dating back to McCulloch's, Turing's, Neumann's and Hebbian era [2][3], when the theoretical foundations of computing and AI were laid by defining basic principles interwoven with neuroscience and psychology. Since then both fields grew tremendously and evolved into full-fledged disciplines, having some collaboration at the periphery, but not mainstream. However, it is a prime time to intensify the interaction within this relationship again [4][5]. Furthermore, the growing empirical evidence of Bayesian decision processes in human sensorimotor control, reasoning and learning mechanisms [6] has triggered an enormous research effort in cognitive psychology. Neuroscientists investigate cognitive control of multi-sensory perception-action couplings in dynamic and rapidly changing environments, which provide important insights for neurocognitive models used in technical system implementations [7]. Research on perception provides mechanisms allowing to capture information, which is relevant, by attention focus and context understanding.

Better understanding biological brains could play a vital role in building intelligent machines. Recent advances in AI have been inspired by studies of neural computation in humans and other animals. Neuroscience could provide a rich source of inspiration for new types of algorithms and architectures, independent of and complementary to the mathematical and logic-based methods and ideas that have largely dominated traditional approaches to AI [4]. Recent studies attempt to discover mechanisms by which the brain implements algorithms with the functionality of backpropagation. Such developments illustrate the potential for synergistic interactions between AI and neuroscience. Leveraging insights gained in neuroscience research could expedite progress in the field of AI. Earlier research in cognitive science followed the approach to reasoning, which uses behavioral rules based on rewards and punishments and is inspired by Behaviorism [8], and have recently refocused onto the Connectionist approach [9][10].

Data science continually makes rapid advances particularly on the frontiers of deep learning, which provide opportunities for a variety of applications [11–13] stretching deep into sectors of economy that have stayed on the sidelines thus far. The volume of available data is growing exponentially, more sophisticated algorithms are being developed and computational power and storage are steadily increasing. The convergence of these trends is fueling rapid technology advances and business disruptions. However, modern AI generally provides solutions fine-tuned to crunch large complex data sets enabling only rudimentary context awareness.

Artificial Neural Networks (ANN) [14] have become very popular recently due to advancements in computing power, availability of big data and developments in deep learning techniques. The great success of Deep Neural Networks (DNN) built largely on the power of GPUs for massive parallel computing. Deep learning derives its power from computational models composed of multiple processing layers able to learn representations of data with multiple levels of abstraction [15][16]. This makes it naturally fit for pattern recognition problems where learning is about discovering features that have high value states in common [10]. More recent advances in deep learning are moving beyond object recognition and towards scene understanding [17][18]. Yet, current deep learning methods excel in recognition [19] rather than understanding tasks, and furthermore are not able to draw causal relationships between objects. Complex scene understanding requires core knowledge about physics [20], compositions and relationships of objects and causality between them [10]. To understand causal relationships between interacting agents in a scene, their intentions and goals, we need core knowledge from social psychology. The mechanism of learning and thinking needs to be local and incremental, based on a generic approach, which starts from a clean slate and evolves over time. A more principled approach to cognition builds models to understand the world [10], as the key to human intelligence is its capability to explain nature, rather than classify or recognize phenomena.

Several concepts for cognitive architectures have been proposed in the past, namely ACT-R [21], Soar [22], ADAPT [23], PSI [24], however the common shortcoming of all is the lack of general design methodology. These approaches lack modeling of cognitive information processing from the ground up. Examples of basic information processing functions are acquisition, processing and transferring, while more abstract and complex ones are analyzing and classification [25]. Other cognitive functions, such as observe, recognize, encode, store, remember, think, problem solving, motor control and language show that beyond formalizing they also combine new information with existing internalized knowledge representation [26].

III. Cognitive products

Cognition implies the ability to understand the underlying nature of things, not only at present but also in the past and in the foreseeable future, and to take this into consideration in decision-making. For this purpose, humans require sufficient, usually not too extensive information, experience, and profound knowledge on the matter as well as an estimation of the consequences of alternative actions. Transferring these capabilities to digital systems could enable new levels of innovative functionality depending on the scale of particular applications, with systems ranging from local man-machine interaction to shop-floor or factory-wide man-to-machine (M2M) communication to management of inter-organizational production processes. This requires the creation of tangible, durable objects consisting of a physical carrier system with embodied mechanics, electronics, microprocessors and software, and equipping them with cognitive capabilities enabled by flexible control loops and cognitive algorithms [27].

In contrast to products operating with deterministic control methods, cognitive products do not only act autonomously, but they do so in an increasingly intelligent human-like manner [27]. Cognitive products could maintain multiple goals, perform context-sensitive reasoning and make appropriate decisions based on complex and uncertain information, which makes them more robust in their adaptation to dynamic environments than other products. Coping with such intelligent, flexible and robust behavior would emphasize the importance of the human factor in smart factories and at the same time could put the human operator into a better position when adapting to highly customized dynamically changing manufacturing processes as compared to fully automated mass production systems. On one hand, the increasing specialization of products and processes requires guidance in task execution, while on the other hand industry requires a continuous, detailed assessment of data in order to optimize product specifications and production processes.

A. Can a machine think?

While the notion of Artificial Intelligence has been around for decades, recent advances in algorithms and processing power combined with the exponential growth in available data are enabling the creation of machines with unprecedented capabilities. While these technologies might not redefine what it means to 'think' they are starting to perform activities long thought to be the sole purview of humans – sometimes at higher levels of performance than people can achieve. Although in some tasks AI outperforms human counterparts [28] machines are still far from general human-level intelligence, which relates to qualitative cognitive aspects of human learning and thinking, such as intuition, inference, imagination, imitation, learning to learn, prediction and planning.

As opposed to narrow (weak) AI, typically developed for a specific application such as object or speech recognition (e.g., IBM's Deep Blue and Watson, Google's AlphaGO [29]), general (strong) AI possesses an understanding of the world and has human-like cognitive abilities. When a general AI is confronted with a new problem it can find a solution based on experience with similar problems by applying, e.g., transfer learning [30][31] or abstract association or based on its understanding of the world independent of the particular task. Knowledge about the world may be simply related to objects size, location, co-occurrences, properties, but also more abstract insights like physical laws, social behavior, and causality. An 'ultimate' test for assessing general intelligent behavior of an AI based on its distinction from a human when inquired by a human observer was proposed already in [32].

Technologies like Cyber-Physical Systems (CPS), Internet of Things (IoT), Industry 4.0 and autonomous vehicles operate in self-contained, distributed and localized manner utilizing resource-constrained devices, which creates scalability issues for deep learning techniques. Therefore, besides flexibility and adaptivity, efficiency becomes a key criterion for future systems. We need a computational cognitive foundation for things that think. For a truly human-like thinking and learning the system should possess causal model of the world describing the structure and the causal relationships between the agents and their environment, rather than merely solving pattern recognition problems. Cognitive systems should be able to perform ground learning starting from a clean slate and evolving on top of born-with theories of core knowledge, e.g., intuitive physics [33] and psychology [34]. They should harness the compositionality, i.e., the construction of new knowledge based on primitive elements, and learning-to-learn in order to rapidly acquire and generalize knowledge to novel situations and processes. These features are necessary for achieving a general-purpose AI flexible enough to adapt to previously unseen scenarios and interactions.

B. Beyond state-of-the-art

We are witnessing an era in which the convergence of algorithmic advances, data proliferation, and tremendous increase in computing power and storage have propelled AI from hype to reality. However, in order to develop truly human-like learning and thinking machines there are open key challenges for AI research, i.e., (i) machine learning requires massive resources (computing power and training data), (ii) models do not generalize well, (iii) processes of training and inference most likely differ from human learning and reasoning.

Within the Smart Movement [35][36] products have been increasingly equipped with electronics, enabling the assessment of isolated environmental data and the interpretation of basic contextual information (e.g., wearable activity trackers, smartphones and watches, etc.). However, these products typically have deterministic and predefined behavior and lack the capabilities required for sustainable and autonomous human-like cognitive functions, such as perception, awareness, learning, reasoning and decision-making. Cognitive products are capable of achieving self-awareness, understand their immediate environment including human collaborators, activities and processes, and can perform goal-oriented complex tasks such as human assistance and guidance, as well as integrate higher-level work-flow information related to environmental states into object models.

Cognitive systems exhibit behavior through perception, action, individual or social interaction with the environment, and depend on standardized networks and interfaces for communication and access to information from distributed and embedded systems. The next generation of products and manufacturing machinery suited for batch and continuous process industries with embedded cognitive functions will enable the following capabilities in an autonomous self-organized fashion

- assistive man-machine collaboration enabling appropriate worker support and guidance in complex processes;
- adaptive control of dynamic M2M networks enabling self-adaptation to work situations, material, human resources and environmental conditions;
- embedded data analytics enabling autonomous sensor-based data collection, data mining and real-time predictive and pro-active planning and decision-making;

- embodiment appropriately related to workers and other cognitive systems in the immediate environment;
- synergistic machine-to-machine organization of production systems.

Further advances of cognitive products could include semantic work-flows and tool description models for (i) work-flow alignment, (ii) quality control, (iii) tolerance range assessment, and (iv) skill, task and overall evaluation. This would require the identification of a formal model for an opportunistic multimodal feedback framework based on the optimization of user, tool, material and environmental parameters. Building on a knowledge database of previously applied strategies a reasoning engine could provide guidance even in previously unseen work-flow situations using context and activity recognition.

C. Embedded AI

Rapid developments in hardware, software and communication technologies have facilitated the emergence of Internet-connected sensory devices that provide ubiquitous observations and data measurements from the physical world. The technology of Internet-connected devices, referred to as Internet of Things (IoT) [37], extends the current Internet by providing connectivity and interactions between physical and cyber worlds. IoT continuously generate data with a variety of modalities and data quality and the intelligent processing and analysis of such data is the key to developing smart applications. As the number of commercial and industrial devices proliferates, connecting them in dynamic networks comprised of intelligent individual components is a key challenge for IoT to realize its full potential [38].

An industrial facility might have thousands of sensors monitoring the status of machines and processes, which however often reside in silos that do not communicate. Some AI solutions are centralized on cloud service architectures, where sensor data needs to be collected, correlated with historical performance data and analyzed to provide actionable information for real-time decision-making. However, in many industrial locations sufficient bandwidth or connectivity cannot be relied upon. Therefore, in order to obtain reliable continuous time-critical decisions we need to embed intelligence at the source of sensing. This requires building smart devices on top of edge computing architectures and equipping them with Artificial Intelligence. To this end, some chip companies work on incorporating conventional AI software in their chips, while others are building advanced cognitive AI solutions that can be embedded in off-the-shelf inexpensive chips. Embedding cognitive capabilities such as perception, awareness, reasoning, learning and decision making into products requires addressing constraints in terms of size and weights, real-time computation, limited processing resources (memory footprint and computing power), low power consumption and low cost. Scarcity of resources hinders autonomous real-time execution of conventional deep learning algorithms on embedded devices due to massive computational requirements. We envision that deep learning will have a pivotal role in realizing a flexible and efficient learning platform for embedded AI. However, industrial design and software need to be optimized to simultaneously meet all of the above constraints, while current machine learning methods still require massive computing power, training data and memory footprint. The next generation of machine learning algorithms need to provide flexible, efficient and incremental learning techniques for resource-constrained environments in order to enable future self-organized autonomous systems. Recent advances in deep learning are already moving beyond object recognition and towards scene understanding, which requires core knowledge about physics, compositions, relationships and causality between objects [39]. If the scene includes agents and humans interacting, percepting and acting, then we also need core knowledge of social psychology for understanding their intentions and goals. For realizing a dynamically evolving low foot-print learning framework, deep learning has to respond to these challenges and answer key research questions such as:

1) Can deep neural networks fit cognitive processes of human brain?
2) How can insights in human perception be applied to AI systems?
3) Can DNN transfer knowledge learned in one task to another?

D. Ensembles of cognitive components

Modern smart factories require the integration of flexible cognitive components enabling implicit supply chain management via vertical integration and quality management via stepwise traceability. Building on the approach of opportunistic sensing cognitive components could advertise their capabilities with respect to both sensing and actuation. Upon localizing each other they could form collective ensembles in self-organized manner and exchange structured data. Furthermore, they could jointly sense their shared contextual state and adapt accordingly by preemptively suggesting usage strategies or best practices to users, or by reactively setting operation parameters to suit particular circumstances. Such ensembles could learn from use and/or misuse of individual tools and take proactive steps to avoid hazardous situations and increase their own life-span. Component and production history awareness could enable the fine-grained modeling, organization and optimization of complex production processes. The ultimate goal is to enable the creation of joint cognitive systems [40], consisting of distributed networks of intelligent devices and human operators.

E. Dependability

The accurate operation of cognitive production tools is of utmost importance even in very harsh production environments as tool downtime or malfunction may lead to reduced productivity, waste products or may harm the worker in safety-critical applications. Certain capabilities related to sensing, localization and communication are particularly vulnerable in harsh environmental conditions such as for example strong electromagnetic fields generated by arc welding. Therefore, highly dependable unified solutions need to be devised, integrated and tested in cognitive tools.

Machines equipped with cognitive abilities could provide higher degree of robustness and dependability by learning to perform complex tasks reliably and accurately in various extreme conditions. In order to achieve that they must take into consideration all available sensory channels and utilize the most appropriate ones. Embedded context and activity recognition based on multi-sensor fusion (RGBD video, motion, orientation and pressure sensors, eye-tracking, GSR, HRV, RFID, indoor localization, etc.) could enable advanced context understanding including presence, activities, needs and skills of workers, work-flows, etc. However, current industrial solutions are limited to recording basic information about specific environmental aspects (e.g., temperature, humidity sensing, etc.). True cognitive products need to advance this state-of-the-art by building on adaptive and robust multimodal sensor networks and distributed data processing algorithms.

IV. Cognitive Architecture

Enabling an advanced level of self-organization, which allows machines to accomplish complex tasks in changing and uncertain environments, maintain multiple goals simultaneously, resolve conflicts between interfering goals and act appropriately in unexpected and previously unseen situations, requires a sophisticated design methodology and appropriate cognitive architecture.

For ensuring robust and reliable behavior of cognitive products we need advanced virtual methods for engineering, tools and models providing fully functional simulation environments. Every cognitive product device generates data, which is fed back into engineering and maintenance systems for continuous product improvement and condition monitoring and therefore requires an individual virtual representation reflecting its context of use. In parallel to virtual methods, modeling and controlling single instances and ensembles of cognitive components require a user-centric product development approach, which takes into account ergonomic aspects and human factors. In order to capture the synergistic interdependence between humans and cognitive products in the context of social interaction and collaboration we need to take into account affective, cognitive and social aspects in interaction design, informed by relevant sociological, psychological, socio-cultural, ethical and legal studies.

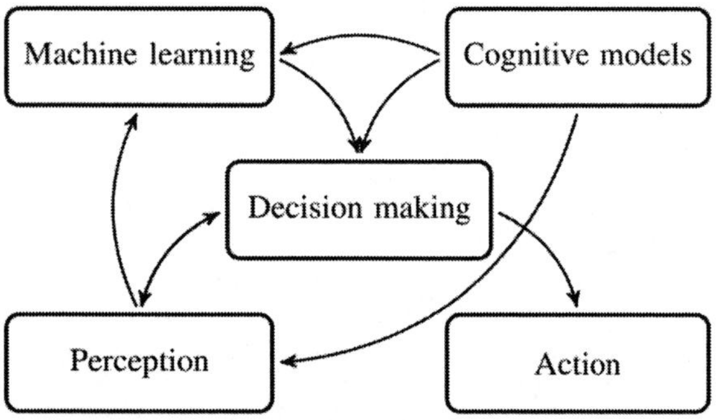

Figure 1. Diagram reflecting the relationships between elements of the Cognitive System Architecture.

A state-of-the-art cognitive system architecture requires a probabilistic approach in order to provide means for integrating perception, learning, reasoning and action in the face of uncertainty. Such an architecture would include a comprehensive repertoire of diverse learning methods capable of generalizing from a very few samples. The acquisition of new skills and activities from little prior experience and a limited number of observations would be facilitated by knowledge representation, learning infrastructure and computational models tailored particularly for low-power sensor-equipped embedded platforms operating in resource-constrained environments.

Cognitive system architectures usually decompose cognition functionally into modules operating in a tightly interconnected mode [41]. The elements describing the conceptual representation of the hierarchical 'human-like' perception–action loop required for realizing cognitive products are shown in Table I.

Creating technical devices that interact with a Human always requires the consideration of the human factor, since the interaction involves two systems that are different by nature, i.e., Biological on one side and Cyber-Physical on the other [42]. Furthermore, enabling a more natural relationship with the user necessitates the integration of sophisticated human-like cognitive functions, such as emotion and intention recognition.

Formal concepts and models of primitive cognitive rules for multi-sensor computational perception, learning and reasoning are inspired by neural processes underlying human cognition and are based on core knowledge theories of intuitive physics and psychology (see Figure 1). They provide a foundation supporting primitives of flexible and efficient learning: descriptive causal model of the world, compositionality and rapid learning-to-learn capability. The aim is to achieve compact representations and optimize inference for execution on embedded devices in real time. Another key criterion is the radical decrease in resource requirements compared to cloud-server based solutions. This requires efficient hierarchical data representations emulating human perception with digital sensors and a new generation of deep learning algorithms and artificial neural networks reflecting the hierarchies of human cognition, distributed and incrementally evolving in nature. Independent cognitive devices would form a network within which they could interact autonomously with each other, providing the basis for the emergence of an even higher intelligent entity.

TABLE I. Elements of the Cognitive System Architecture.

Element	Description
Perception	acquisition of information about the environment and the body of an actor, typically considered in AI an estimation process providing symbolic representation of the world state
Action	process of generating actual behavior in machines in the form of executable control programs derived from precise dynamical system models
Learning	process of acquiring, structuring and reorganizing information that results in new knowledge and leads to behavioral changes, which are measurable and persistent in time
Decision making	process of making inferences and generating representations of conceptual future behavior based on evidence and basic principles using various mechanisms (causal, temporal, spatial, etc.)
Cognitive models	formal models and ingredients of human intelligence reflecting aspects of core knowledge necessary for general-purpose capabilities

V. Concept Devices

In this section we describe a set of specific, yet generic, cognitive features, in the context of two conceptually different prototypes of intelligent production tools. The realisation of these prototypes is ongoing work and therefore their evaluation is not included in this paper. However, with these examples we demonstrate how knowledge transfer could be achieved across a range of cognitive products, ensuring device interoperability and minimizing development costs.

A. Power tool

Let us take the power tool (see Figure 2) as an example of a potential future product with cognitive capabilities. The cognitive power tool is a ubiquitous computing, sensing and actuation device in which sensors are connected in a network, where data analysis is performed in real-time on embedded computing device providing autonomous decision making in a distributed architecture. The cognitive capabilities of the network include state estimation from sensor data, context inference, continuous acquisition, update and use of activity models. The cognitive sensor network has to recognize and understand human actions with respect to tasks and goals, and furthermore estimate and predict user state and future behavior. Certain activities can be performed concurrently and need to be decomposed into primitive actions for classification purposes.

Recent innovations in linear motion and assembly technology enable high-precision measuring systems based on intelligent engineering solutions, opening a variety of opportunities for Industry 4.0 applications. This includes the integration of high-precision digital sensors for torque and angle of rotation acquisition, which provide excellent accuracy, repeatability, durability and process documentation. Both power and control technologies can be fully integrated into the power tool and no external sensors or controls are required during operation. The power tool combines wireless capabilities with state-of-the-art tightening technology, a combination which has the potential to improve efficiency, cycle-times and data collection during the manufacturing process. During each work step

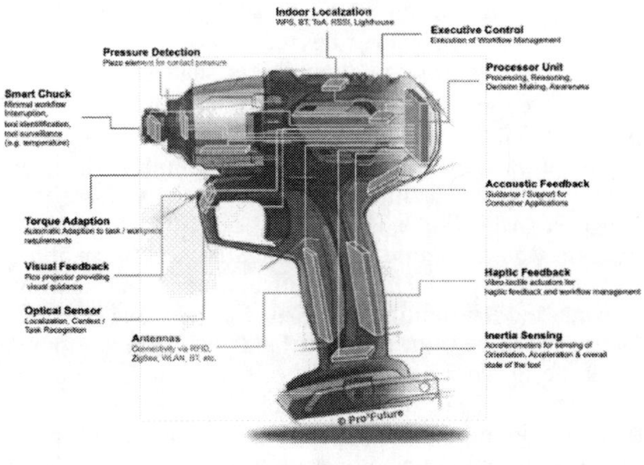

Figure 2. Cognitive components of a conceptual intelligent power tool.

the integrated controller monitors the tightening of variable-speed pump drives and transmits the results over wireless channel to a receiving station. Its decentralized intelligence is integrated in the tool and can utilize product variables such as serial numbers to determine the tightening process recipe for execution. Integrating the control of the tightening process ensures the highest level of reliability even in wireless dead zones. Power tool ensembles interconnected in networks could share tightening data and thus optimize production processes and product quality.

The capabilities of our conceptual cognitive power tool are described in Table II.

B. Head gear

Recent advances in mobile computing, Augmented Reality (AR) and wearable sensors have had a profound impact on assistive technology supporting daily routines of industrial employees. A great effort is dedicated to exploring the benefits of AR, however more advanced developments are typically restricted to the research community and are not commercially available due to various shortcomings. AR solutions have been developed predominantly on hand-held devices, which constrains user movement and ability to interact with the physical world using hands-free operation. More advanced Head-Mounted Displays (HMD) overcome these obstacles by allowing users to follow instructions in hands-free manner while performing an assembly operation.

Google Glass, arguably the most popular HMD, has been utilized in a variety of settings including agriculture, health-care, sports, information retrieval and teleconferencing, to name a few. Smart head-wear devices have also been deployed in industrial environments. However, while large scale developments are under way in this field, the potential and the benefits of the evolving HMD technology in real industrial settings are not completely clear yet.

Recent smart head-wear technologies have targeted a number of areas, including

- aviation – helmet-mounted and cockpit-projected solutions primarily used for military purposes with limited commercialization;

TABLE II. Features of a cognitive power tool.

Feature	Description
Pressure detection	piezo element for contact pressure
Smart chuck	tool surveillance (e.g., temperature) for minimal work-flow interruption
Torque adaptation	based on task and work-piece requirements
Visual feedback	visual guidance on pico projector
Optical sensor	high resolution target localization, context and task recognition
Antennas	communication infrastructure (e.g., RFID, Zigbee, WiFi, BT)
Indoor positioning	localization in industrial environmental settings (e.g., WPS, BT, ToA)
Acoustic feedback	advanced guidance in real-time operation
Haptic feedback	vibro-tactile actuators for work-flow management
Inertial sensing	orientation, position and movement tracking
Cognitive unit	context-awareness, intelligent reasoning and decision-making
Control unit	execution of work-flow management

- consumer – home entertainment and daily activity enhancement (Google, Samsung);
- manufacturing – enhancement of process engineering, logistics and field services (e.g., hands-free maintenance instructions, barcode scanning, warehouse navigation);
- medical/Healthcare – telemedicine and hands-free patient information;
- military – reconnaissance with multi-spectral cameras and thermal night vision;
- sports – display salient information such as track trajectory, temperature, altitude and speed in cycling, sailing and motor sports;
- firefighting – object recognition and flow path tracking using thermal vision and edge detection;
- publishing – instant translation.

The field of HMD is still fragmented with respect to the utilized technology. Commercial products use various connectivity methods, a range of operating systems and a number of primary and secondary input/output devices. No single standard solution exists, which could provide all essential features a factory worker might benefit from in a complex industrial environment in order to increase production efficiency. Existing HMD devices lack comprehensive solutions providing a step-by-step guide to assist workers in the completion of a complex assembly task, instead they usually support a prerecorded video playback or a video teleconference access to relevant experts. Typical features of existing industrial HMD solutions include

- presentation of work instructions related to a particular task, which are overlaid on the real-world scene with spatial and temporal relevance;
- superposition of thermal contour of real-world objects frame-overlaid onto a portable display;
- remote asset access and data visualization;
- connected expertise;
- hands-free interaction using voice control.

Reusing many of the cognitive components of the power tool (see Table II), we could imagine a head-wear device equipped with a smart-phone for localized computation and mirrored visual feedback, as shown in Figure 3. Additional components include a world-view camera for monitoring the environment and gesture control, as well as eye-tracking cameras for attention detection, and multi-directional vibro-tactile feedback.

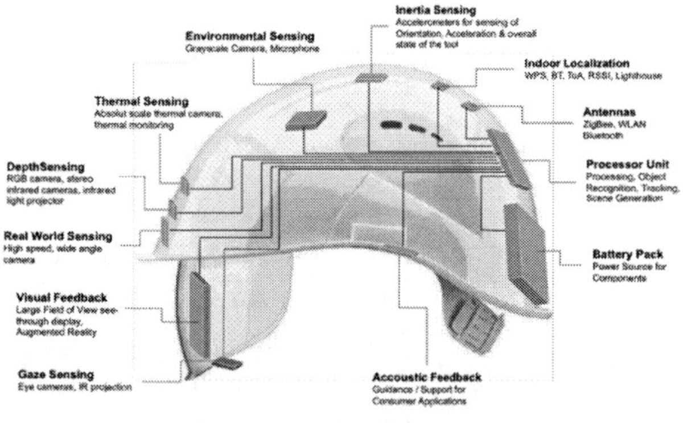

Figure 3. Cognitive components of a conceptual intelligent head gear.

Modern smart-phones are equipped with a variety of unobtrusive embedded sensors (e.g., inertial, infrared, light, proximity, fingerprint, temperature, noise, speech, GPS, etc.), which are widely used for human activity recognition purposes. Data analysis is performed either online in real-time or offline depending on the application and the context. Furthermore, the ubiquity and the significant computational power combined with large built-in memory and low manufacturing cost make smart-phones a very good potential candidate for a head-mounted mini computer, providing a convenient high resolution visual display mirrored in the helmet besides portable sensing and computing resources. Established standards, open source platforms and a variety of connectivity methods make the integration of smart-phones in industrial IT networks easy.

A head-wear with augmented cognitive capabilities could infer the skill or attention level of workers and provide the necessary assistance and appropriate guidance pro-actively. It could anticipate safety critical events and predict human behavior in unstructured and dynamically changing environments, continuously re-training itself also from partial and uncertain information. It could store relevant data locally or remotely and could recall the appropriate piece of information in a timely manner in order to support workers efficiently.

VI. Discussion

In this paper, we have described the basic operational principles of potential future cognitive products, emerging at the intersection of AI, Cognitive and Neuroscience, Control and Information theory, Engineering and Human Factors. Recent developments in AI open up the possibility to advance beyond current standards towards 'Things that think', 'Cyber-Physical Systems' and 'Industry 4.0', which have emerged as keywords for intelligent systems. In this context, we have identified various areas where AI technology could advance the state-of-the-art in cognitive systems. This requires the development of computationally efficient AI algorithms, which could perform real-time inference on resource-constrained embedded devices. We have pointed out a number of research areas, which could provide breakthroughs in this direction such as

- efficient learning from sparse data ('one-shot') [43],
- real-time embedded inference,
- advanced perception and scene understanding.

The integration of cognitive functions could enable future products to interact independently with their environment. This would allow self-organized and self-optimized behavior and would increase significantly their adaptivity and robustness. However, achieving such a high level of autonomous intelligence would require a considerable involvement of non-technical disciplines like cognitive science and neurobiology. Considering the multifaceted nature of this area it is necessary that researchers from different fields collaborate more closely in the design and development of future cognitive products.

The ultimate goal is to enable human-like cognitive capabilities in products by supporting multi-sensor perception of complex environments, storing and recalling information, transferring knowledge in the form of reasoning models to previously unseen situations, human-like decision-making and continuous learning. This would provide autonomous decision-making, flexible adaptation to new tasks in changing environments and workload capacities. Systems that think, reason, make flexible human-like decisions and sense/adapt to the environment will enable seamless interaction with humans resembling smooth and efficient human-human interaction. Empowering production systems and products to adapt, learn, develop and react human-like would enhance production processes and reduce user frustration. This would facilitate the development of human–machine joint cognitive systems in which humans could teach machines to perform specific tasks.

To support human operators in complex work-flows cognitive devices could benefit from their awareness of

- contextual information offered by other devices and via local sensing,
- state of other tools involved in the production process,
- experience and skill level and work-flow complexity,
- cognitive load and level of attention of human operators.

We envision cognitive industrial systems based on manufacturing machinery connected to world-wide online platforms where machines and tools are added and removed in real-time in plug-and-use or plug-and-produce fashion. In a decentralized system architecture systems, processes and services communicate and interact autonomously and solve problems jointly. Industrial utilization typically triggers the enhancement of production tools with cognitive capabilities driven by their application in particular production environments. However, in specific cases such concept devices can be directly transferred to commercial home appliances as well. Cognitive production tools could bring a competitive advantage for industrial players by providing key benefits such as

- learning from past experience to avoid repetition of errors and continuously improve quality and cost,
- worker guidance and support,
- automated tool configuration and adaptation to current work-flows,
- data collection for detailed modeling and documentation of production front- and back-end processes,
- production task awareness to enable flexible adaptation to variations within a single and across different tasks,
- worker skill awareness to enable compensation for lack of skill or attention,
- collaboration between cognitive tools to provide a resolution for deviations in earlier production steps.

New business models and services could make use of the continuous data streams captured in product utilization and production control, paving the way towards a fully automated product-production ecosystems.

VII. Conclusion

We have proposed a generic cognitive architecture, which could provide the foundation for creating future intelligent products and production systems realizing human-like capabilities such as appreciate, learn and plan. The paper sheds light on the important role AI could play in the design and development of cognitive products, and identifies key challenges to be addressed by the AI community in order to fulfil these high expectations. At the same time, cognitive systems could serve as a suitable environment for leveraging advances in AI research and validating their relevance. The paper presents a motivation for integrated future research, and highlights recent progress opening up the possibility for building the cognitive products of tomorrow. In this context, we have identified a number of research areas where major breakthroughs could advance significantly this field. The aim of this paper is to raise the awareness of relevant scientific fields of such joint opportunities in order to foster a highly interactive broader research community.

Acknowledgment

The authors would like to acknowledge support by FFG funded Pro^{2}Future under contract No. 6112792.

References

[1] R. J. Brachman, "Systems that know what they're doing," Intelligent Systems, vol. 17, no. 6, 2002, pp. 67–71.

[2] W. S. McCulloch and W. Pitts, "A logical calculus of the ideas immanent in nervous activity," The bulletin of mathematical biophysics, vol. 5, no. 4, 1943, pp. 115–133.

[3] J. J. Hopfield, "Neural networks and physical systems with emergent collective computational abilities," Proceedings of the national academy of sciences, vol. 79, no. 8, 1982, pp. 2554–2558.

[4] D. Hassabis, D. Kumaran, C. Summerfield, and M. Botvinick, "Neuroscience-inspired artificial intelligence," Neuron, vol. 95, no. 2, 2017, pp. 245–258.

[5] D. L. Yamins and J. J. DiCarlo, "Using goal-driven deep learning models to understand sensory cortex," Nature neuroscience, vol. 19, no. 3, 2016, p. 356.

[6] K. P. Körding and D. Wolpert, "Bayesian decision theory in sensorimotor control," Trends in Cognitive Sciences, vol. 10, 2006, pp. 319–326.

[7] V. Mnih et al., "Human-level control through deep reinforcement learning," Nature, vol. 518, no. 7540, 2015, p. 529.

[8] B. F. Skinner, Science and human behavior. Simon and Schuster, 1953, no. 92904.

[9] J. A. Fodor and Z. W. Pylyshyn, "Connectionism and cognitive architecture: A critical analysis," Cognition, vol. 28, no. 1-2, 1988, pp. 3–71.

[10] B. M. Lake, T. D. Ullman, J. B. Tenenbaum, and S. J. Gershman, "Building machines that learn and think like people," Behavioral and Brain Sciences, vol. 40, 2017, p. e253.

[11] B. M. Lake, R. Salakhutdinov, and J. B. Tenenbaum, "Human-level concept learning through probabilistic program induction," Science, vol. 350, no. 6266, 2015, pp. 1332–1338.

[12] A. Van Den Oord et al., "Wavenet: A generative model for raw audio." in SSW, 2016, p. 125.

[13] L. A. Gatys, A. S. Ecker, and M. Bethge, "A neural algorithm of artistic style," arXiv preprint arXiv:1508.06576, 2015.

[14] F. Rosenblatt, "The perceptron: a probabilistic model for information storage and organization in the brain." Psychological review, vol. 65, no. 6, 1958, p. 386.

[15] Y. LeCun, Y. Bengio, and G. Hinton, "Deep learning," nature, vol. 521, no. 7553, 2015, p. 436.

[16] J. Schmidhuber, "Deep learning in neural networks: An overview," Neural networks, vol. 61, 2015, pp. 85–117.

[17] A. Karpathy and L. Fei-Fei, "Deep visual-semantic alignments for generating image descriptions," in Proceedings of the IEEE conference on computer vision and pattern recognition, 2015, pp. 3128–3137.

[18] S. A. Eslami et al., "Attend, infer, repeat: Fast scene understanding with generative models," in Advances in Neural Information Processing Systems, 2016, pp. 3225–3233.

[19] A. Krizhevsky, I. Sutskever, and G. E. Hinton, "Imagenet classification with deep convolutional neural networks," in Advances in neural information processing systems, 2012, pp. 1097–1105.

[20] P. Battaglia, R. Pascanu, M. Lai, D. J. Rezende et al., "Interaction networks for learning about objects, relations and physics," in Advances in neural information processing systems, 2016, pp. 4502–4510.

[21] J. Anderson et al., "An integrated theory of the mind," Psychol. Rev., vol. 111, no. 4, 2004, pp. 1036–1060.

[22] A. Newell, Unified theories of cognition. Harvard University Press, Cambridge, 1990.

[23] C. Burghart et al., "A cognitive architecture for a humanoid robot – a first approach," in In: Proceedings of IEEE-RAS international conference on humanoid robots (Humanoids2005), 2005, pp. 357–362.

[24] D. Dörner, H. Schaub, and F. Detje, "About the interplay of cognition, emotion and motivation - or: A simple theory for complicated behaviors," In: Sozionikaktuell, no. 2, 2001.

[25] T. Metzler and K. Shea, "Taxonomy of cognitive functions," in In: Proceedings of 18th International Conference on Engineering Design (ICED11), 2011.

[26] G. Strube, Dictionary of cognitive science. Klett-Cotta, Stuttgart, 1996.

[27] T. Metzler and K. Shea, "Cognitive products: Definition and framework," in In: Proceedings of International Design Conference (DESIGN2010). Berlin, Springer, 2010, pp. 865–874.

[28] K. He, X. Zhang, S. Ren, and J. Sun, "Delving deep into rectifiers: Surpassing human-level performance on imagenet classification," in Proceedings of the IEEE international conference on computer vision, 2015, pp. 1026–1034.

[29] D. Silver et al., "Mastering the game of go with deep neural networks and tree search," nature, vol. 529, no. 7587, 2016, p. 484.

[30] A. A. Rusu et al., "Progressive neural networks," arXiv preprint arXiv:1606.04671, 2016.

[31] A. Rusu et al., "Sim-to-real robot learning from pixels with progressive nets," arXiv preprint arXiv:1610.04286, 2016.

[32] A. Turing, "Mind," Mind, vol. 59, no. 236, 1950, pp. 433–460.

[33] D. Buckingham and T. R. Shultz, "The developmental course of distance, time, and velocity concepts: A generative connectionist model," Journal of Cognition and Development, vol. 1, no. 3, 2000, pp. 305–345.

[34] E. S. Spelke, "What makes us smart? core knowledge and natural language," Language in mind: Advances in the study of language and thought, 2003, pp. 277–311.

[35] S. Das., I. R. S. Cook, D., A. Ananda, M. C. Chan, and W. Ooi, "Designing smart environments: A paradigm based on learning and prediction," in Mobile, Wireless, and Sensor Networks, Technology, Applications, and Future Directions. Wiley, 2006, pp. 337–358.

[36] E. Aitenbichler, F. Lyardet, G. Austaller, J. Kangasharju, and M. Mühlhäuser, "Engineering intuitive and self-explanatory smart products," in Proc. 22nd Annual ACM Symp. Applied Computing. ACM Press, New York, NY, 2007, pp. 1632–1637.

[37] J. Gubbi, R. Buyya, S. Marusic, and M. Palaniswami, "Internet of things (iot): A vision, architectural elements, and future directions," Future generation computer systems, vol. 29, no. 7, 2013, pp. 1645–1660.

[38] J. Dean et al., "Large scale distributed deep networks," in Advances in neural information processing systems, 2012, pp. 1223–1231.

[39] E. S. Spelke and K. D. Kinzler, "Core knowledge," Developmental science, vol. 10, no. 1, 2007, pp. 89–96.

[40] E. Hollnagel and D. Woods, Joint Cognitive Systems: Foundations of Cognitive Systems Engineering. Taylor & Francis, 2005.

[41] M. Beetz, M. Buss, and D. Wollherr, "Cognitive technical systems – what is the role of artificial inteligence?" in Advances in Artificial Intelligence, vol. 4667. Berlin, Springer, 2007, pp. 19–42.

[42] D. Fass and F. Gechter, "Virtual environments integrative design – from human-in-the-loop to bio-cyber-physical systems," in 8th International Conference on Applied Human Factors and Ergonomics, Advances in Intelligent Systems and Computing, 7 2018, pp. 168–176.

[43] A. Santoro, S. Bartunov, M. Botvinick, D. Wierstra, and T. Lillicrap, "One-shot learning with memory-augmented neural networks," arXiv preprint arXiv:1605.06065, 2016.

Wearable Augmented Cognition for Improving Medic Performance

An Adaptive Transcranial Cognitive Augmentation Device with Wearable Augmented Reality

Jayfus Tucker Doswell
Juxtopia® Advanced Mixed Reality (JAMR) Lab
The Juxtopia Group, Inc.
Baltimore, USA
e-mail: jayfus@juxtopia.com

Ken Wilson
Trauma and Acute Care Surgery
University of Chicago Medicine
Chicago, USA
e-mail: kwilson9@surgery.bsd.uchicago.edu

Abstract—**Wearable Augmented Reality (AR) combines research in AR, mobile/ubiquitous computing, and artificial intelligence in which an optical see-through Head Mounted Display (HMD) facilitates multi-modal projection of, contextually relevant and computer generated visual and auditory data over physical real-world environments. Through advancements in Brain Computer Interfaces (BCI), wearable AR has capabilities to amplify human cognition by delivering on-demand assistance/training, especially in austere and extreme situations ranging from emergency medical first response and Tactical Combat Casualty Care (TCCC) to public health relief efforts in response to mass casualty events. This Intelligence Amplification (IA) intervention has potential to augment human cognition while wearers naturally interact with their environment. However, research gaps must be addressed to achieve an adaptive and wearable AR BCI that augments human cognition and consequently, improves human performance. This paper presents an innovative wearable AR HMD with an objective for improving human working/long term memory, reduce cognitive load; and contextually adapt to an individual's environment/cognitive/physiological state.**

Keywords-augmented cognition, augmented reality, BCI, context-awareness, cognitive display, intelligence amplification, wearable.

I. Introduction

A. BCI Enabled Wearable Augmented Reality

Wearable Augmented Reality (AR) combines research in AR technologies, mobile/ubiquitous computing, Artificial Intelligence (AI), and human ergonomics in which an optical see-through Head Mounted Display (HMD) facilitates multi-modal delivery of contextually relevant and computer generated visual, auditory, and transcranial data over a physical, real-world environment. Through decades of empirical research, wearable AR has demonstrated capabilities and promise of delivering on-demand assistance and training to humans who operate in austere and extreme environments ranging from emergency medical first response and surgery to Tactical Combat Casualty Care (TCCC) and public health relief efforts. This head worn Brain Computer Interface (BCI) has potential of providing a non-invasive method to augment human cognition and intellectual capabilities while wearers complete complex tasks. More specifically, wearable AR has capabilities to deliver, to humans, contextually aware assistance as multi-modal perceptual cues combining animation, graphics, text, video, and voice, as well as transcranial stimulation and tactile feedback. However, despite many advancements recently demonstrated by wearable AR systems, there are several research gaps that must be addressed in order for wearable AR to achieve an adaptive and wearable BCI that augments human cognition and consequently, improves human performance.

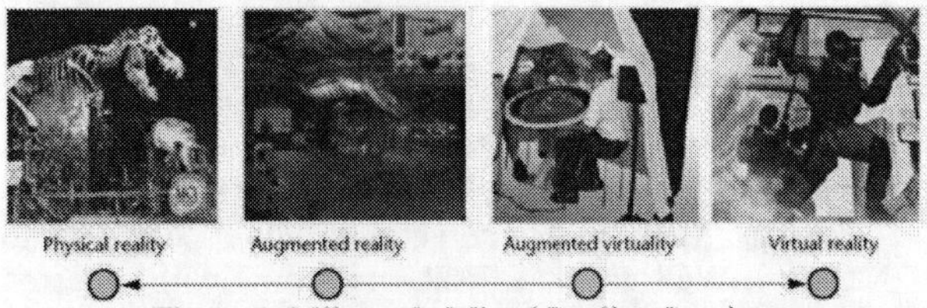

Figure 1. Milgram's Mixed Reality Continuum.

AR falls within Milgram's mixed reality continuum as illustrated in *Figure 1*. In AR, digital objects are added to the real environment. In augmented virtuality, real objects are added to virtual ones. In virtual environments (or virtual reality), the surrounding environment is completely digital [25]. Wearable AR combines research in AR and mobile computing in which a wearable see-through head mounted display (HMD) and increasingly smaller computer subsystem facilitate wireless communications and context-aware digital display [1][10][11]. A Wearable AR-BCI comprises non-invasive sensors with capabilities to digitally collect and interpret neuronal activity to facilitate activities ranging from non-verbal AR interface navigation to brain region assessment of human attention and learning.

B. Cognitive Overload

A primary challenge presented by such advanced BCI-HCI technologies is the development of scientifically-grounded methods for identifying appropriate BCI-HCI presentation, brain input, and multi-modal feedback in order to optimize performance and mitigate cognitive overload. Such multi-modalities must be dynamic, providing the human capabilities to adapt interaction configurations to accommodate various operational and environmental conditions, as well as user cognitive states, which change over time in response to task demands and factors, such as sleep, nutrition, stress, and even time of day. Ideally, interactive technologies should be capable of adapting modalities, in real-time, and in response to task, environmental, and user psychophysiological states.

Cognitive overload may be best described by the *Cognitive Load Theory (CLT)*, which is an information processing theory used to explain the human limits of working memory based on current knowledge of human cognitive architecture [20]. Cognitive architecture refers to the concept that human minds have structures, such as working memory, long term memory, and schemas [24]. In summary, CLT may be described as follows:

1) Working Memory can only handle seven (7) disconnected items at once [24].
2) Overload occurs when Working Memory is forced to process a significant amount of information too rapidly.
3) Long Term Memory is virtually unlimited and assists Working Memory.
4) Schemas are memory templates coded into Long Term Memory by Working Memory.
5) Working Memory is overloaded when its ability to build a schema is compromised.
6) If Working Memory has capacity left over, it can access information from long term memory in powerful ways.
7) Automation (i.e., doing something without conscious thought) results from well-developed schemas due to Working Memory's interaction with Long Term Memory. Well developed schemas come with repeated effort and effective practice. [20]

Furthermore, information that is retrieval from long term memory can be impacted based on external (fast moving or disruptive objects) or internal (physiological) stimuli, which may significantly impact human performance on tasks.

To augment human performance and apply empirically researched understanding of CLT constraints of information storage and retrieval to/from long term memory, an effective contextually intelligent information display is a potentially useful intervention; with the use of AI enabled pictorial mnemonic systems and non-invasive BCI.

Previous research demonstrates that memorization techniques (i.e., mnemonic strategies) has resulted in improvements in humans' ability to recall learned information [7][9][18] from long term memory. Mnemonic strategies are proven systematic procedures for enhancing memory recall [22] and facilitate the acquisition of factual information because they assist in the memory encoding process; either by providing familiar connections or by creating new connections between to-be-remembered information and the learner's information acquisition [21].

According to Bellezza [3], memory experts learn to create mental pictures that endure in the mental space. A medical pictorial mnemonic system has the capability to assist the recall of procedural steps in a single pictorial form, especially if depicted as intuitively formed symbols that are easily and immediately recognizable to the individual user.

A study by Estrada et al. [12], using a pictorial mnemonic system for recalling aviation emergency procedures, discovered that this system facilitated the recall of uncommon, unfamiliar terms and phrases in a population to a level comparable to that of highly-experienced pilots in just one week. The findings highlighted the potential for such a mnemonic strategy to aid in the encoding of information into long-term memory. This encoding and catalytic recall method "chunking" seven (7) pieces of information into a picture format results in decreased human cognitive overload, accelerates human decision making, and measurably augments human task completion performance.

C. *Amplifying Cognition*

The Defense Advanced Research Projects Agency (DARPA) Augmented Cognition (AugCog) and Random Access Memory (RAM) Replay programs were design to extend information processing and management capacity of human-computer symbiotic team by an order-of-magnitude more by developing and demonstrating enhancements to human cognitive ability and memory retrieval in diverse and stressful operational environments. Specifically, these programs sought to develop BCI required to measure and track a user's cognitive state and replay memories, in real-time, utilizing these measurements to augment the user's environment, and then tailor that environment to a particular user's state. The ultimate is to enhance a soldier's operational capability, support reduction in the numbers of soldier's required to perform current functions, and improve soldier performance in cognitively challenging environments. The resulting augmented technology (AR) systems include non-invasive sensors to assess human operators' neurophysiological responses to ongoing events. These measures were then combined with cognitive and contextual models of user intention and task objectives to invoke validated mitigation strategies to enable optimal performance from users, returning users to optimally functional states as needed.

The field of Augmented Cognition (AugCog) has demonstrated the technical feasibility of utilizing psychophysiological measures to support real-time cognitive state assessment and BCI reconfiguration to mitigate cognitive bottlenecks within a wide variety of operational environments. Therefore, Research and Development (R&D) in this domain has spanned a wide range of human-technology platforms and use case paradigms. However, little research has been dedicated to AugCog-based assessments of BCI within the context of AR. Furthermore, Intelligence Amplification (IA) is an AugCog that builds on human intelligence (i.e., that has evolved over millions of years) to adapt neuro-technology to the individual's neuronal state with a programmed goal to measurably amplify the individual's intellectual/cognitive capabilities to perform better than human expected optimal intelligence.

AR provides a complement to human cognitive processes via integrated information access, error potential reduction, enhanced motivation, and the provision of concurrent training and performance. Likewise, Nagao [26] proposed that psychophysiological signals, such as Electroencephalogram (EEG), Electrocardiogram (ECG), and Galvanic Skin Response (GSR) could be used to support personalization of AR interaction. However, subsequent R&D has not fully explored this approach. Other researchers [27] outlined a framework in which physiological measures, such as EEG, heart rate, and body temperature could be used to add intelligence to a wearable BCI, predicting individualized, programmable user behaviors, both offline and online. This functionality was predicted to support faster user response rates, and to support increased freedom and flexibility. This framework also included the option to selectively vary the weights from the various physiological inputs according to contextual factors. Finally, Navarro proposed that the incorporation of technologies, such as AR and multimodal personalized BCI techniques could be used to increase accuracy in dynamic environments, and that this functionality, combined with the adoption of wireless technologies, would support instantiation of this paradigm within increasingly mobile and dynamic contexts. Bonanni, Lee, and Selker [6] provided evidence that multimodal AR based interactions can enhance procedural task performance; and suggested that providing visual cues decreases cognitive load because memory is a more complex process than visual search based on cueing and search principles from attention theory. However, metrics of cognitive load were not directly assessed. Likewise, Kim and Dey [19] demonstrated the effective use of context-sensitive information and a simulated AR representation, combined to minimize the cognitive load in translating between virtual information spaces and the real world. Other researchers proposed the use of VR and AR in combination with hierarchical BCIs and learning models in order to increase BCI usability and interaction with physical and virtual worlds. Specifically, the proposed approach leverages the benefits of two paradigms of Event Related Potential (ERP) stimuli: environmental stimuli and stimuli generated by mental imagery. The goal of this approach was to combine environmental and user-generated inputs within a hierarchical BCI system capable of adapting to individual users.

This paper will discuss cognition BCI gaps (i.e., in Section II); augmenting medical personnel with IA (i.e., in Section III); and researchers conclusion and next steps (i.e, in Section IV).

II. AUGMENTED COGNITION BCI GAPS

A primary BCI gap that must be addressed in order for wearable AR to improve human working/long term memory involves real-time assessment of cognitive workload, real-time adaptive information presentation to mitigate cognitive overload, and non-invasive neuronal interpretation to ascertain attention and learning to activating neurons in the pre-frontal cortex and hippocampus regions. IA and AugCog R&D is grounded in a multi-disciplinary scientific approach to address issues of human-technology interaction through a blending of cognitive science, human factors, and operational neuroscience, and artificial intelligence. While much of the research in this field has focused on the use of physiological assessment metrics to drive real-time adaptive HCI, Tang, Owen, and Biocca [4][5] demonstrated improved task performance using AR and suggested that AR systems can reduce mental workload on assembly tasks. This study also addressed the issue of attention tunneling, indicating that AR cueing has the potential to overwhelm the user's attention, reducing performance by causing distraction from important relevant cues of the physical environment. This phenomenon has yet to be explored using objective measures of user attention and associated cognitive workload. Multiple AR studies have employed the National Aeronautics and Space Administration (NASA) Task Load Index (NASA-TLX) to assess mental workload [4][5][23]. However, the TLX provides only subjective ratings of mental workload and is not assessing in real time during task performance, relying on the user's memory of perceived task demands. Authors proposed a framework and research methodology to support instantiation of an adaptive AR to reduce cognitive load, as well as contextually adapt to an individual's environment or cognitive/physiological state (e.g., stress) using AugCog principles. Specifically, authors propose real-time monitoring and assessment of neurophysiological measures capable of indicating user cognitive workload, and specifically differentiating between verbal working memory and spatial working memory. Within this framework, indices of cognitive workload would drive a closed-loop HCI adaptive AR interface, reducing information presentation to the user during periods of high workload and increasing information as appropriate during periods of low workload. The proposed system would further differentiate between verbal working memory overload and spatial working memory overload, adapting information presentation as necessary to avoid overtaxing one working memory system. The goal of such a methodology is to extend human cognitive capabilities while remotely interoperating with a network of federated computing services.

III. AUGMNENTING MEDICAL PERSONNEL WITH IA

This section provides a use case scenario, selected from the medical domain involving cognitive, psychomotor, and perceptual skills within a dynamic operational environment. Recent wearable AR medical research from Azimi, Doswell, Kazanzides J., [2], demonstrated the use of context-aware wearable AR for use in surgical and trauma medical assistance with future implications of augmenting human perceptual cues with multi-modal cognitive cues.

For example, surgical resection is one of the most common treatments for brain tumors. The treatment goal is to remove as much of the tumor as possible, while sparing the healthy tissue. Image guidance (e.g., with preoperative Computed Tomography (CT) or Magnetic Resonance Imaging (MRI) is frequently used because it can more clearly differentiate diseased tissue from healthy tissue. Most image guidance devices contain special markers that can be easily detected by a computer tracking system. Registering the tracker coordinate system to the preoperative image coordinate system gives the surgeon "x-ray vision." However, this modality can be challenging for the surgeon to effectively use a navigation system because the presented information is not physically co-located with the operative visual display field, requiring the surgeon to look at a computer monitor rather than at the patient. This is especially awkward when the surgeon wishes to move an instrument within the patient while observing the display. Such ergonomic issues may increase operating times, fatigue, and the risk of errors. Furthermore, most navigation systems employ optical tracking, due to its high accuracy, but this requires line-of-sight between the cameras and the markers in the operative field, which can be difficult to maintain during the surgery.

After researchers observed several neurosurgeries, and spoke with neurosurgeons and neurosurgical residents, they identified a need to overlay a tumor margin (boundary) on the neurosurgeon's view of patient's anatomy, which served as a pictorial mnemonic triggering memory recall and visual landmark to cognitively assist surgeons accurately complete a psychomotor procedure. It was also desired to correctly track and align the distal end of the surgical instruments with the preoperative medical images. The aim of the research was to investigate the feasibility of implementing a head-mounted tracking system with an AR environment to provide the surgeon with visualization of both the tumor margin and the surgical instrument in order to create a more accurate and natural overlay of the affected tissue versus healthy tissue and, hence, provide a more intuitive HCI [2].

The resulting wearable AR allows the surgeon to see the precise boundaries of the tumor for neurosurgical procedures, while simultaneously, providing contextual overlay of the surgical tools intraoperatively which are displayed on Juxtopia® optical see-through goggles worn by the surgeon. This AR overlay capability provides the most pertinent information without unduly cluttering the visual field. It provides the benefits of navigation and visualization while being ergonomically more comfortable and intuitive for the surgeon.

The majority of related research has focused on AR visualization with HMDs, usually adopting video see-through designs. Many of these systems have integrated one or more on-board camera subsystems to help determine head pose [13][16][31] and some have added inertial sensing to improve this estimate via sensor fusion [8]. None of these systems, however, attempt to provide a complete tracking system and continue to rely on external trackers.

Combining the aforementioned wearable AR intervention with multi-modal sensors and BCI that track both dynamically changing internal and external stimuli, surgeons may visually monitor the AR display feedback based on their cognitive fatigue and stress level, as well as performance based multi-model cues including, but not limited to, multimedia mnemonics that augment's the surgeon capability to better perform the surgery.

IV. CONCLUSION AND FUTURE WORK

Figure 2. U.S. Army Combat Medic Wearing HoloLens AR Performing Cricothyrotomy.

To prepare young 18-20 year old brains for accelerated learning of combat medic skills (as illustrated in Figure 2) in preparation for delivering accurate clinical proficiency in austere battlefield environments, Dr. Jayfus Tucker Doswell and his research team are applying their preliminary AugCog and IA research to investigate non-invasive BCIs sensors (e.g., EEG, fMRI, etc.) integrated into wearable AR HMDs, and with capabilities to contextually and autonomously extract neuronal data from target brain regions ranging from pre-frontal cortex (attention), inferior frontal junction (visual processing), and hippocampus (memory) to substantia nigra (eye movement and motor planning), and cerebellum (fine motor movement). A primary opportunity presented by such advanced BCI technologies is the development of methods to quantifiably improve human's intellectual/cognitive state to optimally perform better than historically trained persons. Such modality selection methodologies must be dynamic, providing the capability to adapt interaction configurations to accommodate various operational and environmental conditions, as well as user cognitive states, which change over time in response to task demands and factors, such as sleep, nutrition, stress, and even time of day. Ideally, interactive technologies must be capable of adapting interaction modalities, in real-time, in response to task, environmental, and user psychophysiological states. The fields of Intelligence Amplification (IA) and Augmented

Cognition (AugCog) have demonstrated technical feasibility of utilizing psychophysiological measures to support real-time cognitive state assessment and BCI reconfiguration to mitigate cognitive bottlenecks within a wide variety of operational environments.

Researchers will continue to explore how to integrate a dynamically changing BCI sensor device/software framework into a context-aware AR platform [1][2][10][11] to augment human perceptual capabilities and for improving human performance®.

ACKNOWLEDGMENT

This research was supported by the Juxtopia® Advanced Mixed Reality (JAMR) program of The Juxtopia Group, Inc.

REFERENCES

[1] A. Sofolahan, F. Ologhobo, E. Ochieng, D. Gillis, J. Doswell, C. Dickens, "Context-Aware Augmented Reality System: A Medical First Responder Situational Awareness Interface.". Poster Session. Medicine Meets Virtual Reality (MMVR) Conference. Newport Beach, California, 2010.

[2] E. Azimi, J, Doswell, P. Kazanzides, "Augmented reality goggles with an integrated tracking system for navigation in neurosurgery," Conference: Virtual Reality, IEEE Annual International Symposium - VR , pp. 123-124, 2012.

[3] F.S. Bellezza. "The Minds Eye in Expert Memorizers Descriptions of Remembering. Metaphor and Symbolic Activity," 7(3, 4), pp. 119-133, 1992.

[4] F. Biocca, C. Owen, A. Tang, C. Bohil. "Attention issues in spatial information systems: directing mobile users' visual attention using augmented reality. Journal of Management Information Systems, 23(4), pp. 163-184. 2007.

[5] F. Biocca, A. Tang, C. Owen, F. Xiao, "Attention funnel: omnidirectional 3D cursor for mobile augmented reality platforms," In Proceedings of the SIGCHI conference on Human Factors in computing systems (pp. 1115-1122). ACM., April 2006.

[6] L. Bonanni, C.H. Lee, T. Selker. "Attention-based design of augmented reality interfaces," In CHI'05 extended abstracts on Human factors in computing systems. pp. 1228-1231, ACM. April 2005.

[7] R.N. Carney, J.R. Levin, "Promoting Higher-Order Learning Benefits by Building Lower-Order Mnemonic Connections." Applied Cognitive Psychology, vol. 17, pp. 563-575, 2003.

[8] L. Chai, W.A. Hoff, T. Vincent. "Three-Dimensional Motion and Structure Estimation Using Inertial Sensors and Computer Vision for Augmented Reality," Presence. 11(5):474-492, Oct 2002.

[9] B.D. Cox. "Children's Use of Mnemonic Strategies: Variability in Response to Metamemory Training," The Journal of Genetic Psychology, 155(4), 423-442, 2001.

[10] J. Doswell, O. Sampson, M. Jeffrey. "WASA MIST Wearable Assistant for Real-Time Emergency Care Providers," The 15th Annual International Meeting of the American Telemedicine Association, 2010.

[11] J. Doswell, M. Anderson, K. Wilson, P. Kazanzides, "Wearable Augmented Reality for Medical First Response and Situational Awareness," Medicine Meets Virtual Reality (MMVR19) NextGen Conference. Newport Beach, California. 2012.

[12] A. Estrada, J.A. Keeley, P.A. Leduc, J.M. Bass, T.N. Rouse, J.G. Ramiccio, T.L. Rowe, "A novel approach in facilitating aviation emergency procedure learning and recall through an intuitive pictorial system," U.S. Army Aeromedical Research Laboratory Technical Report, No. 2007-07.

[13] H. Fuchs, M.A. Livingston, R. Raskar, D. Colucci, K. Keller, A. State, J.R. Crawford, P. Rademacher, S. Drake, A.A. Meyer, "Augmented reality visualization for laparoscopic surgery," MICCAI, pp. 934-943, 1998.

[14] T. Höllerer, Feiner, T., ""Mobile Augmented Reality," In H. Karimi and A. Hammad, editors, Telegeoinformatics: Location-Based Computing and Services. Taylor and Francis Books Ltd., London, UK, 2004.

[15] T. Höllerer, K. Feiner, D. Hallaway, B. Bell, M. Lanzagorta, D.G. Brown, S.J. Julier, Y. Baillot, LJ. Rosenblum, "User Interface Management Techniques for Collaborative Mobile Augmented Reality". Computers and Graphics;25(5): pp799-810.October, 2001.

[16] W. Hoff, T. Vincent. "Analysis of head pose accuracy in augmented reality," IEEE Trans. Visualization and Comp. Graphics, Vol. 6, 2000.

[17] C.E. Hughes, C.B. Stapleton, D.E. Hughes, E.M. Smith, "Mixed Reality in Education Entertainment, and Training,". IEEE Computer Graphics and Applications. pp. 24-30. November/December 2005.

[18] K.A. Kleinheksel, S.E. Summy, S.E. "Enhancing Student Learning and Social Behavior Through Mnemonic Strategies," TEACHING Exceptional Children, 36(2), 30-35. 2003.

[19] S. Kim, A.K. Dey. "Simulated augmented reality windshield display as a cognitive mapping aid for elder driver navigation," In Proceedings of the SIGCHI Conference on Human Factors in Computing Systems, pp. 133-142, ACM. April, 2009.

[20] Learning and ID. "Cognitive Load Theory" [online] http://im404504.wikidot.com/cognitive-learning-theory. 2019

[21] M.E. Levin, J.R. Levin. "Scientific mnemonomies: Methods for maximizing more than memory". American Educational Research Journal, 27, 1990, 301-321.

[22] M.A. Mastropieri, T.E. Scruggs, "Enhancing School Success with Mnemonic Strategies. Intervention in School and Clinic, 33(4). 1998.

[23] Z. Medenica, A. L. Kun, T. Paek, O. Palinko, "Augmented reality vs. street views: a driving simulator study comparing two emerging navigation aids," In Proceedings of the 13th International Conference on Human Computer Interaction with Mobile Devices and Services, pp. 265-274,. ACM. August 2011.

[24] G.A. Miller, "The magical number seven, plus or minus two: Some limits on our capacity for processing information," Psychological Review. 63, 81-97, 1956.

[25] P. Milgram, A.F., Kishino, "Taxonomy of Mixed RealityVisual Displays," IEICE Trans. Information and Systems, vol. E77-D. no. 12. pp. 1321-1329. 1994.

[26] K. Nagao, "Agent augmented reality: Agents integrate the real world with cyberspace," Community Computing: Collaboration over Global Information Networks, ed. T. Ishida, John Wiley & Sons. 1998.

[27] K.F. Navarro, "Wearable, wireless brain computer interfaces in augmented reality environments," In Information Technology: Coding and Computing. Proceedings. ITCC 2004. International Conference on (Vol. 2, pp. 643-647). IEEE. April, 2004.

A Position for Proactive Cybersecurity Policies for Military BCIs

Ashley Boykin
Capitol Technology University
Cybersecurity Department
Baltimore, USA
e-mail: abboykin@captechu.edu

Jayfus T. Doswell
Juxtopia® Advanced Mixed Reality (JAMR) Lab
The Juxtopia Group, Inc.
Baltimore, USA
e-mail: jayfus@juxtopia.com

Abstract - **More countries are considering equipping their soldiers with Brain-Computer Interfaces (BCI). Hence, these governments will require investment in access control policies that specifically target BCI to prevent the technology from becoming vulnerable to internal and external threats. Authors present a position on the importance of International cybersecurity policies to protect data from BCI and humans.**

Keywords – cybersecurity; policy; government; BCI; brain.

I. INTRODUCTION

Access control policies and management refers to the methods in which users are granted or denied access to users or systems. Its foundation is upholding authentication, confidentiality, integrity, reliability, maintainability, availability and non-repudiation to correctly grant and manage access to a needed resource or system [1].

A. BCI Cybersecurity Overview

The international community has expressed interest in using Brain-Computer Interfaces (BCI)s (BCI) in a variety of industry sectors, ranging from medical and commercial space to military industries. Each of these industries has investigated how technological advancements in BCI can improve human performance in completing tasks more efficiently and at lower costs. For example, BCIs allow improved human capabilities to be enhanced by augmenting human skillset and physical capabilities. However, these technical advancements potentially pose a larger attack surface for cybersecurity professionals to consider. The results of a BCI cyberattack can have devastating and adverse consequences to 1.) BCI wearer's health; and 2.) Provide an attacker with access to critical information ranging from an individual's neurological state; active memory and thoughts; to neurological illnesses/diseases [2].

Hence, understanding the creative capabilities of humans to both create and disrupt BCI infrastructures, it is prudent to take proactive processes for creating policies to, not only bolster a BCIs security mechanisms, but also to enhance BCI access control capabilities to prevent critical data from becoming susceptible to well-meaning colleagues without the appropriate authorization to access the information.

B. Non-Invasive BCI

Across the aforementioned industries, BCIs may be engineered with non-invasive and transcutaneous methods ranging from near-infrared spectroscopy (fNIRS) and electro-encephalogram (EEG) to transcranial magnetic stimulator (TMS) devices. The objective of BCIs is to assist human navigation of computer or other electro-mechanical systems or to extract neurological information from the human. Although fNIRS has positive advantages, such as being low-risk and provides high-spatial resolution, its main drawback is that it is not portable whereas EEG is portable. The disadvantage of EEG is that signals are able to be distorted by surrounding interference [3]. EEG and fNIRS are currently the best options for BCI implementation and research for military implementation.

II. BCI AND CYBERSECURITY

A. HSPD-12 Access Control Guidelines

The Homeland Security Presidential Directive 12 (HSPD-12) was established to streamline the process of access control regarding federal employees and contractors for the United States (U.S.) government. This directive forms the foundation for streamlining access control policies for greater interoperability throughout governmental agencies.

Typically, science innovates faster than policies allow. Therefore, it is a necessity that there are guidelines in place delineating strong access control policies for BCI users that are explored prior and alongside military-wide adoption of BCI for highly-skilled soldiers. Protection against bad actors as well as internal threats must be implemented alongside science, so that researchers will understand what and how to protect a person's BCI and the critical data located within their system.

B. Implementing Access Controls

The best course of action for using fNIRS is a unified physical and logical security system. This is because this method analyzes a current system's capabilities and needs as well as its future needs and goals. Therefore, this access control method will evolve with the BCI's needs. The evolutionary access control will place the foundation for protecting the user and any components required for the BCI to operate successfully within its set of parameters.

C. *Military Medicine Access Control*

Scientists have also discovered that brainwaves are unique to individuals [4]. Thus, it means that brainwaves can be considered a biometric feature to implement within access control mechanisms for wearers in the future. There have been instances where BCIs have proven beneficial to those suffering from neurological conditions. However, BCI cybersecurity researchers must determine, for other reasons, how to protect the identity of BCI wearers who may suffer from cognitive abilities and comorbidities as well as those who have neurological gifts and unique skill proficiency that make the individual a target.

III. CONCLUSION AND FUTURE WORK

In conclusion, strong cybersecurity access control policies must be implemented in governments, around the world, based on how soldiers and peacekeeping units are currently using BCIs and predictive how these specially skilled and protected individuals will use BCIs for battle, training and peacekeeping missions.

The adverse results from a prolonged cybersecurity attack can have devastating results on the wearer's neurological system as well as provide an attacker with access to critical information.

The military's exploration of incorporating BCI comes with a responsibility to ensure the proper access control policies are enabled and enforced alongside the research and development (R&D) phases and prior to implementation. In this way, vulnerabilities can be identified and policies can be created to bolder a user's BCI efficiency as well as its internal and external security.

ACKNOWLEDGEMENT

This research was supported by the Juxtopia® Advanced Mixed Reality (JAMR) program of The Juxtopia Group, Inc.

REFERENCES

[1] CIO Council, Executive Office of the President of the United States. *Federal Identity, Credential, and Access Management (FICAM). Roadmap and Implementation Guidance.* [Online]. Available from https://www.idmanagement.gov/wp-content/uploads/sites/1171/uploads/FICAM_Roadmap_and_Implem_Guid.pdf. Retrieved March, 2019.

[2] J. Minguez and P. Usieto. "Avoiding brain hacking - Challenges of cybersecurity and privacy in Brain-Computer Interfaces." Available from https://www.bitbrain.com/blog/cybersecurity-brain-computer-interface. Retrieved March, 2019.

[3] Grey Matters. Brain-Computer Interfaces (BCI)s. [Online]. Available from http://greymattersjournal.com/brain-computer-interfaces/. Retrieved March, 2019.

[4] B. Armstrong, et. al. "Brainprint: Assessing the uniqueness, collectability, and permanence of a novel method for ERP biometrics," Neurocomputing, vol. 166, pp 59-67, Oct. 2015, doi: 10.1016/j.neucom.2015.04.025.

Algorithm for Classification of EEG Signals in Astronauts

Victor Hugo Ortiz

Biomedical Engineering Department
Tecnologico de Estudios Superiores de Ixtapaluca
Ixtapaluca, Mexico
e-mail: a_biochip@yahoo.com.mx

Jayfus Tucker Doswell

1101 East 33rd Street, B303,
Baltimore, MD 21218, 703-989-1199
e-mail: jayfus@juxtopia.com

***Abstract*—An algorithm is presented for filtering and classification of electroencephalographic (EEG) signals, based on extended Kalman filters and dynamic neural networks. The EEG signals acquisition process is complicated since they have a lot of white noise and because the amplitude and frequency of the different rhythms are in a very small range. The astronaut's brain, when subjected to a microgravity environment, changes its physiology. It is important to analyze these changes because we can analyze: biomechanics, psychological issues, intracranial pressure and using a brain machine interface, among others. The filtering and sorting algorithm are designed based on extended Kalman filters and neural networks. These algorithms are used primarily because of their ease to remove white noise and detect small changes of the different types of rhythms present in EEG signals. Since the presence of EEG rhythms is unknown, an estimator and an observer are designed based on neural networks for the appropriate classification of signals. The neural network algorithm can be adapted to the extended Kalman filter and get one feedback system. The algorithm is used to make more robust the Kalman filter. This algorithm has been able to effectively classify EEG rhythms and which are of interest for biomechanical analysis, and brain machine interface. This algorithm is tested using a database. However, the same proposed algorithm can be used on astronauts in microgravity environments.**

Keywords–Neural Network; Astronauts; EEG Signals.

I. INTRODUCTION

Our brains are changing all the time. Nerves are rearranging themselves and the connections between the nerve cells are reforming as the brain memorizes new information, stores the old and continuously adapts to new situations [1]. New experiences, learning, physiological changes, sleep disturbance and fatigue are among the most influential factors. Sometimes, especially after an accident or a cerebral stroke, the recover power of brain tissue is simply mind-boggling: the remaining healthy tissue can take over the functions of damaged areas. The weightlessness in orbit is also a big change for brains. Not only are there changes in blood circulation and other physical conditions, but the way that cognitive functions of daily life are managed also alter the brain dramatically. Adapting to the multitudinous effects that gravity has on the human body and the way the brain deals with them is perhaps the greatest demand that the nervous system has to face in outer-space. The increased load on the cognitive capacity is accompanied by a multitude of stresses on the brain [2].

A. Extended Filter Kalman

The Kalman filter is an algorithm that is based on the model state space of a system to estimate the future state and future output filtering optimally the output signal, depending on the delay of the samples to be introduced, the filter of the parameter estimator can be used or the filter can be used in the function. In both cases the noise can be eliminated, these equations are widely used because they include statistical probabilities since it takes into account the randomness of both the signal and the noise. Unlike other types of filters that do not require a specific cutting frequency Kalman is based on the characteristic of the noise filter thus allowing across the frequency spectrum [3].

B. Brain Computer Interface (BCI)

BCI systems today are considered a tool with enormous potential for establishing communication alternatives to restore motor functions. There are different types of EEG potentials, which can be classified according to different factors. Brain rhythms can be classified depending on frequency bandwidth and have been designated a Greek letter. [4].

- Delta Rhythm (δ): They are typically between 0.5 and 3.5 Hz and has amplitudes of 20 to 200 μV.
- Theta Rhythm (θ): It occurs in the band of 4 to 7 Hz with amplitudes ranging from 20 to 100 μV.
- Alpha rhythm (α): The alpha rhythm is mainly manifested in the frequency band from 8 to 13 Hz with amplitudes ranging from 20 to 60 μV.
- Mu Rhythm (μ): It manifests in the range of 8-13 Hz and its amplitude is less than 50 μV.
- Beta Rhythm (β): It is an irregular rhythm, with frequencies between 13 and 30 Hz. Its approximate amplitude is between 2 and 20 μV.
- Gamma Rhythm (γ): This rhythm at higher frequencies to 30 Hz and amplitudes manifests between 5 and 10 μV [5].

II. METHODOLOGY

The first step is to obtain EEG signals from different database to show the proposed algorithm. The databases we used were: a database of a group of researchers from different institutions of the European Union [6], Ecole Polytechnique Federale de Lausanne [7] and Graz University of Technology [8].

A. Equation numbers

The electroencephalography study is complicated to perform because the patient must be at rest, the study has a lot of noise and can be confused with any noise rhythm of the EEG signal. For that reason apply extended Kalman filters as they are appropriate filters to eliminate noise caused by the system. Consider the equation of state and output of a non-stationary system with noise form:

$$\begin{aligned} x(k+1) &= A(k)\,x(k) + B(k)\,u(k) + \upsilon(k) \\ y(k) &= C(k)\,x(k) + \omega(x), \end{aligned} \tag{1}$$

Where matrices $A(k)$, $B(k)$ and $C(k)$ are deterministic and are generally variants variables in linear systems with time, $\upsilon(k)$ and $\omega(x)$ are stochastic processes and noise measurement system respectively, which are considered white noise average.

For the classification of signals, we use dynamic neural networks, unaware of how it will end EEG signal acquired have to estimate and observe the different rhythms, dynamic neural networks are suitable for this procedure. The neural network algorithm can be adapted to the extended Kalman filter and get one feedback system, the algorithm with 2 hidden layers is used to make more robust the Kalman filter. This algorithm has been able to effectively classify rhythm signals and which are the rates of interest.

The design idea can be illustrated observers to invariant systems in the time:

$$\begin{aligned} \dot{x} &= Ax + Bu \\ y &= Cx, \end{aligned} \tag{2}$$

A linear observer is designed in the same way as the original system with an additional pending input from the difference between the actual values and the estimated values of the output vector:

$$\dot{\hat{x}} = A\hat{x} + Bu + L\left(C\hat{x} - y\right), \tag{3}$$

Where $\hat{x}_t$ is an estimate of the state vector of the system $L \in \Re^{nxl}$ and is an input matrix. Of course, the vector state observer $\hat{x}$ is available to generate the control action using auxiliary system dynamics.

$$\begin{aligned} \frac{d\hat{x}_t}{dt} &= A\hat{x}_t + W_{1,t}\sigma\left(\hat{x}_t\right) + W_{2,t}\varphi\left(\hat{x}_t\right)u_t + K_1 e_t + K_2 e_t \\ \hat{y}_t &= C\hat{x}_t \end{aligned} \tag{4}$$

Where $\hat{x}_t$ is the state vector representing the neuronal observer estimates brain signals; $\hat{y}_t$ is the output of the neural network corresponding to the differential value of the estimated rate of rhythm signals: μ and β rhythm; A, K_1 y K_2 are the constants appropriate matrices which fit during training, to enhance the process of approximation of the neural network dimensions; $\sigma()$ and $\varphi()$ are vector fields are compounds with standard sigmoid functions; C is assumed that the matrix output previously known; parameters $W_{1,t}$ and $W_{2,t}$ are the weights are adjusted to ensure a good approximation of the neural network to the uncertain nonlinear function. The first is that the adjustment of feedback and the second is related to the effect of the entry in the state estimation process whose time evolution is determined by a special procedure of learning online. The data set available are the rhythms acquired from the BCI, i.e., $y = x$. In this way and in this particular case $C = (1, 0, , 0)$.

III. Results

In this section, we present the EEG signals obtained from each of the databases. These images also reflect the different rates. In Figure 1, we show for the database Europe Union in Figure 2. The database Ecole Polytechnique Federale de Lausanne in Figure 3. the Graz University of Technology.

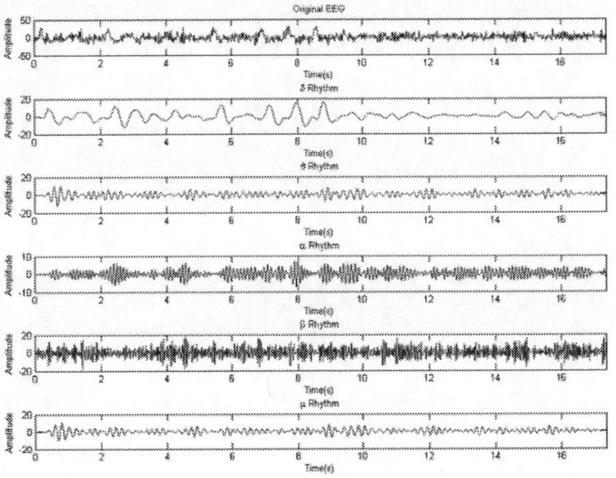

Figure 1. Database of EEG signal, database of the European Union.

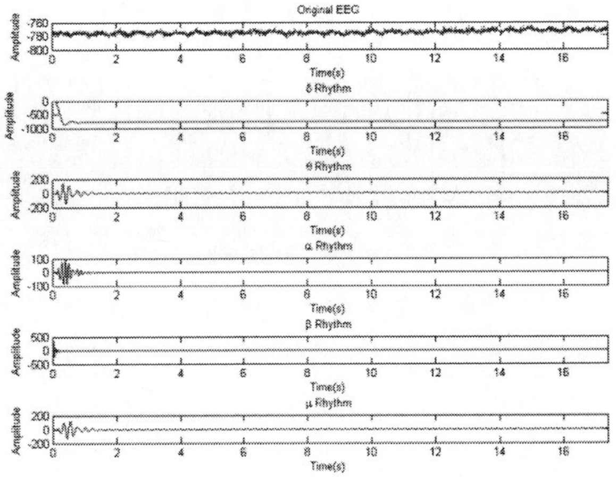

Figure 2. Database of EEG signal, database of the Ecole Polytechnique Federale de Lausanne.

After obtaining signals from the database, we applied the extended Kalman filter to the signal to filter and obtain the rhythm wish, Figure 4 and Figure 5 shows the output of the Kalman filter for rhythms μ and β of first database respectively.

Figure 6 and Figure 7 shows the output of the Kalman filter for rhythms μ and β second database respectively.

Figure 8 and Figure 9 shows the output of the Kalman filter for rhythms μ and β of the third database respectively. Since we have the output of the extended Kalman filter, apply the neural network. The neural network learns from the original network. Specifically, the network learns this is the right pace, we resubmitted another signal type of neural network will

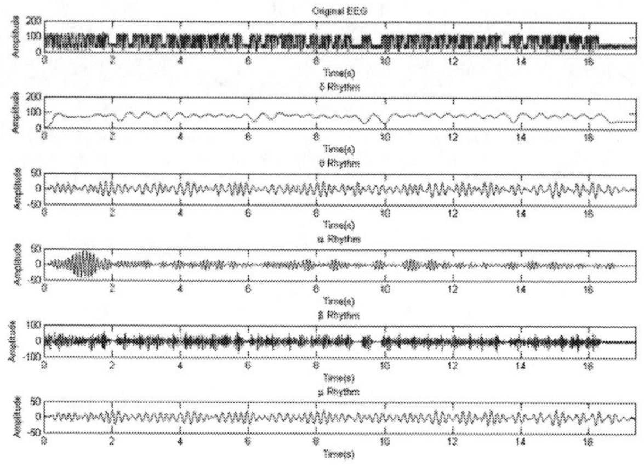

Figure 3. Database of EEG signal, database of the Graz University of Technology.

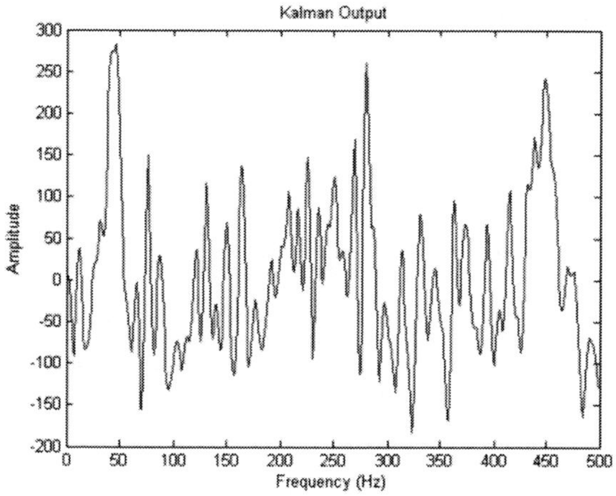

Figure 4. Output extended Kalman filter for μ rhythm, database of the European Union.

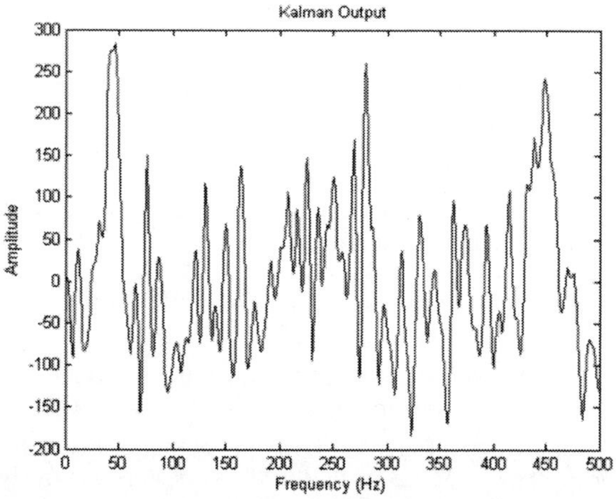

Figure 5. Output extended Kalman filter for β rhythm, database of the European Union.

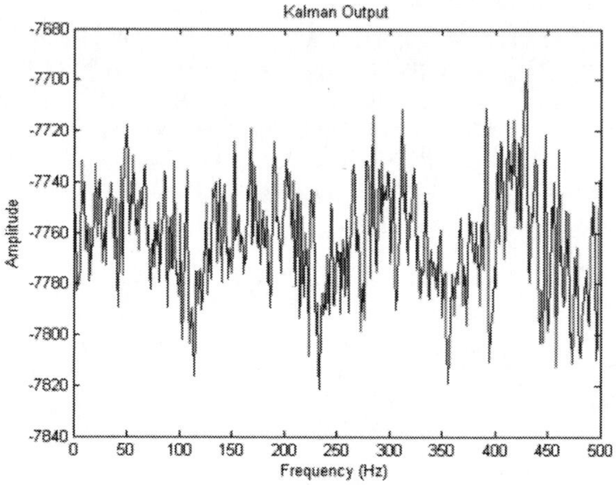

Figure 6. Output extended Kalman filter for μ rhythm, database of the Ecole Polytechnique Federale de Lausanne.

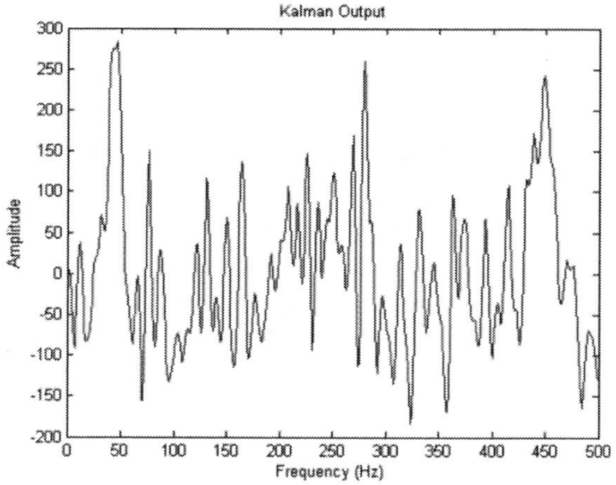

Figure 7. Output extended Kalman filter for β rhythm, database of the Ecole Polytechnique Federale de Lausanne.

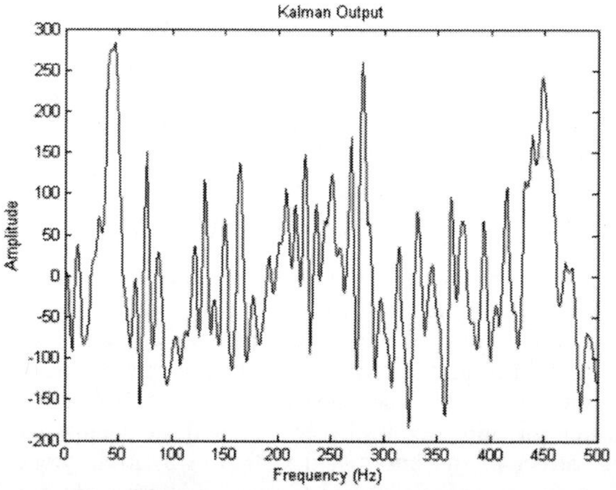

Figure 8. Output extended Kalman filter for μ rhythm, database of the Graz University of Technology.

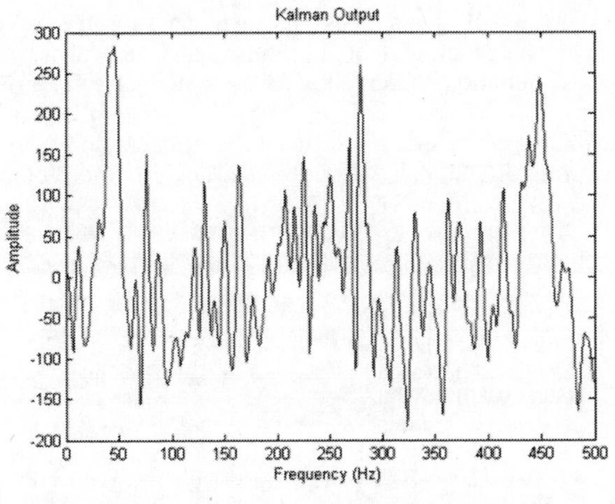

Figure 9. Output extended Kalman filter for β rhythm, database of the Graz University of Technology.

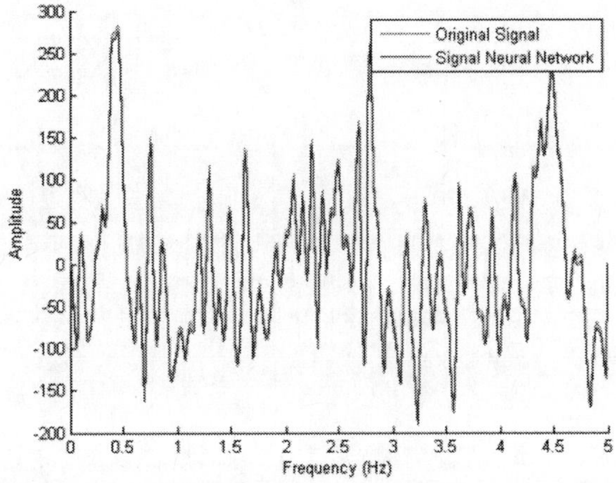

Figure 11. Output neural network for β rhythm, database of the European Union.

take it as another EEG signal. This is the behaviour that we expect as a first test for our classification signals. Because the implementation of the neural network is in matlab takes a long time for the amount of data. In Figure 10 and Figure 11, we show the application of the neural network μ rate signal and β respectively.

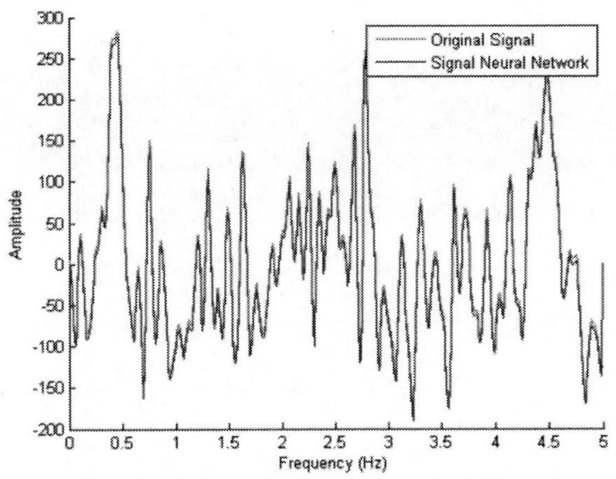

Figure 10. Output neural network for μ rhythm, database of the European Union.

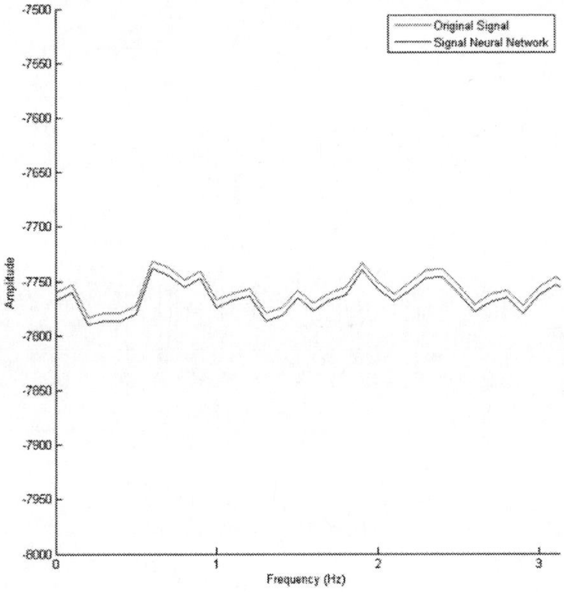

Figure 12. Output neural network for μ rhythm, database of the Ecole Polytechnique Federale de Lausanne.

Figure 12 and Figure 13 shows the output of the neural network for the rhythm μ and β of second database respectively. Figure 14 and Figure 15 shows the output of the neural network for the rhythm μ and β of third database respectively.

IV. Discussion.

When we obtain the signal from Extended Kalman Filter, enters the EEG signal to the system Dynamic Neural Networks. The application of dynamic neural network to μ rhythm. In the figures of the neural network estimation signal (red) is shown, the estimate is appropriate and that would classify the correct signal for the movement of the limbs. The same applies to the β rhythm

The algorithm applied model helped us to estimate the parameters of the neural network, by means of the error matrix K provides us with the estimate of the neural network. The lower the K matrix best estimate of the neural network. Another important parameter is to calculate the matrix of the weights W. The weights are given us the speed with which estimates the network, this data is important because it also indicates the computational cost of the algorithm.

V. Conclusion

The proposed algorithm is able to identify EEG signals in the first instance removing noise that provides acquisition

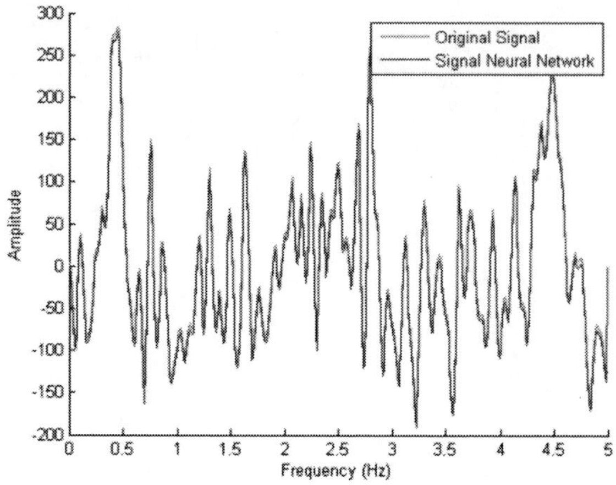

Figure 13. Output neural network for β rhythm, database of the Ecole Polytechnique Federale de Lausanne.

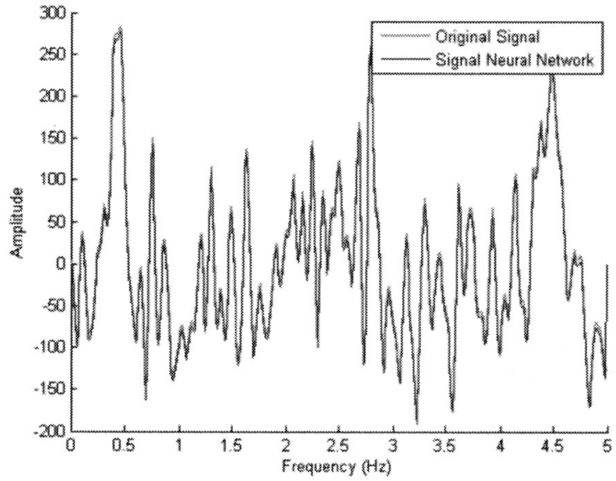

Figure 14. Output neural network for μ rhythm, database of the Graz University of Technology.

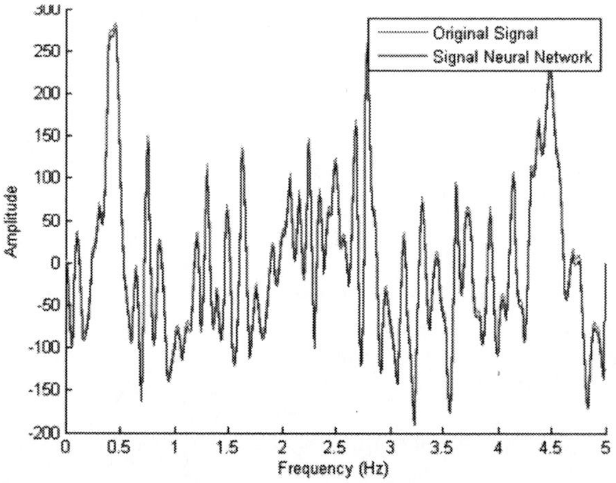

Figure 15. Output neural network for β rhythm, database of the Graz University of Technology.

system which guarantees that we can get the rhythm we want. The other part of the algorithm is the observer of the neural network, which showed us that it is able to learn the correct signal (required rhythm). This system could be used in microgravity environments for astronauts and who wish to acquire EEG signals where system noise is more common.

REFERENCES

[1] "ESA Paolo," 2011, URL: https://www.esa.int/Our_Activities/Human_and_Robotic_Exploration/MagISStra/Studying_Paolo_s_brains [accessed: 2019-03-10].

[2] L. Rossini, D. Izzo, and L. Summerer, Eds., Brain Machine Interfaces for Space Applications: enhancing astronaut capabilities. Elsevier, 2009, ISBN: 9780123748218.

[3] Y. Wang, K. Veluvolu, and M. Lee, "Time-frequency analysis of band-limited EEG with BMFLC and Kalman filter for BCI applications," Journal of NeuroEngineering and Rehabilitation, vol. 10:109, 2013, pp. 1–16.

[4] D. Krusienski, G. Schalk, D. McFarland, and J. Wolpaw, "A μ-Rhythm Matched Filter for Continuous Control of a Brain-Computer Interface," IEEE Transactions on Biomedical Engineering, vol. 54:02, 2007, pp. 273–280.

[5] J. E. Hall, Ed., Guyton and Hall textbook of medical physiology. Elsevier, May 2016, ISBN: 9781455770052.

[6] "Data base European Union," 2018, URL: http://bnci-horizon-2020.eu/database/data-sets [accessed: 2019-03-10].

[7] "Data base Ecole," 2018, URL: http://mmspg.epfl.ch/page-58318-en.html [accessed: 2019-03-10].

[8] "Data base GRAZ," 2018, URL: https://bci.tugraz.at/ [accessed: 2019-03-10].

Neural Network-Based Reasoning for Solving the Tower of Hanoi

Sanghun Bang
Laboratoire Cognitions Humaine
et Artificielle (CHArt)
University Paris 8
Saint-Denis, France
Email: sang-hun.bang@univ-paris8.fr

Charles Tijus
Laboratoire Cognitions Humaine
et Artificielle (CHArt)
University Paris 8
Saint-Denis, France
Email: charles.tijus@univ-paris8.fr

***Abstract*—In this paper, we propose a reasoning solution, which can infer the rules of game, such as Tower of Hanoi. Neural networks require large amounts of data to improve performance. However, human intelligence requires only a simple exposition. The goal of this paper is to learn to solve a Tower of Hanoi without much learning. We collect sequential data from participants' experiments that are supposed to solve the Tower of Hanoi. And then, we observe relations between different objects and their actions to establish our reasoning model. We train our reasoning model to solve the Tower of Hanoi. Finally, we show that our reasoning model can infer the rule of game through observations from objects, their relationships and actions.**

Keywords–Reasoning;Inference;Neural Networks; Machine Learning;Tower of Hanoi.

I. INTRODUCTION

From a psychological point of view, the reasoning of human being can be considered as the process of drawing conclusions. Human beings' endeavors to solve problems or to make decisions are goal-oriented [1]. Reasoning has long been regarded as exclusive domain of the human being. It was one of the most difficult areas to implement mechanically. Because we need to understand contextual meanings, such as texts and images, and we have to consider contextual relationships that change depending on the situation, even with the same information. Therefore, reasoning has received a lot of attentions in the last few decades [2][3]. In recent years, advances in deep learning, especially the evolution of learning algorithms, are leading to rapid research and development of artificial intelligence in the field of reasoning [4]. In this paper, we pay our attention to a matter of reasoning about objects, relations and interactions. This task is a matter of reasoning about things and relationships in order to solve problems. The French mathematician Edouard Lucas introduced the Tower of Hanoi (TOH) puzzle in 1883. Figure 1 shows a standard example of Tower of Hanoi. There is a pile of different size disks on the right peg. The largest disk is at the bottom of the peg and the smallest at the top of the pile. The goal of TOH is to move the whole stack of disks from the right peg to the left peg. There are three rules as constraints: One disk at a time should be moved, in a location, the smallest disk is the one to take and a large disk cannot be placed on top of a smaller one. In this paper, our hypothesis is that we can infer the rule of game through observing the movements of the participants action. In order to test this hypothesis, we carry out an experiment for which participants were given two successive tasks: to solve the three-disk Tower of Hanoi task, then to solve this problem with four disks. Based on the acquired data, we observed relations between different objects and their actions to establish our reasoning model. As we know, neural networks require amounts of data to improve performance. But, in this paper we tried to infer the solution of Tower of Hanoi without much learning. We trained with 3 disks and predicted out model with 4 disks.

II. REASONING MODEL

As mentioned at the introduction, only one disk at a time can be moved, a disk can only be moved if it is the top disk on a pile, and a larger disk can never be placed on a smaller one (See Figure 1). From the rule of game, we can infer this participant's action. How can we make such inference possible without any information about the rule of game ? We have received great inspiration from Interaction Networks(Ins) [5] and Relation networks(RNs) [6]. These models, which have a neural network architecture, are very helpful for inference learning by observing from objects, their relationships and actions.

Figure 1. The smallest disk in the four is at the top, and participant grabs it and moves it.

As with the Relation Networks [6], we assume reasoning of rule that depends on the relations $\mathcal{R}$ between objects. According to our sequential data, relation ($\mathcal{R}$, with elements r) is consist of location, and inclusion relation. For example, the smallest disk is the relation with other disks (Ex:The smallest disk is in contact with the second smallest disk.). In the case of the Tower of Hanoi with 3 disks, we have six objects (3 disks, 3 pegs) with a vector of 3 features encoding properties, such as the object's position (beneath and on) and inclusion relation. We can express the smallest disk like this, $o_1 = (o_1^{beneath}, o_1^{on}, o_1^{inclusion})$. We are interested in models generally defined by the composite form $f \cdot g$, where f is a function that returns a prediction y. The function g_ψ is defined to operate on a particular factorization of D

(ex: $g_\psi(D) \equiv g_\psi(o_1^1, o_1^2, ..., o_i^1, ..., o_m^n)$). As shown in Figure 2, there is the smallest disk on the second small disk. In this case, there is a relation with the disk below. It means $g_\psi(o_1, o_2) = beneath(o_1, o_2)$. But, there is not the disk on the smallest disk. For inclusion, There are four disks in peg1. But the peg2 and peg3 do not have a disk.

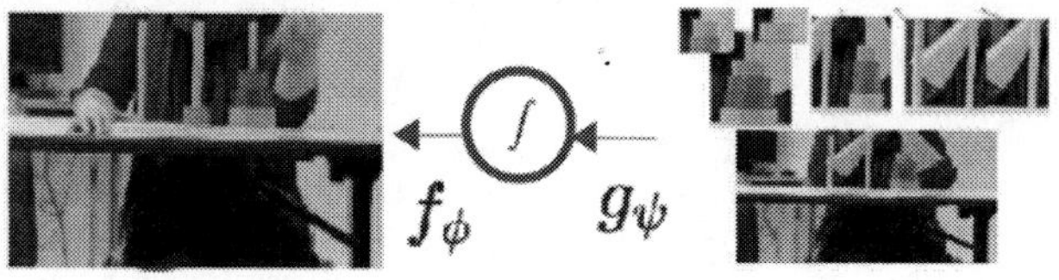

Figure 2. Model type

The model we want to predict is given by $y = f_\phi(\sum_{i,j} g_\psi(o_i, o_j))$ where f_ϕ and g_ψ are Multi-Layer Perceptron. We optimize this model by means of training. Finally, our model gives us probabilities about whether we can move the disk in each different situation or not.

III. Experiments

A. Experiment: Tower of Hanoi

We recruited 14 participants (Average age 41, Standard Deviation=8.51). The blind group consisted of 6 women and 1 man (Average age 39, Standard Deviation=6.65). The sighted group consisted of 6 women and 1 man (Average age 43, Standard Deviation=10.30). Sitting down at the table, the participants were then given four disks of the Tower of Hanoi that they had to solve. The instructions were given to the participants. The participants were requested to solve the four disks TOH as we collected their solution. Through these research experiments, we have obtained the sequential data concerning about the solution of Tower of Hanoi.

B. Experiment: Reasoning model

The model has 5 input units, one or two hidden layers and one output unit. There are different neurons (5,10) in each layers. Rectified linear activation functions are used in each hidden layer and a sigmoid activation function is used in the output layer, for binary classification. Reasoning model with different architectural variations was trained to find the rule of Tower of Hanoi. The model with different number of neurons reaches a cross entropy loss below 0.6. However, the fourth model (MLP:5 inputs, two hidden layers with 10 neurons, 1 output) performed well as compared to other models.

As we can see in Figure 3 and Table I, the test accuracy with 3 disks for the first and fourth model are 95.24% and 100%, respectively. When we try to infer the rule of game for The tower of Hanoi with 4 disks, we find our reasoning model achieves 75% prediction accuracy for the first model and 96.67% for the fourth model.

IV. Conclusion

Human being's reasoning and thinking do not require much learning data. Human intelligence requires only a simple exposition [7]. Based on this idea, without much learning data, we propose a reasoning model that can infer the rule of the game through observing the characteristics, relationships, and actions of objects. In particular, the objective of Tower of Hanoi is to find the solution in a way that is the shortest possible movement. For future work, we will apply our model to find the shortest path of Tower of Hanoi. Furthermore, after proving the effectiveness of this model, we will apply it to explore the more complicated tasks.

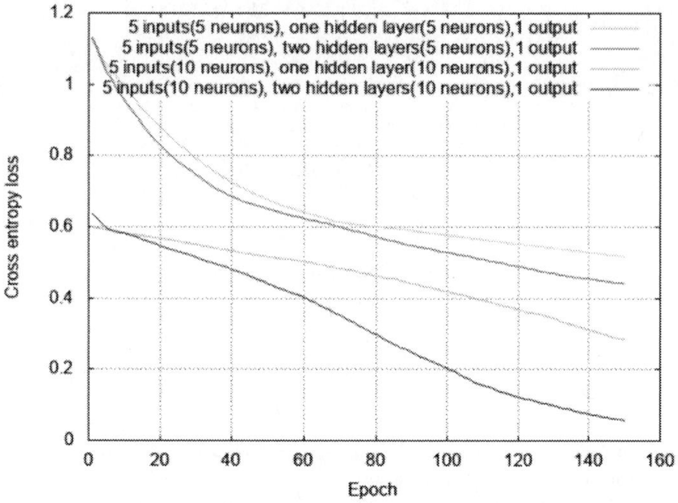

Figure 3. Reasoning model with different number of neurons was trained to find the rule of TOH.

TABLE I. MODEL PERFORMANCE FOR TOWER OF HANOI WITH 3 DISKS (TRAINING) AND 4 DISKS (PREDICTION)

	Accuracy	
Model	training(%)	prediction(%)
Five inputs (5 neurons), one hidden layer (5 neurons)	95.24	75
Five inputs (5 neurons), two hidden layers (5 neurons)	90.48	76.67
Five inputs (10 neurons), one hidden layer (10 neurons)	90.48	71.67
Five inputs (10 neurons), two hidden layers (10 neurons)	100	96.67

Acknowledgment

We would like to thank Mathilde Malgrange and the participants for participating in the experiment.

References

[1] J. P. Leighton and R. J. Sternberg, The nature of reasoning. Cambridge University Press, 2004.

[2] M. Minsky, The society of mind. New York : Simon and Schuster, 1986.

[3] E. T. Mueller, Commonsense reasoning: an event calculus based approach; 2nd ed. Waltham, MA: Morgan Kaufmann, 2015.

[4] A. Kumar et al., "Ask Me Anything: Dynamic Memory Networks for Natural Language Processing," arXiv.org, Jun. 2015, p. arXiv:1506.07285.

[5] P. Battaglia, R. Pascanu, M. Lai, D. J. Rezende, and K. Kavukcuoglu, "Interaction Networks for Learning about Objects, Relations and Physics," 2016, pp. 4502–4510.

[6] D. Raposo et al., "Discovering objects and their relations from entangled scene representations," CoRR, vol. abs/1702.05068, 2017. [Online]. Available: http://arxiv.org/abs/1702.05068

[7] R. B. Zajonc, "Mere Exposure: A Gateway to the Subliminal:," Current directions in psychological science, vol. 10, no. 6, Jun. 2016, pp. 224–228.

Capturing Knowledge for Multimodality Processing:

Interpreting Brain Vascular Imaging and its Description

Julia M. Taylor Rayz
Computer and Information Technology
Purdue University
West Lafayette, Indiana, USA
email:jtaylor1@purdue.edu

Vitaliy L. Rayz
Biomedical Engineering
Purdue University
West Lafayette, Indiana, USA
email:vrayz@purdue.edu

Victor Raskin
Linguistics & CERIAS
Purdue University
West Lafayette, Indiana, USA
email: vraskin@purdue.edu

Abstract—**Advancements in medical imaging led to increased amount of image data that needs to be post-processed and examined in order to determine a pathology and provide diagnosis. In particular, post-processing and analysis of magnetic resonance images of blood vessels in the brain requires advanced tools capable of representing the vessels network in 3D and eliminating errors caused by image artifacts and noise. An approach based on the knowledge of the anatomy and functions of the brain vasculature is considered. While state-of-the-art tools are designed to evaluate image intensity, the knowledge-based framework can use the information on the underlying vascular structures to map imaging data to ontological representation, thus allowing for annotation possibility and textual description understanding, as well as detect errors and separate them from abnormalities caused by vascular disease.**

Keywords-Ontology; Knowledge Representation; Medical Imaging; Blood vessels; cerebral circulation.

I. INTRODUCTION

The paper proposes using an ontology as the basis of relevant knowledge for the domain. It assembles and neatly arranges, in an online resource that could be open to use by any health professional, all knowledge and experience that is available to an experienced physician "intuitively," thus upgrading any less experienced medical practitioner's ability to diagnose and treat the patient. Needless to say, while the ontology is open to any user, an individual patient's data are duly protected as required by the relevant laws.

For any individual domain, the ontology is an easy and affordable extension of the existing general and previously extended ontology. The extension is implemented semi-automatically, with the computer formatting the entry and *prompting* a moderately trained user for questions about the linguistic meaning of terms. The previous extensions, to the banking industry, information security, and to feelings in general and humor research in particular, all resulted to the addition of under 400 new concepts, usually developed as new branches and leaves under one existing concept (BANK, SECURITY, and FEELING, respectively).

The ontology in our Ontological Semantic Technology approach is much more than a typical government or industry ontology for various areas: those are often an inventory of terms, usually aiming in standardizing them and focusing on objects rather than objects and events, linked with an abundance of properties. It is common for many published ontologies to have hardly any properties beyond subsumption, which establishes the hierarchy.

The standard procedure starts with what was referred to in the 1980s as knowledge engineering that led to the creation of expert systems. The crucial difference is that we are aware of the semantics of the collected material rather than the syntax-oriented and, therefore, failing expert systems. We do have an expert in vascular system among us, so the following sections of the paper were written in the process of conversing with him or drafted by him. But, the standard extension procedure could have started from a well-indexed textbook or reference book. Another significant advantage is that, within our approach, any acquisition is guided by the ontology that, logically and consistently, develops the new branches and leaves where they belong.

The purpose of any ontological extension is to identify all the events and objects in the domain and the multiplicity of properties that link them to each other. The objects and events are the nodes in an ontology, and the links are its named edges. The central concept for this extension is, of course, blood VESSEL.

The paper is organized in the following order: section II introduces blood vessels from a human perspective and describes what a system should know about them; section III describes how this knowledge can be represented for computational purposes; section IV goes further into the details of ontological representations, describing the salient features that are useful for processing. Finally, section V demonstrates what happens when an image is analyzed.

II. BLOOD VESSELS 101: WHAT KNOWLEDGE SHOLD BE CAPTURED

A blood vessel can be characterized by its anatomy and function. In the current clinical practice, clinical decisions are often based on medical images visualizing vascular anatomy, thus neglecting valuable information that could be inferred from functional data. Vessel anatomy can be characterized by its location and geometry, with the former describing whether it is an artery or vein, and where it is located in the circulation. This also defines the "parent" vessel and the branches, i.e., a vessel from which the vessel of interest originated and all vessels emanating from the vessel of interest. Longer vessels, such as an internal carotid artery, are subdivided in segments, in order to precisely locate the regions of interest. The geometry is defined by the diameter, length, and tortuosity of the vessel – these can obviously vary for different segments of the same vessel. The purpose of circulation is to quickly deliver oxygen from the lungs to all the cells of various organs and tissues, thus large vessels delivering blood to a particular region of the body divide into subsequent branches with smaller diameter but larger cumulative area. This typically results in a gradual decrease of the vessel diameter (but not necessarily length!) as we proceed through the circulation. The vessels or their segments located closer to the heart are called "proximal", while those further away are called "distal". It should be noted that this is defined by the vessel relative location and not by the direction of blood flow. The vessels that are located above are called "superior" while those below are called "inferior". Finally, the vessels closer to the front of the body are named "anterior" and those closer to the back are "posterior".

A vessel affected by cardiovascular disease typically has a local change in its diameter, such as an abnormal constriction, named "stenosis" or dilation, named "aneurysm". Medical images showing stenosis may indicate atherosclerotic plaques obstructing blood flow and potentially decreasing the amount of blood delivered to the distal vascular territory supplied by this vessel. An aneurysm of a brain vessel may grow and rupture, causing hemorrhage in the brain.

The functional information can be obtained with advanced images that can either visualize the transport of an injected contrast agent or directly measure blood flow velocities. These characteristics of the vessel include the blood flow rate, the pulsatility of the flow (how much it is changing through the cardiac cycle), the velocity distribution in the vessel or simply the average or maximum velocity, and the pressure drop, i.e., the difference between the pressure at two different points in the vessel. For example, a stenosis resulting in a minimal pressure drop is likely to present less risk than that causing a larger pressure drop, even if both are characterized by the same degree of the vessel's obstruction. In addition, there are numerous flow-derived metrics that can characterize the vessel's function and, in some cases, help with diagnostics and risk stratification of patients. These include wall shear stress -- a frictional force exerted on the vessel wall by flowing blood, flow residence time -- the relative time blood dwells at a given location and other, more complex flow descriptors.

A healthy vessel is characterized by approximately the same or gradually changing diameter and relatively smooth distribution of velocities, faster in the core of the flow and slower near the wall. This also results in a very minimal pressure drop along the vessels and an optimal range of wall shear stress for all arteries of similar size. A diseased artery, affected by a stenosis or aneurysm is characterized by local changes of the diameter and curvature, as well as by complex flow patterns affecting other flow-derived descriptors. A narrowing of the vessel results in a high velocity jet and region of disturbed, slowly recirculated flow. The flow residence time in these disturbed regions is typically increased. These features may cause various image artifacts, such as a loss of signal or insufficient resolution to detect the smaller section of the diseased vessel. An aneurysm is also characterized by disturbed flow with jets and regions of flow recirculation, affecting wall shear stress and flow residence time. This may, in turn, affect the quality of medical images, e.g., cause the loss of MRI (Magnetic Resonance Imaging) signal in regions of stagnant flow which occur in larger aneurysms.

Depending on the size of blood vessel or whether it is affected by disease, the flow through it may be also "Newtonian" or "non-Newtonian". Since blood is not a homogeneous fluid but a suspension of cells in plasma, blood viscosity (resistance to flow) depends on the interactions of these cells. In a vessel that is comparable in size to these cells or in regions of disturbed flow, blood viscosity can increase due to aggregation of cells. In addition, blood may form clots consisting of aggregated cells and cell fragments. Blood clotting is important for preventing leaks through injured regions of the vessel wall. At the same time, a clot formed in a vessel may travel to the smaller vessel downstream and block it, causing a stroke.

It should be mentioned that the vessels are also characterized by the wall thickness and properties. While vessel walls in the brain are typically too thin to be detected with existing imaging modalities, it is crucial to understand their anatomy and function in health and in disease. A vessel wall is composed of three layers with different characteristics and properties. The inner layer, the intima, is a layer of endothelial cells providing a barrier between the flowing blood and stationary tissue. The other two layers, media and adventitia, are composed of elastic tissue reinforced by collagen fibers which determines its elastic properties. A diseased vessel may contain plaques with necrotic (dead) tissues, calcifications and intraplaque hemorrhage. Advanced vessel wall imaging techniques, such as those developed by David Saloner at UC San Francisco [1], aimed at detecting various components of the wall. A healthy wall thickness is typically 10% of the vessel's diameter, while a diseased wall can be either abnormally thin or inflated. While a healthy wall is compliant, and moves corresponding to heart pulse, a diseased wall may become rigid, affecting both the flow and pulse wave propagation.

III. Ontological View

We take a general ontology that we have developed [2] as a reference point. Our general ontology contains concepts and their properties and has been formally described in its crisp [3]-[5] and fuzzy [2], [6], [7] flavors. Here, we will continue with the fuzzy approach, and we will demonstrate that it is most suitable for this domain. As [2] states, given a set of objects D, where D is the disjoint union of D_c (concepts) and D_d (literals), and given its interpretation function $\mathcal{I}$, for every fuzzy concept C, object x is an element of C with some degree $\mathcal{I}[C](x) \rightarrow [0, 1]$; for every relation R, $\mathcal{I}[R](x, y) \subseteq D_c \times D_c \rightarrow [0, 1]$; for every attribute A; $\mathcal{I}[A](x, a) \subseteq D_c \times D_d \rightarrow [0, 1]$.

We assume that $x \in C$ if $\mathcal{I}[C](x) \rightarrow (0, 1]$. With this in mind, the following is true for concepts C_1 and C_2:

$\mathcal{I}[C_1\ C_2](x) = \max\{\mathcal{I}[C_1](x), \mathcal{I}[C_2](x)\}$;

$\mathcal{I}[\text{and}\ C_1\ C_2](x) = \min\{\mathcal{I}[C_1](x), \mathcal{I}[C_2](x)\}$;

$\mathcal{I}[((C))](x) = \max_{y \in C}\{\mathcal{I}[R](y, x)\}$;

$\mathcal{I}[(R(\text{and}\ C_1\ C_2))](x) = \min\{\mathcal{I}[(C_1)](x), \mathcal{I}[(C_2)](x)\}$;

$\mathcal{I}[R(C_1\ C_2)](x) = \max\{\mathcal{I}[R(C_1)](x), \mathcal{I}[R(C_2)](x)\}$;

$\mathcal{I}[C_1(R(C_2))](x) = \min\{\mathcal{I}[C_1](x), \mathcal{I}[R(C_2)](x)\};$

$\mathcal{I}[C(R_1(C_1))(R_2(C_2))](x) =$
$=\min\{\mathcal{I}[C(R_1(C_1))](x), \mathcal{I}[C(R_2(C_2))](x)\};$

A. Vessel domain ontologies

Many terminological descriptions of blood vessels that resemble ontologies exist today. We take an approach here that an ontology should capture most useful properties of the domain of application, and thus, a hierarchy with a handful of properties is not an ideal ontological representation. With this in mind, lattices of blood vessels' anatomy are a useful starting point.

The second point worth making is that we are only interested in the details of the cerebral vessels, which means that while we cannot completely discard the rest, a special attention is paid to the description of the brain area. Finally, we treat an ontological hierarchy as a good starting point due to its mathematical properties, such as inheritance. We will assume, then, that it is sufficient to describe properties of a parent concept in this paper with a full understanding that they will propagate to the children concepts. We assume that inheritance of properties is carried though IS-A relationship. We also allow transitive and symmetric properties in our representation:

$\forall c_1, c_2 \in C, r_s \in R: c_1(r_s(c_2)) \Leftrightarrow c_2(r_s(c_1))$, where c_1, c_2 are concepts and r_s is a symmetric property;

$\forall c_1, c_2, c_3 \in C, r_t \in R: c_1(r_t(c_2)), c_2(r_t(c_3)) \Rightarrow c_1(r_t(c_3))$, where c_1, c_2, c_3 are concepts and r_t is a transitive property.

We are going to start with anatomical description of the vessel and then continue with its functional characteristics.

B. Anatomical Properties of Blood Vessels

As mentioned before, anatomical characteristics can be described in terms of location and geometry. While the location of the vessel may be reflected in its name, it is still crucial to represent this information mathematically. We thus have the following location properties, all with a domain of the vessel:

- RELATIVE-LOCATION-TO-HEART, with a range of {proximal, distal};
- RELATIVE-VERTICAL-POSITION, with a range of {superior, inferior};
- RELATIVE-FRONTAL-POSITION, with a range of {anterior, posterior};
- RELATIVE-SIDE-POSITION, with a range of {left, right};
- INFLOW-VESSEL, with a range of names of vessels that (blood) flow into a given one;
- OUTFLOW-VESSEL, with a range of names of vessels that (blood) flow out of a given one.

Both INFLOW-VESSEL and OUTFLOW-VESSEL properties are transitive.

Geometry properties can be summarized as follows:

- DIAMETER, with a range of being dependent on a particular vessel, relative to the aorta of that individual;
- LENGTH, with a range of being dependent on a particular vessel, not relative to the aorta;
- TORTUOSITY, with a range of true of false, dependent on a particular patient, rather than on a type of a vessel.

DIAMETER and LENGTH must be greater than zero.

Based on the properties above, the following concepts can be defined:

- STENOSIS: a portion of artery of variable length where diameter of the lumen is decreased relative to the diameter the proximal or distal segment of the same vessel;
- ANEURYSM: a segment of a vessel with a significantly dilated diameter, relative to proximal or distal diameter of the same vessel.

An ANEURYSM has additional properties that a healthy vessel does not need to have, such as:

- diameter of a neck of an aneurysm (NECK-DIAMETER), which is a diameter of the opening between the aneurysm and a parent vessel;
- number of lobes (LOBES-NO), which is a number of separate convex shapes in an aneurysm;
- volume of an aneurysm (VOLUME);
- area of an aneurysm (AREA), measured by wall surface area;
- height of an aneurysm (HEIGHT), which is a maximum distance from the neck to the wall.
- diameter of the aneurysm (DIAMETER), which is the largest dimension between any two points in the aneurysm;
- aneurysm angle (ANGLE), which is an angle between its diameter and flow direction;

The range of all of these additional properties is a rational number. Additionally, two types of aneurysms can be described: a SACCULAR aneurism is an aneurysm that appears on one side of a vessel; and a FUSIFORM, which bulges out on circumference of the vessel. It is possible to create new child concepts for these two types or create a property, reflecting its relative location as a property, TYPE, with the range corresponding to the type names.

C. Functional Properties of Blood Vessels

Functional properties of vessels correspond to properties that are usually captured with advanced imaging methods. These properties, while descriptive of a vessel, may be selectively obtained. However, it should be noted that the values correspond to each voxel of an image, and thus, each vessel is explicitly represented in three dimensional coordinates. The properties that describe the vessels are then spatiotemporal distributions with values in each of the (existing) points in the coordinates, not the properties of vessel as a hole. The properties of interests are:

- blood flow velocity (VELOCITY);
- blood flow rate (FLOW-RATE): exists in a given cross-section, not in a voxel ;
- pulsatility of the flow (PULSATILITY): how much it is changing through the cardiac cycle;

- pressure (PRESSURE): pressure measurement at any point in a vessel;
- wall sheer stress (WSS): a frictional force exerted on the vessel wall by flowing blood;
- flow residence time (FRT): the relative time the blood dwells at a given location.

It is tempting to consider mereology (a study of parts and holes) when considering mathematical properties of the descriptions above. However, for the purposes of this paper, it is sufficient to treat each of these points independently, although in reality there is a strong dependence between them.

IV. ACCEPTABLE RANGE OF VALUES

While location features of blood vessels are tedious to construct, there is no mystery to their verification of correctness: any anatomical atlas can be constructed for information as to whether something is correct or not. For example, if one is to describe branches of BASILAR-ARTERY, and fill its location properties, one would describe them as:

- LEFT-ANTERIOR-INFERIOR-CEREBELLAR ARTERY
- RIGHT-ANTERIOR-INFERIOR-CEREBELLAR ARTERY
- LEFT-SUPERIOR-CEREBELLAR ARTERY
- RIGHT-SUPERIOR-CEREBELLAR ARTERY
- LEFT-POSTERIOR-CEREBRAL ARTERY
- RIGHT-POSTERIOR-CEREBRAL ARTERY

Since all of these are branches of the BASILAR-ARTERY, the flow of all of the above vessels would be provided by the BASILAR-ARTERY, and thus, BASILAR-ARTERY is an INFLOW-VESSEL for each of them, and each of them is an OUTFLOW-VESSEL for BASILAR-ARTERY.

A. *Geometric Properties of a Concept VESSEL*

Selecting the correct range of values of the geometric properties for a given vessel is slightly more complex. We will start with a description of DIAMETER values for a vessel. These values are best described as fuzzy membership functions [8], where a perfect range corresponds to a maximum value of membership function, but then there is a gradual decline in the values that corresponds to less than maximal, yet still acceptable membership value. We will call these acceptable values a HEALTHY fuzzy set. There are some deviations from healthy range, some more severe than others, but, these values should still be physically possible. We will call this an unhealthy range, corresponding to UNHEALTHY fuzzy set. Finally, there will be some values that can only be achieved as a result of a measuring error or an artifact of a method, we will call this set ARTIFACT set. A graphical representation is shown Figure 1.

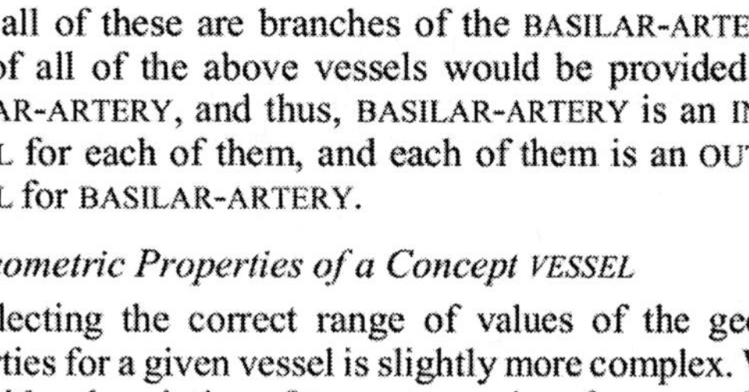

Figure 1. Fuzzy sets as DIAMETER values (sets are not drawn to scale)

HEALTHY = {x, $\mu_{HEALTHY}(x)$ | x∈X}, where X is all possible values received for a given property.

UNHEALTHY = {x, $\mu_{UNHEALTHY}(x)$ | x∈X}, where X is all possible values received for a given property.

ARTIFACT = {x, $\mu_{ARTIFACT}(x)$ | x∈X}, where X is all possible values received for a given property.

$$\mu_{HEALTHY}(x) = \begin{cases} 0, (x < h1) \; or \; (x > h4) \\ \frac{x-h1}{h2-h1}, \; h1 \le x \le h2 \\ 1, \; h2 \le x \le h3 \\ \frac{h4-x}{h4-h3}, \; h3 \le x \le h4 \end{cases}$$

By convention, a trapezoidal fuzzy set HEALTHY can be expressed as [h1, h2, h3, h4].

$$\mu_{UNHEALTHY}(x) = \begin{cases} 0, (x < u1) \; or \; (u4 < x < u5) \\ \frac{x-u1}{u2-u1}, \; u1 \le x \le u2 \\ \frac{x-u5}{u6-u5}, \; u5 \le x \le u6 \\ 1, \; (u2 \le x \le u3) \; or \; (u6 \le x \le u7) \\ \frac{u4-x}{u4-u3}, \; u3 \le x \le u4 \\ \frac{u8-x}{u8-u7}, \; u7 \le x \le u8 \end{cases}$$

We will notate UNHEALTHY as [u1, u2, u3, u4] ∪ [u5, u6, u7, u8].

$$\mu_{ARFIFACT}(x) = \begin{cases} 0, (x < a2) \; or \; (x > a1) \\ \frac{x-a1}{0-a1}, \; x \le a1 \\ 1, \; x = a1 \; or \; x = a2 \\ \frac{a2-x}{a2}, \; a2 \le x \end{cases}$$

The range of acceptable values of inflow vessel have to be propagated to the outflow vessel. The values can be assumed to be the same, unless the inflow vessel is branching out into a number of outflow vessels. In the described example of BASILAR ARTERY, it has 6 branches that serve as its outflow vessels: LEFT-ANTERIOR-INFERIOR-CEREBELLAR ARTERY, RIGHT-ANTERIOR-INFERIOR-CEREBELLAR ARTERY, LEFT-SUPERIOR-CEREBELLAR ARTERY, RIGHT-SUPERIOR-CEREBELLAR ARTERY, LEFT-POSTERIOR-CEREBRAL ARTERY, RIGHT-POSTERIOR-CEREBRAL ARTERY. Common sense dictates that the diameter of these arteries should not be the same, and thus it is important to provide a model that is close to a real world. We will take a previously defined HEALTHY fuzzy set [h1, h2, h3, h4] as a starting point. We will assume that each of the branches *i* have their own $HEALTHY_i$ [$h1_i$, $h2_i$, $h3_i$, $h4_i$] fuzzy set such that for any branch *i*, $h1_i$<h1, $h2_i$,<h2 $h3_i$<h3, $h4_i$<h4. Moreover,

$$(h2 - h1)^2 \le \sum_i (h2_i - h1_i)^2 \approx 1.2(h2 - h1)^2.$$

Thus, the DIAMETER values of the branching vessels can be verified compared to the parent vessel.

LENGTH and TORTUOSITY values of vessel are independent on factors other than the actual vessel. While the LENGTH still varies from person to person, and should be described as a fuzzy number, there are no other dependencies other than that of a TORTUOSITY.

B. Geometric Properties of the Concept ANEURYSM

Let us now consider the properties of SACCULAR and FUSIFORM aneurysms. As stated earlier, the difference between these types is that the former appears to the side of the vessel, and the latter to bulges out on the circumference. Most properties defined for an aneurism are applicable for both types, however some differences should be pointed out.

The first properties, NECK-DIAMETER, describes an opening between a parent vessel and an aneurysm. It follows from a definition of FUSIFORM aneurysm that its NECK-DIAMETER could be equal to the diameter of the vessel, whoever this parameter is not typically used in medical practice. Similarly, HEIGHT is not of much use for FUSIFORM aneurysm, although, technically, could be defined. A NECK-DIAMETER and HEIGHT of the SACCULAR aneurysm can vary and thus are useful parameters.

Number of lobes is typically applicable to SACCULAR aneurysms, but there is no reason why it would not be applicable for both. VOLUME and AREA are useful parameters for both types, and can vary in values. A DIAMETER of an aneurism should not be confused with a DIAMETER of a vessel. Since DIAMETER of an aneurysm is defined as a largest distance between any two points of an aneurysm, it is always greater than the vessel DIAMETER for FUSIFORM aneurysms. However, it is possible that it could be greater or less than the vessel DIAMETER for SACCULAR aneurysms.

With these restrictions in mind, the next section will demonstrate how an ontology could be used to annotate an image.

V. INTERPRETING AN IMAGE

Figure 2 shows an image used by [9] as an example of image segmentation errors. While it is possible to assume from this picture that an aneurysm is connected to two arteries, the ontology would reject such interpretation.

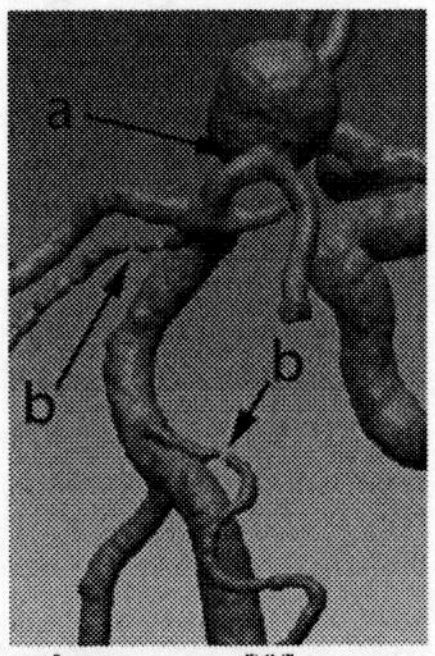

Figure 2. Image segmentation errors [9]: separate blood vessels are blended together a) cerebral aneurysm pressing on posterior cerebral artery; b) two disconnected arteries.

Before we get to a reasoning step, however, let us consider information presented to us. There are 8 vessels that can be identified "under" the aneurysm in this image. Let us start at the bottom of the figure, with the large vessel at the center, let us identify it as v_1. There is another vessel on the left of v_1, let us call it v_2, that merges with v_1 to form v_3 (in Figure 2, v_3 actually looks like a continuation of v_1). A fourth vessel, v_4, branches off v_3. Since we know that a diameter of a vessel has to be greater than 0, v_4 should not have an empty segment next to the right b-arrow. A similar error is seen where another vessel, v_5, branches off v_3. Three more vessels branch off of v_3, we will call them v_6, v_7, v_8. The following can be observed:

- v_1 and v_2 flow into v_3, which means that
  - v_1 and v_2 are INFLOW-VESSELs for v_3,
  - and v_3 is an OUTFLOW-VESSEL for v_1 and v_3
- v_3 flows into v_4, which means that
  - v_3 is an INFLOW-VESSEL for v_4,
  - and v_4 is an OUTFLOW-VESSEL from v_3;
- v_3 flows into v_5, v_6, v_7, v_8, which mean that
  - v_3 is an INFLOW-VESSEL for v_5, v_6, v_7, v_8;
  - and v_5, v_6, v_7, v_8 are OUTFLOW-VESSELs for v_3
- since INFLOW-VESSEL and OUTFLOW-VESSEL properties are transitive, we can conclude that
  - v_1 and v_2 are INFLOW-VESSELs for v_4, v_5, v_6, v_7, v_8
  - v_4, v_5, v_6, v_7, v_8 are OUTFLOW VESSELs for v_1 and v_2

Looking at the location properties, and comparing them with possible ontological interpretations, v_1 corresponds to LEFT-VERTBRAL-ARTERY, v_2 corresponds to RIGHT-VERTBRAL-ARTERY, v_3 corresponds to BASILAR-ARTERY, v_4 corresponds to POSTERIOR-INFERIOR-CEREBELLAR-ARTERY, v_5 and v_6 to LEFT and RIGHT SUPERIOR CEREBELLAR ARTERIES, v_7 and v_8 to LEFT and RIGHT POSTERIOR CEREBRAL ARTERIES.

Let us now address the geometric properties. All of these vessels have TORTUOSITY value of false, with the exception of v_4. The diameter calculation for healthy vessels should be as follows:

$$1.2^{*}\ \text{DIAMETER (BASILAR-ARTERY)}^2 \approx$$
$$\approx \text{DIAMETER(RIGHT-POSTERIOR-CEREBRAL-ARTERY)}^2 +$$
$$+\ \text{DIAMETER (LEFT-POSTERIOR-CEREBRAL-ARTERY)}^2$$

While the total area of the branches should exceed that of the parent vessel, an abrupt increase in the area could make the vessel unhealthy, at the flow would separate from the wall resulting in a swirl or recirculation.

Finally, there is an aneurysm that is seemingly located on a side of v_8, thus it is a SACCULAR aneurysm. Its DIAMETER is considerably greater than the DIAMETER of v_8. Its NECK-DIAMETER appears to be quite large, and a person not familiar with brain vessel anatomy may not detect that it is also connected to another, yet unlabeled, vessel. A person familiar with anatomy (or a computer program?) may detect the connection. It follows that this SACCULAR aneurysm is connected on its two sides to two arteries, which is not possible according to our current definition. Further analysis could indicate that even if it was possible for an aneurism to be connected to more than one vessel, there is no blood-flow either from v_8 to the unlabeled artery with aneurysm or from it to v_8. Such determination can be done through transitive properties INFLOW-VESSEL and OUTFLOW-VESSEL, thus flagging the imaging error, which, in this case, is due to an artifact. In reality, the aneurysm is supplied by the anterior cerebral artery; the large aneurysm size resulted in its wall contacting the v_8, without any flow exchange.

VI. CONCLUSION

The knowledge-based approach for visualization and analysis of MR angiography data was formulated and verified on an example dataset containing cerebral aneurysm. This approach can help in reliable representation of the vascular anatomy in 3D, thus helping in flow analysis and treatment planning. Moreover, the knowledge-based methods can be invaluable for automatic screening of large image datasets in order to flag pathologies that require human intervention.

REFERENCES

[1] G. Zhu, et al., High resolution imaging of the intracranial vessel wall at 3 and 7 T using 3D spin echo MRI, *Magnetic Resonance Materials in Physics, Biology and Medicine*, 2016.

[2] J. M. Taylor and V. Raskin, "Fuzzy ontology for natural language," *NAFIPS 2010*, 2010.

[3] C. Hempelmann, J. M. Taylor, and V. Raskin, "Application-guided ontological engineering," *IC-AI 2010*, 2010.

[4] J. M. Taylor, C. Hempelmann and V. Raskin, "On an automatic acquisition toolbox for ontologies and lexicons in Ontological Semantics," *IC-AI 2010*, 2010.

[5] J. M. Taylor, V. Raskin, and C. Hempelmann, "From disambiguation failures to common sense knowledge acquisition: a day of life in an ontological semantic system," *2011 IEEE/WIC/ACM International Conferences on Web Intelligence*, 2011.

[6] J. M. Taylor and V. Raskin, "Understanding the unknown: Unattested input processing in natural langauge," *FUZZ IEEE'11* 2011.

[7] J. M. Taylor and V. Raskin, Computing with nouns and verbs, *FUZZ IEEE'12*, 2012.

[8] L. A. Zadeh, Fuzzy Sets, *Information and Control 8(3),* 1965

[9] J.T. Rayz, V. L. Rayz and V. Raskin, Cognitive imaging: Using knowledge representation for reliable segmentation of MR angiography data, *ICCI*CC 2017*, 2017.